OAKWOOD LIBRARY OF RAILWAY HISTORY

The East Kent Railway

Volume Two:
Nationalisation, the Route,
Rolling Stock and Operation

by
M. Lawson Finch & S.R. Garrett

THE OAKWOOD PRESS

British Library Cataloguing in Publication Data
A Record for this book is available from the British Library
ISBN 0 85361 609 4

Typeset by Oakwood Graphics.
Repro by Ford Graphics, Ringwood, Hants.
Printed by Cambrian Printers, Aberystwyth, Ceredigion.

> *If you want to take a ride*
> *with your bonny buxom bride,*
> *if you've something really*
> *nice you want to say.*
> *You can change at Shepherds Well*
> *for Timbuctoo or Neuve Chapelle,*
> *on the East Kent Railway.*
>
> *J. Kelly,*
> *Porter,*
> *Staple*
> *1922/1923*

With thanks to Richard Harffey from whom this was received on St Patrick's Day 1960.

Front cover: Golgotha tunnel was the main civil engineering feature of the East Kent Railway. One of British Railways dwindling band of 'O1' class 0-6-0 locomotives emerges from the tunnel heading towards Tilmanstone. *Colour-Rail*

Rear cover: A selection of East Kent Railway tickets. *Ken Elks*

Published by The Oakwood Press (Usk), P.O. Box 13, Usk, Mon., NP15 1YS.
E-mail: oakwood-press@dial.pipex.com
Website: www.oakwood-press.dial.pipex.com

Contents

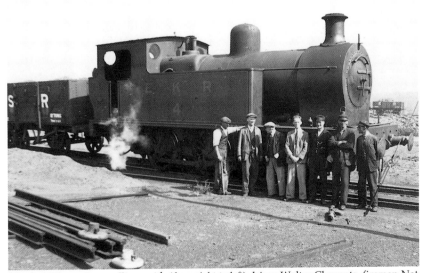

No. 4 at Tilmanstone colliery with (*from right to left*) driver Walter Clements, fireman Nat Sedgewick and guard Percy Buttifint together with colliery staff captured by the camera of Dr J.R. Hollick.

A scene at Shepherdswell during British Railways' brief passenger-carrying days. EKR No. 6 has not changed at all but carriage No. 5 and brakevan No. 34 (now 54873) carry markings 'FOR USE ON THE EAST KENT SECTION ONLY'.

'O1' class 0-6-0 No. 31425 pauses on the siding connectiing the East Kent to the main line yard. All East Kent stock has been removed but the locomotive shed is still intact.

Chapter Thirteen

The East Kent Railway since 1948

Although much of the EKR disappeared in the early years of its new ownership it is remarkable that part of the line survived in active operation for almost as long under British Railways as it had existed as an independent railway. If the period of operation by the East Kent Contract & Financial Company is excluded then the section from Shepherdswell to Tilmanstone Colliery was actually operated longer by British Railways than by the East Kent Light Railways Company. That this section has gone on to survive the closure and obliteration of Tilmanstone Colliery and has resumed operation as a preserved railway is even more remarkable.

There was little immediate sign in 1948 that the EKR had become the East Kent Section of the Southern Region of British Railways. The same locomotives continued to be based at Shepherdswell locomotive shed. The recently acquired bogie carriages continued in use still lettered EAST KENT RAILWAY albeit with white stencilled notices on the lower body sides reading 'FOR USE ON EAST KENT SECTION ONLY'. Even the timetable remained the same. Admittedly the older carriages and wagons were soon broken up or taken away and 'British Railways' began to appear on posters and notice boards, but to all intents and purposes the railway continued much as before.

The value of the EKR, shares and debentures was eventually settled on the 24th September, 1948 when it was agreed to pay £2 10s. 0d. in British Transport Commission stock for every £100 of Ordinary Shares and £55 for every £100 of Debenture Stock. In setting this price the Tribunal expressed doubts that the recovery of Tilmanstone Colliery would bring any serious benefit to the railway as the colliery could always restore the ropeway to working order. The Tribunal considered the debentures to be '. . . an investment the full interest upon which is by no means secured' and the shares to be '. . . an equity with only a remote chance of any dividend'. This was not entirely the end of the matter as interest had accrued on the debentures during the first half of 1948. The *Railway Gazette* for 5th November, 1948 therefore reported that: 'The Commission has decided to pay such further interest as will . . . be equal to the amount of interest which has accrued for the half-year to 30th June, 1948, on the British Transport stock to be issued in satisfaction'.

If there were doubts about the value of increased coal traffic there were certainly no illusions about the value of the passenger traffic which continued to dwindle. A·contributor to the *Railway Observer* reported that in September he had found no notices warning of the closure of the line and that the staff were still dismissing any possibility of the end of passenger services as rumours. The notices must have gone up shortly after his visit as the passenger service ceased on 30th October, 1948. Peter Bowden recalls travelling on that day: 'I went on the outward trip all the way with a friend, but it was simply an ordinary run with Engine 2, carriage and goods brake. There was not even any shunting *en route* and certainly no bands or fireworks! I have my ticket - an SR paper - fare

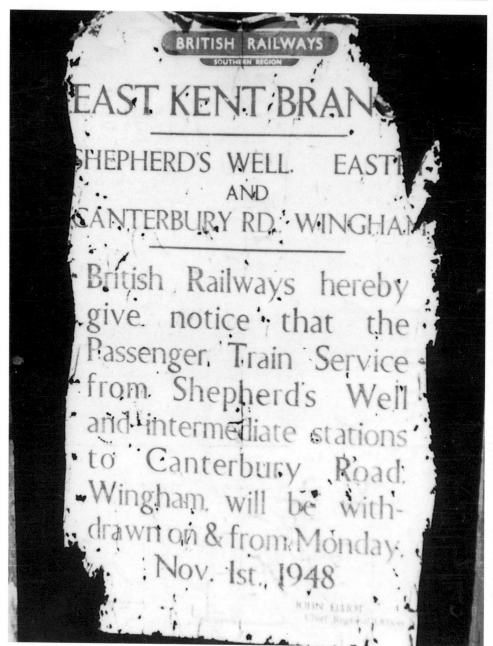

Closure notice still displayed at Shepherdswell in 1950.   *M. Lawson Finch Collection*

THE EAST KENT RAILWAY SINCE 1948

1s. 2½d. I doubt if the return journey had any passengers at all'. Tom King was the driver on this last passenger train.

Shepherdswell locomotive shed closed with the end of passenger services and the surviving EKR locomotives, Nos. 2, 4, 6 and 1371, went to Dover. No. 4 was provisionally allotted the number 30948 and was partially dismantled at Dover, presumably with a view to carrying out repairs. These must have proved more extensive than could be justified as No. 4 was withdrawn together with No. 1371 in January 1949 and taken away to Ashford for scrapping. No. 6 did not long outlast its companions and was withdrawn for scrapping in February 1949. No. 2 caused some interest in the first half of 1949 by appearing on shunting duties around Dover in what remained of its EKR livery. Later in the year No. 2 went to Ashford for overhaul and emerged in October 1949 in British Railways livery as No. 31383. In this guise it returned to Dover to work on the railway until withdrawn in April 1951, along with 13 other members of the 'O1' class.

With the closure of Shepherdswell Shed the goods and coal traffic on the railway had become the responsibility of the dwindling pool of 'O1' locomotives allocated to Dover. One of these was No. 1379 which was observed at Shepherdswell by a surprised Mr J.G. Sharland on Sunday 17th July, 1949. Not only was it unusual to find traffic of any sort on the railway on a Sunday but No. 1379 was engaged in propelling a four-wheeled luggage van and a main line corridor coach along the line and into Golgotha tunnel. Distant whistling later indicated that it had emerged from the tunnel and was heading for Eythorne but whether it went any further and to what purpose can only be guessed at.

A report in the *Railway Observer* of a visit to Shepherdswell on 26th September, 1949 revealed that the locomotive shed was still intact but contained nothing more interesting than a 'decrepit open goods wagon'. The yard contained about a dozen other wagons but the only real sign that the line was still in use was the presence on the erstwhile passenger platform of a number of parcels awaiting delivery to Wickhambreux, presumably via Wingham. The running line was reported to be in very poor condition with rotten sleepers and missing keys. All carriages had been removed or broken up.

A number of other changes had taken place since Nationalisation some of which cannot be accurately dated. At Wingham Canterbury Road the line was cut short of the level crossing and the rails lifted beyond this point. However, the station building on the old passenger platform had been retained for the management of the remaining goods business.

At Staple British Railways demolished the wind pump and connected the water tank to the mains supply. At Eastry the run-round loop was turned into a siding by the simple expedient of removing the point connection at the Richborough end of the loop. The final changes of significance were at Shepherdswell where the locomotive shed and its associated workshops were demolished. The circular corrugated iron hut behind the Shepherdswell passenger platform also disappeared at this time, together with its heaped contents of EKR paperwork.

Two additions were made to the Shepherdswell scene by British Railways in the form of lineside notices. One was placed alongside the start of the sharply

Track being removed from beyond the level crossing at Canterbury Road in August 1949. The station buildings remained in use as an office for the goods traffic.   *K. Graham Barlow*

The locomotive shed has gone and the track is about to be lifted in this Shepherdswell view of May 1953.   *B.S. Plummer*

curved connection between the main line goods yard and the EKR yard and read 'ALL ENGINES HEAVIER THAN C CLASS ARE PROHIBITED FROM WORKING BEYOND THIS POINT' whilst a similar sign alongside the EKR line a short distance before the level crossing instructed that 'ALL ENGINES HEAVIER THAN O CLASS ARE PROHIBITED FROM WORKING BEYOND THIS POINT'. Although British Railways may have considered replacing the 'O1' locomotives on the railway with 'C' class locomotives it does not seem that this was ever attempted and the Tilmanstone Section remained the preserve of the 'O1' class until diesels took over. The 'C' class were more powerful locomotives but they were not so much younger than the 'O1' class that the investment necessary to accommodate them would have been justified. A proposal to replace the 'O1s' with ex-Lancashire & Yorkshire Railway 0-6-0s was also rumoured at this time.

The general goods traffic continued to decline and it was decided to close all but the section of line between Shepherdswell and Tilmanstone. Regular traffic officially ceased on the section between Eastry and Richborough Castle siding on 27th October, 1949 but the official closure of this section did not take place until 1st January, 1950. Even this date does not seem to have been too rigorously observed as traffic seems to have continued well into 1950 at least as far as Poison Cross for an adjoining nursery. Regular traffic between Eythorne and Wingham was intended to be withdrawn on 31st December, 1950 but this was postponed until Wednesday 28th February, 1951. There seems to have been some confusion locally as to whether the line was still open or not and motorists who had taken to disregarding the signs warning of level crossings had several narrow escapes. The actual closure was no better attended than had been the end of passenger services as the following article from the *Kentish Gazette* attests:

BOUGHT THE STATION - EAST KENT'S LAST TRAIN

The East Kent Light Railway ceased to function on Wednesday evening when Engine '31425' hauled the last goods train into the tiny 'terminus' at Wingham.

For 55-year-old Richard Harffey, 28 years the station master, booking clerk and porter, that was not the end of his long association with the 14 ft x 16 ft station building. When he heard that the railway was to be closed he bought the wooden structure and is going to put it in his garden at Winterton, Canterbury Road, Wingham, as a garden shed.

A World War I veteran of the Royal Engineers, he lost his leg at Ypres and joined the railway in 1922 when he married Florence Pay - a Wingham girl.

Mr Harffey started at Wingham, but went on to Staple where he remained for about five years. In 1929 he was given the post at Wingham as station master which he retained until the closing on Wednesday. With 10 years to go for his pension, Dick Harffey hopes to get a ticket-collector's job elsewhere.

Every afternoon his spaniel, Jill, would stroll down to the station to keep her master company, and even she was strangely subdued on Wednesday evening.

THE ONLY MOURNER

Only one member of the public turned out to see the exodus of the 'East Kent' - 70 year-old Douglas Stoddart - of Canterbury who cycled from his home in Stodmarsh Road.

Mr Stoddart, an organ and pianoforte tuner - he built the organ in St Augustine's College 45 years ago - makes a hobby of railways and swears the country would be better off if rail transport took the place of road haulage.

Life definitely improved for the East Kent's platelayers under British Railways. This Wickham motorised 13 hp trolley replaced the back-breaking pump trolleys that they had previously had to use. These photographs date from 1951.   *David Kevan*

'It's a terrible thing to see this old railway go.' he told a *Kentish Gazette* reporter. Asked if he included nationalised railways in his remarks, Mr Stoddart replied 'Nationalisation! It's no good on railways or anywhere else.'

Driver Wally Clements and Fireman Smith, of Dover, drove 31425. Mr Clements, who had driven East Kent locomotives since 1926, has pictures on the walls of his home of all the old EK engines.

As he watched the last train come into the station, Mr Harffey collected together the station's goods and chattels for dispatch to Shepherdswell.

During the War the Army ran mobile 12-inch siege guns up the line to Staple, where the RAF stored thousands of bombs until a Luftwaffe bomb 'persuaded' them that Staple was no longer healthy.

Last load on Wednesday was 14 bags of seeds for Mr Deverson, and for Parsons & Sons of Wingham.

Twenty minutes later '31425' blew her whistle and pulled the trucks up the hill towards Staple and Mr Harffey went home - with Jill. The 'East Kent' was finished.

The April 1951 *Railway Observer* reported that on 22nd February wagons were still to be found in the sidings at Wingham, Staple and Eastry South and at Hammill Brickworks. 'O1' No. 31434 was running the daily goods service but its load only consisted of a brakevan carrying packages. A further visit on the 3rd March found that all rolling stock had been cleared. The same article mentions that Poison Cross continued to receive and dispatch traffic for the adjoining nursery right up until closure. The official closure from Eythorne to Wingham was announced on 1st July, 1951.

Effectively the EKR was now purely a mineral branch to Tilmanstone Colliery although some non-colliery traffic is known to have continued to operate to Eythorne. A report in the December 1951 *Railway Observer* recorded that 'O1' No. 31434 had been seen collecting two wagons of sugar beet from Eythorne on the 25th October. There was even evidence of a train having recently travelled up the Richborough branch as far as Roman Road. The same edition also reported that most of the EKR track was still intact, even on the Richborough branch, although the sidings at Richborough had 'long gone'. It is not clear which sidings this refers to but the Richborough Castle sidings seem the most likely candidates.

The Richborough branch was lifted during 1952 and a visit to Sandwich Road on 21st December, 1952 suggested that the section from here to Eastry had only recently been lifted. Level crossing warning signs were still in position and at Poison Cross the sleepers had not yet been lifted nor the track in the level crossings. A report in the May 1953 *Railway Observer* stated that the Wingham branch was still intact but that the 'Sandwich Road branch' had been lifted. There was a certain irony in the lifting of the Richborough branch in 1952 as the demolition of the Tilmanstone ropeway to Dover also began in that year.

In December 1952 the section between Eastry and Eythorne still had its track and even sported EKR trespass warnings and mileposts. Platforms still existed at Eastry, Eastry South, Knowlton and Elvington but their nameboards had been removed. Eythorne was still intact and kept its nameboard, buildings and signals.

During 1953 plans were announced by the National Coal Board to invest up to £7 million in the Kent coalfield. These plans included the erection of new Koepe winding gear at Tilmanstone Colliery and the sinking of a new shaft to the Mill Yard seam to replace the workings on the Beresford seam which was

'O1' class 0-6-0s Nos. 31434 and 31430 between Tilmanstone and Eythorne on 11th August, 1953. The train includes a returning empty van and flat wagon as well as loaded coal wagons - a reminder that Tilmanstone received goods traffic as well as dispatching coal.

An unidentified 'O1' class descending from Golgotha tunnel *en route* to Tilmanstone with one loaded van and a good number of empty coal wagons.

running out. It was intended that the Mill Yard seam workings would eventually link Tilmanstone with Snowdown Colliery and that all coal produced would be brought to the surface at Snowdown. Had this scheme been completed it would, of course, have rendered the remaining section of the EKR redundant. Nor would there have been any joy for the railway in the announcement that a fifth colliery would be sunk in the coalfield, as this was intended to be sited near to the coast to exploit the coal reserves beneath the Channel. It is clear that Richborough Port, which the Coal Board had inherited, did not figure in their plans for the coalfield either as the site was put up for sale in October 1953. Fortunately, for the railway at least, the Coal Board's plans were only implemented to the extent of modernising the existing pits and the link to Snowdown was never carried out.

By June 1953 the lifting of the Wingham branch had reached a point mid-way between Wingham Colliery Halt and Staple. Lifting was in the hands of Geo. Cohen's 600 Group and was carefully planned. Each morning a train of empty wagons would be propelled to the current end of the line where a lorry-mounted crane travelling along the trackbed would load the track materials onto the wagons. Gradually the crane would advance, the train would retreat and the railway would disappear - as systematic as rolling up a very long carpet. It was a slow business since the track could not be lifted more quickly than it could be loaded onto the waiting train. By September 1954 demolition had reached Knowlton but we have not been able to find the exact date for the completion of demolition beyond this point.

Meanwhile the daily traffic to and from Tilmanstone Colliery remained in the hands of Dover's remaining band of 'O1s' Nos. 31258, 31425, 31430 and 31434. The closure in January 1954 of the Headcorn Extension of the Kent & East Sussex branch released further 'O1s' but only one of these, No. 31065, was selected for allocation to Dover.

1954 also saw the final chapter written in the history of the Concessions Group. When the Concessions Companies had sold their mineral interests to PDL they had acquired a right to charge super-royalties on every ton of coal raised in the pits that were to be built. In the event no new pits were ever built on the lands acquired from the Concessions Group but super-royalties were still payable on coal from Snowdown Colliery. By 1951 only the Kent Coal Concessions Company survived of all the enterprises that Arthur Burr had founded and the National Coal Board began negotiations to buy out the remaining interests of this company by a 'once and for all' payment. The result was that by 1954 Kent Coal Concessions was in a position to liquidate its assets and wind up its affairs. After paying off its creditors the company had £40,421 18s. 4d. to distribute to its shareholders. Although the face value of shares issued amounted to £134,503 10s. 0d. the return to shareholders was probably the healthiest that any Concessions Group company ever paid.

On 5th April, 1954 Stonehall & Lydden Halt on the Dover to Canterbury main line was closed. This had served the small village of houses originally erected to house miners at the Stonehall Colliery and was located at the point where EKR Railway 13 from Guilford Colliery to Stonehall would have joined the main line. Some of the colliery buildings still survive here.

Stephenson Locomotive Society special at Eythorne on 9th May, 1957. Note that the passing loop is still laid with spiked flat bottom rails while the running line has chaired track.

The other end of the same train. The six coaches of this special easily exceeded the length of Eythorne's platform.   *H.C. Casserley*

As the 1950s progressed the railway attracted less and less interest amongst enthusiasts and published accounts of its working virtually disappear. Interest in the Line was re-awakened in 1957 when the Stephenson Locomotive Society organised a trip to Tilmanstone as part of a railtour around much of the old London Chatham & Dover Railway system. For the Tilmanstone section of the tour the six-coach train was 'topped and tailed' by 'O1s' Nos. 31434 and 31425. The inclusion of a buffet car in the train was probably the first instance of catering facilities on the railway.

The 'O1s' were now beginning to show their age and alternative forms of motive power were under consideration. On 9th July, 1957 an 0-6-0 Drewry diesel-mechanical locomotive, No. 11220, took one of the return workings between Shepherdswell and Tilmanstone. This locomotive had spent a week in May on the Kent & East Sussex but only seems to have made the one test trip to Tilmanstone. It is unlikely that this type of locomotive, later designated class '04', would have been suitable for regular use on loaded coal trains up the gradient to Shepherdswell. It may have been hoped to use the type for shunting and thus replace some of the duties performed by the 'O1s', although by this date the National Coal Board were doing much of their own shunting with their own Hunslet diesel.

A trackbed walk between Wingham and Eastry in August 1957 revealed that all track had been removed even at the level crossings. Platforms only survived as mounds of earth and a number of embankments had been demolished and cuttings filled in. Quite a lot of the route had obviously been sold off to adjoining land owners. The body of the old Cheshire Lines Committee carriage, EKR No. 3, still survived as a bungalow at Staple but at Eastry the bridge over the Selson Road had been demolished and the site of the station had been cleared.

A similar walk between Shepherdswell and Eastry in October 1957 found that most of the line between Shepherdswell and Eythorne had been relaid with concrete sleepers, except for the section through Golgotha tunnel. At Eythorne the old main line had been lifted although its course was clearly marked by ballast. About 200 yards beyond the Eythorne level crossing the track of the main line was still in place and remained so to the point at which the northern connection from Tilmanstone Colliery had once existed. A platform still existed at Elvington but beyond this point the Tilmanstone spoil tips were rapidly encroaching on the course of the line. The route beyond the old North Bank Junction was in much the same condition as the route between Wingham and Eastry, with portions of land sold off and the platforms at Knowlton and Eastry South demolished.

On Saturday 23rd May, 1959 another railtour over the railway was organised by the Railway Enthusiasts' Club (REC) and consisted of 'O1' No. 31258, two non-corridor coaches and a van for bicycles. The tour started from the down platform of Shepherds Well main line station before reversing into the 'Southern' goods sidings. It then drew forward and made its way round the sharp curve into the East Kent yard and reversed into the old East Kent passenger platform. This must have been the first passenger-carrying train to have used this platform since passenger services ceased in 1948. The train then proceeded to Tilmanstone Colliery where No. 31258 ran round its train before returning to Shepherdswell where it again ran round, presumably in the main

'O1' class No. 31065 with a loaded coal train heading for Shepherdswell in July 1959. This locomotive was the only 'O1' to survive and may now be seen on the Bluebell Railway.

'O1' class 0-6-0 No. 31258 employed on a demolition train in August 1954.   *Norman Cavell*

line goods yard. The Tour then proceeded via Kearsney, Martin Mill, Deal and Betteshanger Colliery to Minster before returning to terminate in the bay platform at Kearsney.

The REC Railtour took place against a background of growing fears for the future of the Kent coalfield. Figures released by the National Coal Board in January 1959 showed that the coalfield had lost £3,000,000 since Nationalisation. Betteshanger Colliery was particularly uneconomic, losing £1 1s. 0d. for every ton raised. There was, however, some cause for hope for the future as construction of a new power station had started at Richborough for which the coal at Betteshanger would prove particularly suitable. It would be some time though before the power station was completed and it was feared that work at Betteshanger might be suspended in the meantime. Betteshanger did not close but there was certainly no more talk of new pits being sunk in East Kent after 1959.

In September 1959 the *Railway Observer* reported that the use of diesel-electric shunters, with the exception of Nos. 15201-3, had been authorised for the East Kent line and conjectured that the 'O1's would soon be withdrawn. The end was not long in coming. In September 1960 the *Railway Observer* reported that the East Kent was now worked by 350 hp diesels. It was now possible to work the line with only one locomotive whereas the steam diagram had required two locomotives. The remaining 'O1's, Nos. 31048, 31065 and 31258, would be retained temporarily for shunting at Dover and one Monday turn at Shepherdswell. It is not clear when 'O1' working ceased altogether on the railway but No. 31048 was withdrawn and scrapped in October 1960, No. 31258 lasted until February 1961 and No. 31065 lasted until June 1961. Even then she was set aside at Ashford marked 'Condemned but not to be cut up' and thus survived to be purchased for preservation.

The passing of the 'O1s' came at a time when there was a possibility of increased activity on the railway. Falling coal sales had not been matched by any reduction in production in the Kent coalfield and the pits were having difficulty finding space for the unsold coal. In 1960 the National Coal Board identified the site of the EKR yard at Shepherdswell as an ideal location for storing this coal and relieving the congestion at the pitheads. Bulldozers moved onto the site and cleared any surviving traces of the locomotive and carriage sidings. At this point the residents of Shepherdswell erupted in protest at the prospect of dust and dirt from the tips. All work ceased while the question of planning permission was investigated. Fortunately 1960 saw much of the surplus coal sold and the plans to store it at Shepherdswell faded away.

Life on the railway changed little as the 1960s passed. Traffic to and from Tilmanstone Colliery continued in the capable but somewhat unexciting hands of the 0-6-0 diesel-electrics, later classified class '09'. Towards the end of the decade variety appeared on the line. A proposal to run a locomotive-hauled electric multiple unit on the branch as part of a Branch Line Society tour was unsuccessful, but on 19th November, 1967 a tour train did visit the line made up of Mark I carriages 'topped and tailed' by 'Crompton' Bo-Bo diesel electrics Nos. D6595 and D6585. A similar train using 'Cromptons' D6566 and D6568 ran over the branch on 3rd March, 1969 as part of the Locomotive Club of Great Britain's 'Invicta' Railtour.

BR class '73' electro-diesel No. 73108 crossing the road bridge on the Tilmanstone branch in July 1983. The bridge had been strengthened for these 75 ton locomotives.   *Norman Johnson*

One of the items of rolling stock brought to Shepherdswell by the preservation society in its early years was this Fowler 0-4-0 diesel-mechanical locomotive, Works No. 4160002 of 1952, seen here in August 1990.   *S.R. Garrett*

During 1968 approaches were made to both British Railways and the National Coal Board by the Kent & East Sussex Railway Association whose application for a Light Railway Order to re-open the Kent & East Sussex Railway had been refused. There was a very real possibility that the Association would have to find a new base for its operations at short notice. Both Shepherdswell and Tilmanstone were being considered as possible alternatives. Neither British Railways nor the NCB felt able to accommodate the KESR stock on the railway but, fortunately, legal action and negotiation eventually secured the Kent & East Sussex line for preservation.

On 27th July, 1969 Chislet Colliery closed as a result of geological difficulties. Although the Kent coalfield was by now recognised as being one of the most expensive areas operated by the National Coal Board there seems to have been no intention at this time to close the remaining pits. Investment continued in the coalfield to reduce the costs of coal production. One of these improvements was the replacement of much of the mineral branch to Betteshanger Colliery in 1976 by a conveyor belt system. Presumably Tilmanstone was considered too distant from the main line to consider a similar system. Instead a £200,000 programme began in 1977 to upgrade the rail facilities at Tilmanstone. As a result it became possible to increase train loadings and eventually to replace the diesel shunters used on the branch by class '73' electro-diesels. These could use their 600 hp diesel engines between Shepherdswell and Tilmanstone and then operate at 1,600 hp picking up electric current from the third rail on the main line. It was no longer necessary to allocate a locomotive to the branch as the electro-diesel could shuttle the 21 ton wagons to Shepherdswell 10 at a time and then depart with the complete train. In 1981 most of Tilmanstone's output was being carried to the RPCM cement works at Halling but by 1983 Tilmanstone was almost exclusively devoted to supplying Kingsnorth power station with pulverised coal fuel.

Tilmanstone Colliery and the railway serving it might have carried on in this fashion for some time but for the declaration of the National Coal Strike in 1984. Traffic on the line ceased on 1st March, 1984 and was never resumed. Tilmanstone did not re-open when the strike ended and was officially closed on 24th October, 1986. The site has been cleared completely since closure. Snowdown Colliery was closed a year later on 23rd October, 1987. Betteshanger Colliery did resume production but was itself closed in August 1989, a clear indication that Tilmanstone and Snowdown would not have survived for long even if there had been no strike.

This would have been the end of the story had it not been for the formation of the East Kent Railway Society with the aim of purchasing the line from Shepherdswell to Tilmanstone '. . . to construct a museum railway showing what it was like to travel on a Colonel Stephens type light railway'. By 1990 the Society had secured a lease on part of the site at Shepherdswell and on 24th June, 1995 an inaugural service ran from Shepherdswell to Eythorne formed of a two-car class '108' diesel multiple unit. It is hoped to re-open a further stretch of line to the site of Tilmanstone Colliery in due course.

Holman Stephens was once asked about the business side of his railway operations. He is reported to have replied, 'I don't make a lot of money but I get a lot of fun'. Long may the fun continue.

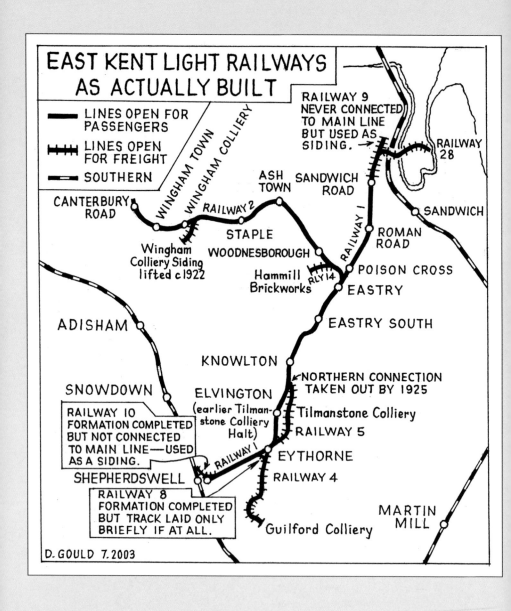

Chapter Fourteen

The Line as it was

Shepherdswell

Mention the name Shepherdswell to minor railway enthusiasts and you will be told that it was the terminus of the East Kent Light Railway. You may possibly also be told that it was the name of the adjoining station on the main line from Canterbury to Dover. Beyond this your informant is unlikely to go. Curiously when an effort is made to describe the place and its history without delving too deeply into parochial matters very little else seems to have been recorded.

Shepherdswell lies exactly six miles due north of the coast at a point about two miles east of Folkestone. The main line station stands close to the northern mouth of Lydden tunnel, 1 mile 609 yards long. During the boring of this tunnel, opened in 1861, a very small pocket of coal was found although the importance of this discovery was not appreciated at the time.

The name of the village has changed a number of times over the years. Very early on it was known as Siebertswould which later became Sibertswold meaning Sibert's Downs. Sibertswold still has official status but locally the next stage was to become Shebbert's Well. With the coming of the London Chatham & Dover Railway the village's station was named Shepherd's Well and remains so to this day, although local practice and the EKR favoured the single word Shepherdswell.

The main line at this point is some 300 feet above sea level and the connecting spur and EKR station and sidings are for the most part at around this level. The EKR track nevertheless has to climb up to the Eythorne Road at the far side of the site by the foot of what is known as North Bank.

As can be seen from the plan of the site, the EKR station platform is located on a spur almost at a right angle to the main line. It was originally intended to construct a Dover-facing junction with the main line but this would have interfered considerably with the SECR's goods yard and down platform. It is tempting to suppose that the platform spur was originally laid in as part of this junction and that the connecting portion was never completed. This is unlikely as a connecting curve from the East Kent platform to the SECR would have been too sharp to operate. It is more probable that the spur was added as an afterthought at the closest convenient point to the main line station.

The platform spur has always had a parallel siding, mainly used for stabling empty stock, which may have originally been intended to form a run-round loop when finance permitted. This was never done and running round has always required the use of one of the loops on the main running line. However, since such an operation would get in the way of the more remunerative business of coal traffic, the East Kent tended to avoid running round altogether. Instead passenger trains would halt at the entrance to the yard where the carriage brakes would be applied. The locomotive would then uncouple and run to the locomotive sidings.

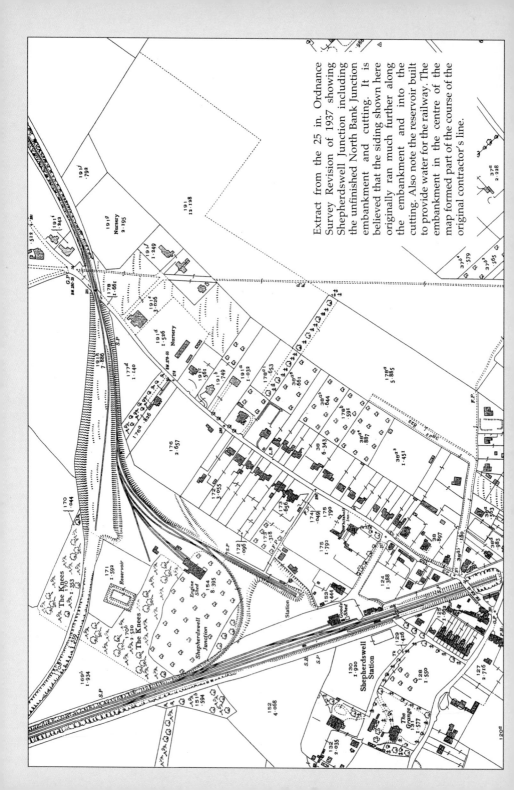

Extract from the 25 in. Ordnance Survey Revision of 1937 showing Shepherdswell Junction including the unfinished North Bank Junction embankment and cutting. It is believed that the siding shown here originally ran much further along the embankment and into the cutting. Also note the reservoir built to provide water for the railway. The embankment in the centre of the map formed part of the course of the original contractor's line.

An aerial view of Shepherds Well main line station and Shepherdswell EKR station and yard in 1968. The course of the incomplete connection to the main line can be made out running across the top of this view.

Simmons Aerofilms

Shepherd's Well station in SECR days looking towards Lydden tunnel.

M. Lawson Finch Collection

The original layout of Shepherdswell station and yard in the early 1920s. Points to note are the two buildings on the platform flanking the approach footpath, the engine shed extension under construction, the presence of three locomotives, Nos. 4, 3 and 5 and what appears to be the wreck of two Tilmanstone colliery wagons to the left of bogie carriage No. 1. The northern embankment appears to be occupied by contractor's tipping wagons.

Colonel Stephens Railway Museum

The points were then set for the platform road, the carriage brakes would be released and the carriage would run down the gradient into the platform road by gravity. On the last train of the day it seems to have been a point of honour to complete this task with maximum speed and to have the train and station locked up in the least possible time. Despite the obvious risks involved the only serious smash occurred during World War II when a train was propelled into the platform road without taking account of the presence there of a train of War Department stock. During the 1930s it was not uncommon for trains to ignore the platform altogether and to start from the running line itself. The late Dr Ian C. Allen used to recall his surprise at being invited to leave the platform and make his way across the tracks to join the train in the yard.

Shepherdswell station was quite well equipped with buildings in view of the shortage of passengers presenting themselves there. In 1920 there were two small wooden sheds on the platform, one on each side of the platform entrance, which presumably did duty as booking office and waiting room. When a new footpath was built providing more direct access to the platform from the main line station a new wooden building was erected at the near end of the platform. This consisted of two sheds facing each other with a roof and rear wall filling the gap between them. This style of building was used elsewhere on the line but the building created at Shepherdswell had a less makeshift appearance than the others. A timetable was displayed on one end for the use of intending passengers. Passengers relenting of their intention to travel could take advantage of the invitation displayed on one corner of the building: YOU MAY TELEPHONE FROM HERE. In the absence of a coin box it was necessary for the booking clerk to ascertain the cost of calls from the operator.

Behind the platform stood a round corrugated iron building with a conical roof. An identical building stood in the goods yard at Wingham Canterbury Road and further examples were used on the Shropshire & Montgomeryshire Light Railway as offices and camping huts. They were War Department surplus bargains snapped up by the prudent Holman Stephens. The Shepherdswell specimen was painted red and had a vent at the apex of its roof that suggested the possibility of housing poultry. The building seems to have served at first as a waiting room and then as a depository for a decaying mass of old company papers of all descriptions. Today these would be furiously haggled over by collectors but in those days one only glanced in and wondered.

The main office for the whole line, apart from the general offices at Tonbridge and the premises of the various Secretaries, was a long wooden building set on blocks and sited on a bank looking down on the platform. This was reached by a cinder path from the booking office. Behind the office building and concealed amongst the trees was a brick building with a corrugated iron roof. This was provided with two sets of double doors and inside were two inspection pits. It had originally served as a garage but later became a dry store for wooden patterns. These included a pattern for a locomotive cylinder block providing for two inside cylinders complete with both piston valve chests. Nearby stood a wooden 'bungalow' let to one of the railway's staff.

The actual junction with the SECR was a sharply curved Canterbury-facing line joining one of the main line company's sidings at a point 273 yards north of

8160 SHEPHERD'S WELL

Shepherdswell platform in 1926. The new station building erected at the western end of the platform was accessed directly from the main line station by a cinder footpath.

Shepherdswell platform in 1948 with a clear view of the round corrugated iron shed.

Shepherdswell platform from across the tracks in 1936, giving a clear view of the line's office building looking down on the platform.

The Shepherdswell 'garage'. At one time it housed Arthur and Malcolm Burr's motor cars but was later used for pattern storage.

This was the sharp curve connecting the main line yard to the East Kent. The sign prohibiting engines heavier than 'C' class was erected by British Railways but there is no evidence that 'C' class locomotives ever made their way onto the East Kent.   *B.S. Plummer*

The main line end of the 'high capacity' route to the East Kent which was never completed.
                                                                                    B.S. Plummer

the SECR station. The sharpness of this curve always restricted the classes of locomotives that could work onto the East Kent.

At the boundary point on this line a large notice board was maintained which warned that no vehicles were to pass that point without authority. The general practice was for through wagons to be shunted onto the line by an engine of one company and to be collected by an engine of the other. This procedure led to a number of instances of minor disagreement between the servants of the two companies concerned. One day the EKR single coach train arrived at Shepherdswell where the driver observed that a lengthy rake of empty coal wagons was occupying the connecting line awaiting collection and transfer to Tilmanstone. The driver lost no time in dropping his coach off and coupling up to the wagons. Although the train was somewhat longer than usual it surprised the driver that his engine failed to move when he opened the regulator. This was not, however, an unusual event on the East Kent so the driver adopted his usual tactics for such situations. This consisted of easing the wagons back so as to create some slack in their couplings, the trick then being to snatch the train into motion with a rapid opening of the regulator. With a practised hand the regulator was flung open at the appropriate moment and, much as expected, the engine surged forward. What was less expected was that the locomotive's progress was accompanied by a frightening splintering sound as one of the wagons disintegrated into scrap. Apparently the Southern driver had been admonished the previous day for passing the sign without permission. On this occasion he was sitting in his cab taking no chances and his locomotive with its brakes full on was still coupled to the far end of the train!

Another tale in the same vein concerned the day that a Southern driver sent three wagons round the curve onto the EKR without prior notice. They would normally have come to rest on the running line to be collected in the usual manner. On this occasion, however, the East Kent locomotive happened to be standing on the running line at the other end of the curve while its crew ate their breakfast on the footplate. Upset at the rude interruption to his meal by the sudden impact of the unexpected wagons, the driver seems to have lost his usual composure and promptly shot the wagons back whence they had come. Unfortunately this was done at greater speed than was safe for the curve and the wagons came to grief as they spread themselves generously over Southern Railway property. At this point our informant's narrative closed so that the names of those involved remain a mystery.

Curiously a much easier alignment for the connection to the main line had long existed but was never used. This was by a siding which trailed into the running line immediately beyond the Eythorne Road from an embankment which led back to the SECR formation some 600 yards north of the existing junction by means of a cutting. This was authorised as Line 10 in the original Light Railway Order and would not only have provided an easier link with the SECR but would, if completed as planned, have provided a marshalling area on top of the embankment eight tracks wide. In the absence of any substantial development of the coal traffic the East Kent decided that further investment in this link was unnecessary. A signal cabin had been built by the Southern on the up side of the main line to control the junction with this line, but it was never

Shepherdswell yard *c.* 1933 with locomotives Nos. 6 and 4 between duties. The earlier extended engine shed is still standing as is the row of cisterns to water the locomotives. As usual the carriage siding is filled with surplus stock.

Shepherdswell yard *c.* 1947 showing the replacement engine shed. The cisterns have gone with water now supplied from a reservoir behind the trees on the right. The carriage fleet is now much reduced.

brought into operation and was eventually dismantled in 1948. For most of its life it was used as a store by lengthmen. Track was originally laid for the entire length of the embankment and through the cutting up to the SECR siding but no connection was ever made. Much of this track was subsequently lifted and the remaining length was used to store empty stock and in later years to break up withdrawn stock. It was known as North Bank siding.

The main operational feature of Shepherdswell Yard was the presence of two parallel sidings joined at each end to the running line, effectively two running-round loops. In theory these enabled incoming wagons to stand on one loop and outgoing loaded wagons to stand on the other. But actual practice was often complicated by the presence on one or both of the loops of the East Kent's own internal wagons and vans. Integrating the collection and onward dispatch to Tilmanstone of empty coal wagons with the assembly and outward dispatch of loaded coal wagons, while handling the railway's own internal traffic and the general goods traffic onto and away from the railway must have called for some intricate shunting. This would have become even more complicated during the period when coal from Snowdown was transported through to Richborough. One can see why the railway tried to avoid having to run-round passenger trains in addition to the above movements, though there was an additional crossover between the running line and the inner loop siding in the early days which was obviously intended for just this purpose. It should be added that in the absence of any sort of goods dock or loading platform the passenger platform could serve this purpose between passenger turns.

A point on the outer goods loop served a single siding that was used for the storage and repair of carriages and wagons. A point at the start of this siding served three further sidings roughly parallel with each other and with the goods loops. One of these was used for the storage and repair of locomotives whilst the other two ran into the locomotive shed. In the early days a hoist was provided shortly before the two locomotive shed sidings diverged. In later years lifting was carried out by jacking and packing assisted by the use of the railway's rail-mounted crane.

Originally there was a small wooden locomotive shed capable of holding only two engines. In 1920 a somewhat taller extension was added in front of this enabling a further two locomotives to be housed under cover. This was also built of wood and was without doors. On several occasions the end of the original shed had to be rebuilt as a result of wagons being propelled through it. By 1934 the original shed had been demolished and a wood-framed structure clad with corrugated asbestos began to take its place. This had been completed by 1936. It was then the turn of the 1920 extension to be demolished and a slightly longer structure to the same dimensions as the replacement for the original shed was built in its place. This work was completed by the end of the year and gave the railway a remarkably smart and commodious building capable of housing all the railway's locomotives under cover.

'Smart and commodious' could hardly describe the various workshops around the locomotive shed. 'Makeshift and cluttered' would describe them better. Built onto the northern side of the locomotive shed was a long brick building housing the railway's main workshop and smithy. This building also

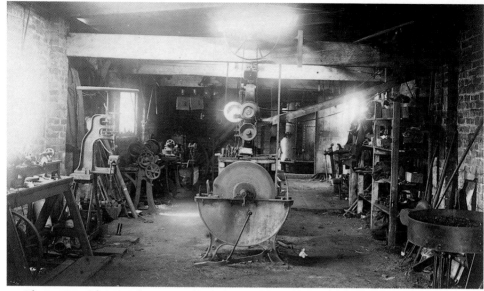

The interior of the workshop built alongside the engine shed. The vertical boiler at the rear drove the various items of machinery by a complicated system of belts and shafts.

Colonel Stephens Railway Museum

0-6-0T No. 4 working hard to lift its train of empties away from Shepherdsell yard. Wagons stored on the North Bank siding are just visible behind No. 4's train.   *Dr Ian C. Allen*

housed a vertical boiler which drove most of the workshop equipment by a series of belts. The boiler also supplied power for the railway's electrical needs by means of a dynamo. Unfortunately the boiler was rarely able to maintain working pressure for any sustained period. This was not only unfortunate for the workshop but also for the adjoining carpenter's shop whose circular saw was driven by a further belt running from a drive wheel on the outside of the workshop wall. An even more peculiar feature of the carpenter's shop was that it was built above a large sunken water tank, the presence of whose contents was all too apparent to anyone working there. This tank supplied water to a collection of cisterns mounted on wooden trestles alongside the line outside the locomotive shed. These provided the locomotives' water supply. During the 1930s these were replaced by a covered reservoir built on higher ground behind the yard. The reservoir was fed with water from a deep well by means of an 8 hp Lister oil engine and was able to supply water by gravity to two standpipe water cranes, one alongside the locomotive siding and one alongside the running line. Just behind the row of cisterns were two further ramshackle wooden buildings. One was the platelayers' headquarters and the other was described to the company's insurers as 'the open-fronted fitters' shop'. To complete the scene the area between the locomotive shed and the carriage siding was usually occupied by spare pieces of trackwork, bridge girders, gates and fencework awaiting erection and parts of locomotives under repair or in course of demolition.

All in all Shepherdswell had a great deal to interest the observer. There may have been long periods of inactivity between the arrival and departure of trains but there was quite often a locomotive in steam over by the shed. With luck a little shunting might be in progress and the cries of the pointsman, clanging of buffers and bustling of the duty shunting engine were borne clearly across the still air of the surrounding woods.

During the years before 1939 a visit to Shepherdswell usually included a view of engine No. 4 standing in the sidings some way off awaiting its next trip to Tilmanstone. A feather of steam would just be visible at her safety valves from which emanated an insistent high-pitched buzzing which seemed to reach the ear from all directions simultaneously. Many years ago a very young and serious lady said she thought that this noise was made by the 'sun shining on the engine'. Be that as it may the noise was not unpleasant and to those whose senses feel pleasure in such a setting this was in every way a most satisfying scene.

Shepherdswell to Eythorne

Trains leaving Shepherdswell did so on a climbing gradient to the Eythorne Road. Shortly before reaching the road a sign was erected by British Railways on the right-hand side of the line reading 'ALL ENGINES HEAVIER THAN 'O' CLASS ARE PROHIBITED FROM WORKING BEYOND THIS POINT'. On the left hand side of the line the North Bank siding eased down to meet the running line just beyond the ungated level crossing. The line climbed a little further and

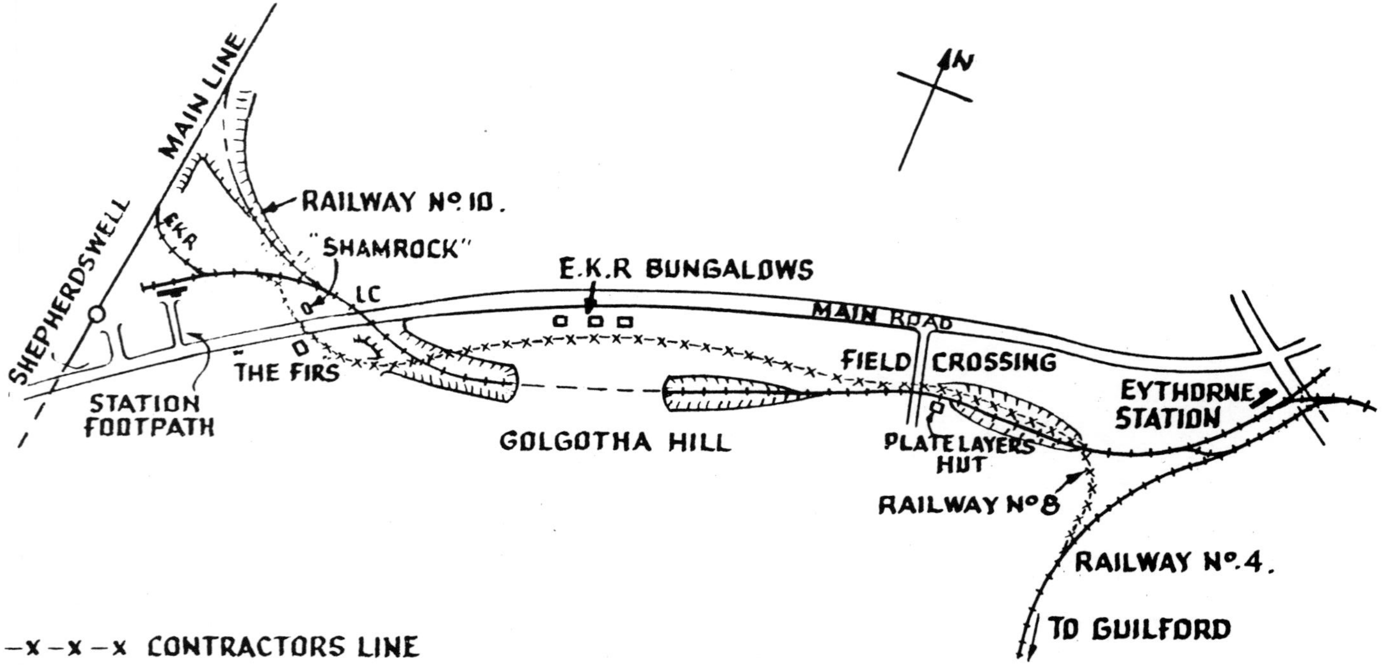

M. Lawson Finch

DIAGRAM OF CONTRACTORS LINE

−x−x−x CONTRACTORS LINE

MAIN LINE

SHEPHERDSWELL

RAILWAY Nº 10.

"SHAMROCK"

E.K.R

LC

THE FIRS

STATION
FOOTPATH

E.K.R BUNGALOWS

MAIN ROAD

FIELD CROSSING

GOLGOTHA HILL

PLATE LAYERS
HUT

RAILWAY Nº 8.

EYTHORNE
STATION

RAILWAY Nº 4.

TO GUILFORD

N

then began a steady descent as it entered the cutting taking it to Golgotha tunnel. The cutting was built with steep sides through the chalk and was notorious for the frequency of chalk falls. Had the line ever been doubled it would have been necessary to carry out very substantial additional excavation.

The formation of the cutting widens as it approaches the western portal of the tunnel which was built to accommodate double track. The bricks used to construct the portals and to line the tunnel came from the Pluckley brickworks, purchased by Kent Coal Concessions to provide bricks for the railway and the various collieries it was to serve. However, for economy's sake the tunnel was only fully lined for a short distance at each end. Between these two points a shoulder of chalk was left standing on either side to support the brickwork lining the roof. On the left-hand side refuges are cut into the chalk for the safety of platelayers and others working in the tunnel. On the right-hand side the formation of the second line that was never built is still occupied by massive blocks of chalk. The tunnel is 477 yards long and falls steadily throughout its length at 1 in 100. This called for hard work by locomotives hauling loaded coal trains to Shepherdswell and conditions on the footplate were unenviable to say the least. It is recalled by staff that one heavily-loaded train once came up through the tunnel double-headed with the crew of the second engine only able to avoid asphyxiation by lying on the footplate with sacking over their heads.

The railway also owned the land above the tunnel and the initial temporary contractor's line passed over the hill in order to connect Tilmanstone with the main line as quickly as possible. It is apparently still possible to trace the track of the contractor's line by the presence in the soil of a densely compacted pathway of hardcore that formed the original trackbed. In the 1930s the railway put some of its property above the tunnel to good use by erecting three 'bungalows', which were let cheaply to members of the railway's staff who could not otherwise find affordable accommodation within easy reach of the line.

The tunnel's eastern portal was succeeded by a further length of cutting but this was generally more shallow and less afflicted by falling chalk than that on the Shepherdswell side. At this point the falling gradient went from 1 in 100 to 1 in 75 for a short distance. The cutting runs for about 600 yards and ends shortly before an occupation crossing. It is believed that this is the point where the permanent line joined the tracks of the temporary line trailing in from the left and this was also the point where Railway 8 would have set off to the right to complete a triangular junction with Railway 4, the Guilford branch. A quarter-mile beyond this the line passes Eythorne Court on the left and shortly afterwards enters Eythorne station.

Eythorne (1 m. 52 ch., 30 l.)

Eythorne station was actually located in Lower Eythorne, the proper settlement of Eythorne being on higher ground to the south. Eythorne is pleasantly located but has few claims to historical fame. The *Homeland Handbook* for 'Dover, Kent, With Its Surroundings', published in 1915, had only this to say about Eythorne: 'To the North West of Waldershare, about a mile and a half

Top: The Shepherdswell end of Golgotha tunnel showing the steep sides to the cutting. Winter frosts could cause serious falls of chalk in this cutting. One of the East Kent bungalows can be seen above the tunnel mouth.

Centre: The cutting at the Eythorne end of Golgotha tunnel was shallower than at the other end. The silhouette of the uncut blocks of chalk within the tunnel can just be made out.

Right: The East Kent never needed to double its tracks through Golgotha tunnel so the uncut chalk remains there to this day. *S.R. Garrett*

from its church, is Eythorne, noted for its healthy air and the delightful prospects from the gently rising hills'. For the railway enthusiast Eythorne not only offered glimpses over the skyline of the Tilmanstone winding stocks but should have become one of the focal points of the EKR network. However, new collieries and the like were not universally welcomed by everyone. *Black's Guidebook to East Kent*, also published in 1915, said of Eythorne: '. . . a fine farmhouse is on the right, ½ mile short of the village; and the hideous chalk "spoil banks" of Tilmanstone Colliery are painfully conspicuous in front'.

Two branches ran off the EKR at Eythorne, to Tilmanstone and Guilford respectively. The Guilford branch only ever carried construction and demolition traffic but could have carried coal from Maydensole or coal to Stonehall if Railways 12 and 13 had been built, as well as traffic from the Alkham Valley if Railway 23 had been built. There was also the possibility of traffic to Deal and coal from Ripple if Railways 11, 16, 19 and 37 had been built. Even the Tilmanstone branch had originally been intended to run beyond Tilmanstone Colliery to the outskirts of Northbourne where the coal eventually mined at Betteshanger might have been mined instead. There is also the possibility that Railway 12 might have been extended beyond Maydensole to link up with the Martin Mill Tramway, and so bring the EKR to Dover Harbour, or that Railway 23 could have linked up with the Channel Tunnel beyond Drellingore. The grand total of all these railways is in the region of 35 miles about half of which were authorised and all of which would have met at Eythorne.

Alas, there were never to be any day returns from Wingham to Paris via Eythorne and the station managed happily with its single 200 ft platform on the left-hand of the line. This had a brick face and was surfaced with cinders. For many years a single siding at the rear of this platform sufficed, but a second siding was laid in alongside this for the War Department's use during World War II. Shortly before these sidings a point gave access to a loop on the right into which the Guilford branch ran. The loop and the 'main line' continued alongside each other across the ungated level crossing beyond the end of the platform. The Tilmanstone branch then veered off to the right to link up with the loop line, while the main line ran straight ahead before beginning a steady curve to the left. It can be seen that the loop was built to serve the operational needs of the Tilmanstone branch rather than the main line. Quite how all the other proposed branches and their traffic would have fitted into the relatively limited confines of the Eythorne site is unclear. For some time Eythorne was shown in the timetables as 'Station for Guilford Colliery'.

In the 1920s the platform was served by a pair of small wooden buildings. One was horizontally boarded and stood lengthwise along the platform while the other was vertically boarded and stood at right angles to the platform. There was also a small brick building alongside the level crossing. In later years Eythorne acquired one of the only two brick station buildings on the railway. This was a more substantial version of the platform building at Shepherdswell, effectively consisting of two end rooms with a sheltered waiting space between. During World War II the platform was reduced to half its previous length in order to create space for access to the new siding.

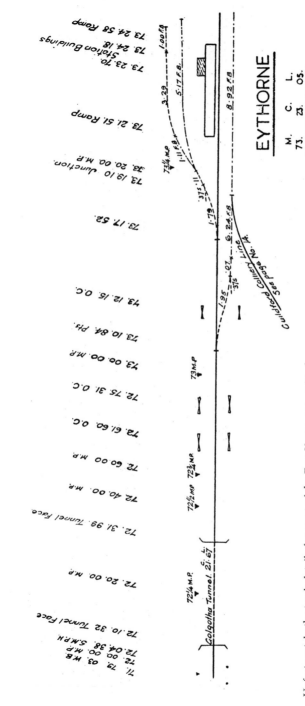

Unfortunately the track details for most of the East Kent were omitted from the Ordnance Survey Revision of 1937/38 as they were lost during bombing of Southampton. Fortunately British Railways drew up detailed diagrammatic plans of the railway in 1948. Mileage is shown from London (Victoria).

Eythorne station in the 1920s with the original wooden station buildings.

Colonel Stephens Railway Museum

Eythorne station looking towards Tilmanstone in 1939 with a brick station building.

Eythorne station in the 1950s showing how much the platform was shortened during World War II.

The branch to Tilmanstone is shown veering off to the right beyond the level crossing. The wooden shed behind the signal in the centre of this view was built to house the motorised trolley pictured on page 242.

Before the platform was shortened the station possessed three wooden post signals, one at each end of the platform and another at the divergence of the line to Tilmanstone. The first to go was the one at the Shepherdswell end of the platform to make way for the siding and the other two were replaced in the 1940s. The remaining platform signal was replaced by a shorter lattice post signal and the Tilmanstone branch signal was replaced by a tubular metal post pattern. Both of these had been removed by 1954. Eythorne was for many years the end of the first block section and it was here that the tablet was handed in and the key taken out.

Eythorne to Eastry

Three-quarters of a mile beyond Eythorne was the 100 ft-long brick-faced platform of Elvington Halt (2 m. 28 ch. 11 l.). Tilmanstone Colliery could be seen away to the right. This halt was shown on the earliest maps as Tilmanstone Colliery Halt and was referred to in the first timetable of 1916 simply as Tilmanstone Colliery. It remained so described until 1926 when it briefly bore the title Tilmanstone Halt. In 1927 it became Elvington Halt.

These changes were due to the vagaries of the passenger traffic to the Colliery. Up to the end of World War I it seems that the mine workers had to alight at Tilmanstone Colliery Halt and then enjoy a 10 minute walk to the pit head. In 1918 a platform was constructed in the Colliery yard and certain trains either terminated or started from here. These trains were specifically for the colliery workers and employed the older carriages acquired from the Kent & East Sussex and the London Chatham & Dover four-wheelers. The decrepit state of these carriages was mitigated by the cheap fares available on these trains. Since the Tilmanstone branch had never been passed for passenger traffic it was convenient to retain the name Tilmanstone Colliery for the halt and to show the trains actually destined for the real colliery as terminating or starting at Eythorne with an ambiguous footnote, 'Runs to or from Tilmanstone Colliery when required'.

During 1925 the effects of a bus service operating from Dover to the colliery were beginning to be felt and the rail traffic began to decline. In 1927 the name Elvington was adopted after the nearby miners' housing estate begun by the Burrs and extended by Tilden Smith. Workmen's trains continued to run into the Colliery yard until 1929 when the service ceased altogether. This resulted from the colliery ceasing its £1 daily subsidy for the workmen's service, which may in turn have been the result of the railway adding the following gratuitous footnote to its entry in *Bradshaw*: 'Do not run during stoppages at Tilmanstone Colliery'. This was a period of considerable acrimony between the railway and the colliery owing to the latter's construction of its ropeway to Dover.

Neither Elvington nor the yard platform was ever staffed but Elvington was at least provided with a small open-fronted shelter clad and roofed in either corrugated iron or asbestos. This appears to have been a later addition and deviated from the normal range of wooden sheds and chalet-type structures usually found on the line. The shelter appears to have been removed or to have

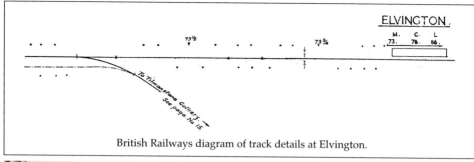

British Railways diagram of track details at Elvington.

Elvington Halt after closure. The wooden waiting shelter had gone long before passenger services ceased.   *M. Lawson Finch Collection*

Holman Stephens (*third from left*) on a visit to Elvington miners' village.
                                          Colonel Stephens Railway Museum

fallen down before 1948 as it does not appear on the plans drawn up by British Railways in April of that year. Originally it was intended to name the halt as Elmton after a nearby farm.

About half a mile beyond Elvington the northern end of the Tilmanstone Colliery branch curved in alongside the main line and at one time formed a junction here facing Eastry. This had originally been laid in to carry coal from Tilmanstone to Richborough for onward transport by sea. The long delayed completion of the Richborough branch left this connection with little purpose and it was lifted at some time in the 1920s. The junction is clearly shown on the 1920 Railway Clearing House map of Southern England. The Railway Clearing House also quoted mileages to Tilmanstone Colliery from both directions. In July 1943 the railway Directors received a request from Tilmanstone Colliery to reinstate the junction at the Colliery North Bank and to put in a connection with the Southern near Richborough. The Directors advised the colliery to approach the Ministry of War Transport to finance the project. Nothing more was heard of this matter.

The junction took the form of a spur from the Colliery branch connecting to a long loop on the main line. The loop was provided with a short shunting neck at its southern end. The Colliery branch itself continued to run parallel to the main line for a considerable distance. On a surviving plan this parallel section is referred to as LONG SIDING HOLDING EMPTY WD WAGGONS. This was a reference to the ROD vans that were purchased by the colliery with a view to conversion into spoil wagons. The scheme was apparently unsuccessful as they stood on this section of line for a period well into the 1930s when they were presumably scrapped.

Just over a mile beyond Elvington stood Knowlton Halt (3 m. 40 ch. 24 l.). In the October 1916 Timetable this was named as Tilmanstone Village & Knowlton Halt. It was in fact almost midway between these two villages and somewhat closer to Tilmanstone than Elvington was when it was known as Tilmanstone Halt. In the 1917 Timetable it had become Knowlton and remained so from then on. No mention is made of this halt in Major Pringle's inspection of the line in September 1916. It would not, however, have taken long to construct as it consisted of a short platform faced with sleepers and a tiny shelter of singular appearance. This was an open-fronted wooden shed with the roof extending over the front to provide a rudimentary awning as a sort of reminder of the correct thing to be found at more substantial establishments. The awning was renewed once or twice in the halt's lifetime. With each renewal the saw-toothed edging acquired a much coarser pitch due, no doubt, to the increasing tempo of modern times. A similar structure was erected at Ash Town.

According to Len Lawrence, a member of the railway's staff, most of the wooden buildings up and down the line were supplied by Messrs Brisley Bros of Ash. It is a tribute to their workmanship that most of them outlasted the railway. Specific examples of these buildings were those at Eythorne, Staple and Wingham. It should be noted that the East Kent moved buildings from station to station as necessity demanded.

Knowlton was the somewhat inconvenient alighting point for Betteshanger House, the seat of Lord Northbourne on whose land the Betteshanger Colliery

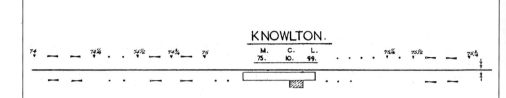

British Railways diagram of track details at Knowlton.

Knowlton Halt in 1926.   *M. Lawson Finch Collection*

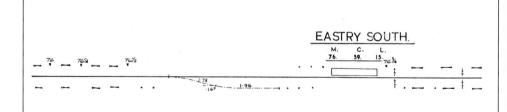

British Railways diagram of track details at Hernden siding and Eastry South.

was later built. Whilst there is no evidence that Lord Northbourne ever made use of the halt, it was generally believed that it was established as a diplomatic gesture towards the noble gentleman. In the absence of such august patronage Knowlton attracted little custom from the general public. This is not surprising when it is considered that the *ABC Railway Guide* for May 1935 gave the population of Knowlton as 16.

Beyond Knowlton the line eased down into a secluded valley. The course of the line is still clearly visible from the lane running along the ridge of the eastern flank of this valley. It is easy to conjure up the delightful prospect of a short mixed train, headed perhaps by locomotive No. 3, pacing easily through the meadows. Passing the village of Hernden on the left the line encountered a spur of higher ground through which a cutting was excavated. Emerging into full view at the end of this cutting the line threw off a short siding to the right. This was Hernden siding. The installation of this siding was approved by the Board of Trade in January 1918 out of consideration for the needs of local farmers. It could hold about six wagons and stood alongside a quarry-like excavation in the chalk hillside. It received regular loads of fertilisers, seeds and other farming essentials. In the season large quantities of sugar beet were shipped out and even larger quantities of oats destined for the breweries at Burton-on-Trent. Besides catering for agricultural traffic the siding was also used for the delivery of granite to be fashioned into paving setts by the inmates of the nearby Eastry Workhouse.

Just beyond Hernden siding the line crossed the road to Eastry. On the opposite side of this road the platform of Eastry South Halt (5 m. 8 ch. 60 l.) was located on the left-hand side of the line. Unfortunately, a sharp bend in the road on the Eastry side and the combined effect of the cutting, roadside hedges and the sharp angle of approach on the Hernden side made the level crossing here the scene of a number of accidents. The halt was not opened until 1925. Its wooden platform with its one plank seat was never staffed, nor was any passenger shelter ever erected.

Beyond Eastry South the line had another half-mile to run before reaching Eastry station. This final stretch ran through irregularly contoured land and required some excavation of cuttings. During the railway's lifetime this was an open and sometimes windswept stretch but the trackbed is now quite well wooded.

Eastry Station (5 m. 47 ch. 96 l.)

Eastry, 5 miles from Shepherdswell, was possibly the most important passenger station on the EKR after Shepherdswell. Had the passenger service on the Richborough branch ever developed it might have become an important passenger junction but the few trains that did run through to Sandwich Road were really only extensions of trains that would otherwise have terminated at Eastry. It would have taken an extremely patient passenger to have contemplated travelling from Sandwich Road to Ash or Wingham via Eastry as the train would first return to Shepherdswell before setting out again for Wingham.

Hernden siding looking towards Eastry. The siding is unusually well filled.
Colonel Stephens Railway Museum

Eastry South Halt with few concessions to passenger comfort.

Eastry is of considerable archaeological and historical importance. It was once the home of the Kings of Kent and the surrounding area is rich in Roman and Saxon remains. For the railway its importance was to be found in its not inconsiderable population for the area, 1,457 in 1935, and a modest selection of shops which drew in some passenger traffic from the other villages through which the railway passed. It must be admitted that we are not talking of crowds of passengers here, but of the difference between trains with some passengers and trains with none.

The attractions of Eastry to the travelling public were diminished by the fact that it was a station built strictly for the able-bodied. Not only was it no nearer to the heart of Eastry than was Eastry South, but the only access to the station was by a steep footpath down to a narrow lane, lacking any sort of pavement, and subject to surface water in wet periods. Unsuspecting passengers who placed faith in the railway's timetable description 'Eastry for Sandwich' would have needed even greater reserves of energy for the brisk walk of over two miles to the latter destination.

Eastry was never lavishly equipped but at opening in 1916 it was as basic as any of the other stations on the line. It possessed a brick-faced platform, 170 feet long, on the right-hand side of its single line, a double-ended wooden platform building similar to that at Shepherdswell and no sidings. Since some trains terminated here from the earliest days it is probable that these would proceed down the Sandwich Road branch as far as Eastry (Goods) to run round in the loop there. This would also have enabled vans and wagons to be delivered to and collected from Eastry (Goods).

The problem was solved by the installation of a passing loop in or about 1920. This was accompanied by the installation of a second-hand lever frame to control the points and signals. The state of this frame gave Colonel Mount some concern when he inspected the site in 1925 as it was insecurely mounted and its locking was defective. The frame was housed in a wooden shed that was burned down in or about 1937 and replaced by a new shed with a pent roof. An old van body stood close to the signal cabin, presumably for the use of the permanent way gangs who kept two lengthmen's trolleys at the station. The platform was equipped with two oil lamps, the usual style of rudimentary plank seat and, somewhat incongruously considering the difficulties of access to the station, a porter's hand truck.

Eastry was well equipped with signals. Approaching the station there was a tall signal post on the left-hand side with two arms, the upper arm was for the platform line and the lower and somewhat shorter arm was for the loop. On the right-hand side was a signal for the platform line. Just beyond the far end of the platform was another pair of signal arms on a single post. The upper arm was for the Wingham branch and the lower arm, of a corrugated pattern, was for the Richborough branch. There were further signals on the two branches protecting access to the junction.

By 1951 British Railways had removed the points at the far end of the loop leaving the loop as a siding. It may have served some purpose as a storage siding during the demolition of the line but, in the absence of road access to the station, it would have been of little use for goods purposes.

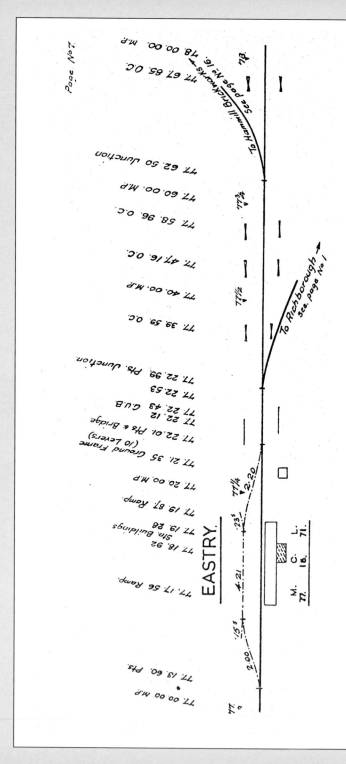

Page No 7.

British Railways diagram of track details at Eastry. For diagram purposes the line to Wingham is shown as running straight ahead with the Richborough line curving to the right. In reality the Wingham line curved to the left and the Richborough line ran straight ahead.

Eastry station with its original signal cabin. The Richborough line runs straight ahead while the Wingham line curves to the left. *M. Lawson Finch Collection*

Eastry station with the later signal cabin. The wooden footway across the tracks leads to a steep path down to the adjacent road - the only means of access to the station. *M. Lawson Finch Collection*

Looking back at Eastry station from beyond the bridge over the Selson Road. The bridge was built for two tracks but only ever carried one.   *M. Lawson Finch Collection*

View of the junction beyond Eastry. Defective interlocking meant that trains for Wingham were sometimes directed onto the Richborough branch instead.   *R.F. Roberts*

Above: 0-6-0ST No. 2 stands on the bridge at Eastry.

Left: Something of a luxury at a station without proper access - EKR sack barrow at Eastry.

Ralph Gillam Collection

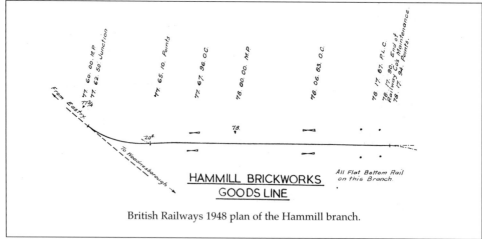

British Railways 1948 plan of the Hammill branch.

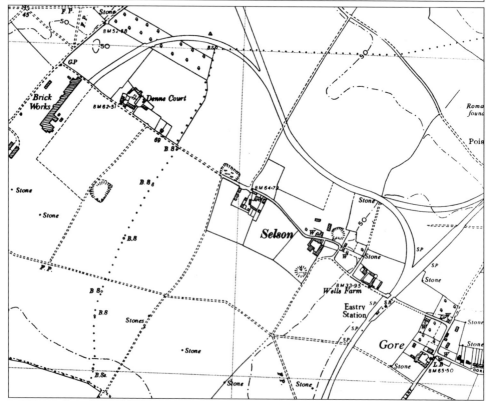

Extract from the 25 in. Ordnance Survey Revision of 1937 (track details missing) showing the trackbed of the Hammill branch curving away from Railway No. 2, *top centre*. The map also shows part of the course of the uncompleted triangle at Eastry.

Just beyond the station was a bridge over the lane between Eastry and Hammill. This was built for two tracks although only one was ever laid. In 1916 the tracks were supported between the brick abutments on heavy timber beams which were subsequently replaced by girders. There were metal handrails on either side of the bridge. This was the only bridge on the passenger-carrying section of the railway, although a very similar structure was to be found on the Tilmanstone branch.

Almost immediately beyond the bridge the Wingham branch veered off to the left while the Richborough branch set a straight line towards Poison Cross. Both branches were raised on substantial embankments which are still standing today providing homes for a substantial population of rabbits. For the purposes of this description of the line we shall take the left-hand fork and head for Wingham.

Between Eastry and Staple

The terms 'Overland Route' and 'Paddy Line' seem to have been applied variously to the full length of line from Eythorne to Wingham and to just the section between Eastry and Wingham. The origin of both terms is obscure though guesses can be made. The Wingham branch would have provided access to Canterbury and the outside world 'overland' as opposed to the access by water that could have been obtained by the Richborough branch. For 'Paddy Line' a variety of suggestions can be made. Trains serving collieries have been known as 'paddy trains' the length and breadth of the country. Equally there may have been an influx of Irish workmen into the area for the construction of the railway and the collieries and there was certainly a continuing Irish association with Staple station in particular. The term 'Overland Route' seems to have been confined to the railway's staff whilst 'Paddy Line' was in general use throughout the neighbourhood.

The Wingham branch curved sharply to the left immediately beyond the road bridge outside Eastry station. Originally it was planned to follow an easier curve and the junction would have been about mid-way between Eastry and Eastry South but this was one of the sections of the original proposals to be deleted following objections. Since no new Eastry-facing connection was ever proposed to the Light Railway Commissioners it has been argued that this section of line was never actually authorised. It was, however, inspected and approved by Colonel Pringle in 1916 and the authorities never seem to have questioned its legality.

About half a mile from the junction a short line branched off to the left. This was originally built to serve Woodnesborough Colliery but only came into its own with the construction in 1926 of the Hammill Brickworks on the colliery site. This branch was renowned for the 'elephant grass' covering its tracks, which gave the innocent observer the impression that EKR trains were in the habit of abandoning the rails and striding off through the fields. The branch was just under half a mile long and curved through nearly 90 degrees to reach the old colliery site. It was a surface line and climbed steadily to the mid-point of the

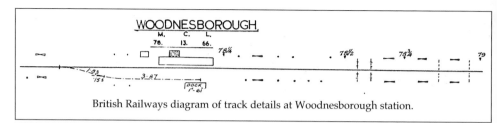

British Railways diagram of track details at Woodnesborough station.

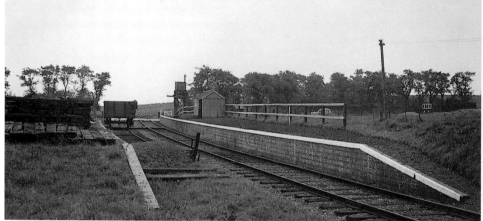

Woodnesborough station looking towards Eastry. Note the location of the water tank next to the level crossing, and economical 'buffer stop' beside the goods platform.   *M. Lawson Finch Collection*

Woodnesborough station with original water tank. The photograph shows how the siding was accessed from points on the Eastry side of the level crossing. The van conceals the loading bank which stood opposite the station building.

curve and then descended to cross the Selson Road on the level. It was sometimes necessary for locomotives hauling wagons from the brickworks to take a number of runs at the gradient before being able to mount the summit on the branch. The constant snatching and bumping of wagons during this process tended to damage the bricks with which they were loaded and may account for the brickworks' preference for road transport. The railway's tracks officially ended on the colliery side of the level crossing, though it is likely that the sidings on the colliery site were laid by the railway rather than by the brickworks. A photograph taken in 1927 to show the progress of the new buildings for the brickworks shows these sidings as having recently received attention and there is no way of telling quite what the original layout here was. It was intended at one time to continue this line all the way to Snowdown Colliery.

Returning to the Wingham branch, this ran through the Selson cutting and emerged alongside clay pits dug for the brickworks before entering the Prince of Wales cutting, named after the nearby public house. Beyond this cutting the line doubled and crossed over Mornington Road to enter Woodnesborough Halt (6 m. 42 ch. 91 l.). This name was once Winsborough and it is a pleasing experience to hear the dialect of the locality in which 'Woonsboro', 'Oonsboro' and 'Winsboro' satisfy such needs as arise. The area, as at Eastry, is rich in Roman remains.

The halt is not actually in the village of Woodnesborough and it was originally intended to name it Dreynold's Drove after a nearby road. This road has itself undergone some transformations of name and now appears on maps as Drainless Drove. The halt was actually opened as Woodnesborough & Hammill Platform but soon became Woodnesborough Colliery Halt and finally became Woodnesborough Halt from about 1925. Some caution is required in interpreting references to stations as, until the opening of the Sandwich Road branch to passengers in 1925, the Roman Road Halt on that line was known as Woodnesborough Road (Goods). It should be added that although Woodnesborough was always spelled in full in timetables the station nameboard actually read 'WOODNESBORO'.

It seems certain that Woodnesborough Halt was intended to have a passing loop as it was built with two platforms. However, the line into the second platform remained a simple goods siding throughout its life with the short platform alongside it serving as a loading dock. In May 1919 the 1.40 pm train from Shepherdswell was shown in *Bradshaw* as terminating at Knowlton rather than Eastry where it would only stop if signalled to do so. This was probably a typographical error as it is the only known example of Eastry serving as a conditional stop.

Woodnesborough was typical of many East Kent stations in that the siding parted from the running line before crossing the road into the station. This was presumably a means of safeguarding a double right of way across the road should there ever be any need to double the line. It also meant that any shunting of the siding involved more interference with road traffic than was strictly necessary and must have contributed to the local prejudice against level crossings. To make matters worse Woodnesborough was equipped with a locomotive water tank which was placed at the level crossing end of the

Above: The station building at Woodnesborough
was a single-ended version of the building
at Eastry.   *Ralph Gillam Collection*

Right: Watering Wingham-bound trains
at Woodnesborough required the train to
stand on the level crossing. This 1939 view
shows the later water tank equipped with
a hose rather than the chute previously
employed.   *C.C. Bowker*

platform. Whilst it was fine for locomotives returning from Wingham to take water here, it was a different matter if the locomotive was coming from Eastry as its train would remain parked across the level crossing until the locomotive's thirst had been satisfied.

The main platform at Woodnesborough was 200 feet long and faced with brick. There was a small wooden station building with a covered extension to serve as an open-fronted waiting shelter. The water tank previously mentioned stood on a rather makeshift arrangement of wooden piles and trestles which was replaced by a more purposeful structure in the 1930s. Two oil lamps and the nameboard completed the equipment of the halt. When the RAF took over Staple station in 1940 the station agent and porter from Staple were temporarily moved to Woodnesborough.

Beyond Woodnesborough Halt the line ran in a north-westerly direction through fairly level land. Moat Farm siding (7 m. 45 ch. 59 l.) branched off to the right about a mile beyond Woodnesborough. This siding was built with the original line about 1914 and may be the 'Farm Siding' mentioned in Colonel Pringle's Inspection Report, though this honour might equally go to Poulton siding further along the line. Both sidings appeared on the company's publicity maps from 1917, but curiously Moat Farm siding was incorrectly located between Ash Town and Poulton siding on these maps. Both sidings disappeared from the maps about 1930 although they continued in existence until the closure of the line.

The siding was only 130 feet long and was situated between the running line and a stream or ditch which then passed under the running line. This required the ditch to be covered, bridged would be too grand a title, to provide road access to the siding. The siding was used for the dispatch of fruit, potatoes and sugar beet and for the reception of agricultural manure and shoddy, a waste product from the wool industry which was used to improve the soil. Some coal also came into this siding. It is alleged that a heavy gun was twice fired from this siding out into Pegwell Bay causing concussion damage to local windows and roofing tiles. This may, however, be another case of confusion with Poulton siding.

Beyond Moat Farm siding the line began to curve in a more westward direction and after about ¼ mile Ash Town Halt (7 m. 71 ch. 37 l.) was reached. Despite serving one of the larger centres of population in the vicinity, 2,094 inhabitants in 1935, the halt had no road access and could only be reached by a footpath through the meadows. The instructions for reaching the station when asking in the town would go, 'Turn right at Vye's the Chemist, turn down Pudding Lane, right across the meadow and there you are'.

When opened in 1916 the halt consisted solely of a brick-faced platform. An open-fronted wooden waiting shelter, similar to that at Knowlton, was later added. Curiously the *Railway Clearing House Station Handbook* claimed that Ash Town possessed facilities for the dispatch of cattle and horses. If the possession of a platform was the criterion for this traffic then the same could be said of all the other stations on the East Kent.

The halt was first known as Ash Platform but was soon renamed Ash Town. This would not only distinguish it from Staple & Ash, the next stop on the line, but would also avoid confusion with Ash in Surrey. However, tickets with the

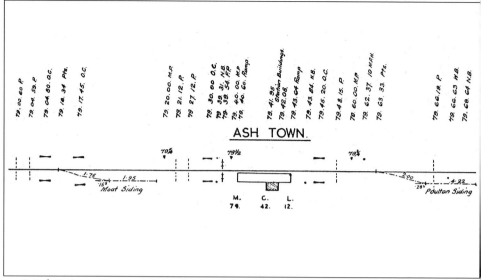

British Railways diagram of track details at Moat siding, Ash Town and Poulton siding.

Like Eastry the station at Ash Town was only accessible by footpath, though this was at least a level promenade through the meadows rather than a scramble up an embankment.

Ralph Gillam Collection

simple Ash designation remained in use for many years. It should be noted that the Southern Railway had a Brewery siding known as Ash Road siding, Sandwich, and that the East Kent's own Sandwich Road Halt was actually located on Ash Road.

Ash itself has a great deal of interest. It is a pleasantly straggling village with a fine restored church. The tower and lofty spire are of the Perpendicular style whilst the remainder is Early English. It consists of a nave with aisles, chancel and transepts. The East window is by Willement and there is a good memorial window to the Coleman Family in imitation of 15th century stained glass. The monuments are also of interest, particularly an altar tomb with effigies of a knight and lady showing the change of costume from chain mail to plate armour.

Like a number of places at which the East Kent stopped in this area, Ash was once noted for its windmills of which it had three. One of these was Mount Ephraim Mill, a post mill with a roundhouse, which was clearly visible from the train. It was built in 1795 and worked until 1929. Sadly it was blown down in a storm on the night of 21st October, 1955. Another mill, built around 1736, once stood north of the church and the third, of which little is known, stood on the edge of the sandpit behind the Red Lion Inn.

Asha, from which the name is thought to derive, appears once to have been a Saxon settlement, a cemetery of that date having been explored at the Wingham end of the village. A number of relics and ornaments were obtained. There are also traces of ancient earthworks about half a mile to the south-east. On a more basic note the South Eastern Survey by Richard Wyndham, published in 1940, contained this note: 'John Coat, butcher, makes the finest brawn in England - ORDER MORE.'

Unfortunately, as with so many wayside stations on the East Kent, Ash seems to have lured few railway enthusiasts to alight at its remote platform and few photographs of the halt ever seem to have been taken.

Just a quarter of a mile beyond Ash stood Poulton Farm siding (8 m. 12 ch. 58 l.). Again it is not clear if this was the 'Farm siding' referred to in Colonel Pringle's Inspection, but local opinion had no doubts that both sidings were built with the line in its very first days and that both sidings were used for storing empty wagons during the construction period.

The original siding here ran off to the right and came to a stop at Poulton Lane. The siding was 270 feet long. During World War II the Royal Artillery had a second siding constructed on the left-hand side of the line. This parted from the running line just after the original siding and also ran up to Poulton Lane. It was necessarily shorter than the original siding. The 12 in. gun was stationed on the new siding, which ended in a buffer stop, and the vans housing the gun crews were stored on the Farm siding. A sandbagged dugout was constructed against the buffer stop at the end of this siding. The new siding was removed at the end of the war.

Very little is recorded regarding the original siding and we have not been able to trace any photographs of it. Like Moat Farm siding it was mainly used for the delivery of shoddy, stable manure and coal to the local farms and for the collection of sugar beet, potatoes and fruit. This service was greatly missed when the line closed.

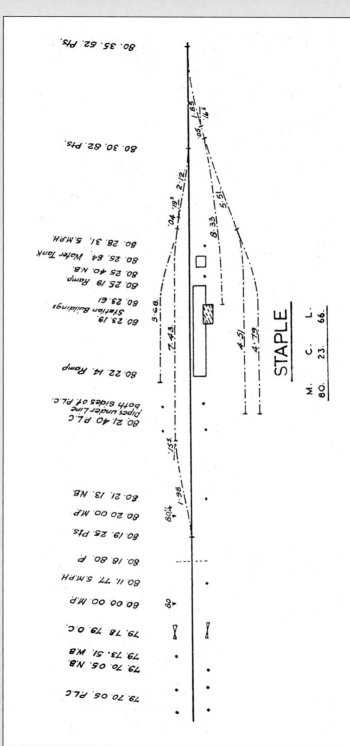

British Railways diagram of track details at Staple. This was lavishly provided by East Kent standards.

For farmers who were too remote from the farm sidings or from the railway's stations it is said that wagons or vans were sometimes left at convenient points on the running line for loading between trains. The evidence for this lies in statements and recollections of farmers loading wagons 'straight from the fields'. This extremely dangerous practice may only have taken place between the last train on Saturday and the first train on Monday when no trains usually ran. There is no record of any accident arising from such circumstances so it is hard to confirm that it actually did take place. Obviously there would be no official record!

Beyond Poulton Farm siding the line pursued a level and gently curving course for just under a third of a mile before coming to Staple station.

Staple Station (8 m. 52 ch. 91 l.)

This station was originally named Staple & Ash at the time when Ash Town Halt was simply Ash Platform. The station was mid-way between the villages of Staple and Ash and its real location was the hamlet of Durlock. EKR staff preferred to use the title Durlock when referring to the station. The small village of Staple, population 456 in 1935, was about three-quarters of a mile to the south of the station. It seems to have avoided the attention of the local guide book writers and gazetteers apart from a reference in 1882 to the fact that it '. . . has a burial chapel for the Groves Family and some monuments to that of Lynch'.

When opened in 1916 there was a 100 ft platform and a small wooden station building. Colonel Pringle's Report of 1916 makes no mention of sidings or of a passing loop but it is clear that if these were not originally here they were added soon afterwards. The running line divided into a passing loop before crossing the road and entering the station. Besides the main passenger platform which seems to have been extended beyond its original length there was a shorter platform alongside the loop line. As at Woodnesborough this was used as a goods loading dock. On the southern side of this platform, and served by a siding trailing back from the Wingham end of the loop, was Setterfield's coal yard whose address was given locally as Windmill Siding, Staple. Two further sidings trailed back behind the passenger platform where there was a very spacious yard. These sidings were said by staff to have been installed in 1927 for coal storage, possibly in connection with the application made in that year to build Line 36 which could have brought coal from Chislet Colliery through Staple on its way for export via Richborough. It was also believed by staff that it was intended to carry both sidings across the road by a second double level crossing to rejoin the running line on the Ash side of the road. This would have facilitated the crossing of long coal trains in either direction. In the event the extension to Chislet never took place and the sidings were used for whatever traffic presented itself.

Extra siding space at Staple was certainly needed as the station had developed into the main railhead for agricultural produce on the railway. During the period after World War I this traffic grew to such an extent that 15 to 20 wagons of fruit and vegetables might be loaded in a day. On occasions

Staple station *c.* 1933 showing the Lloyds Aeromotor windpump, the old LCDR carriage body used as offices in preference to the brick station building, the corrugated iron warehouse occupied by C.W. Darley and the second platform used as a loading bank.
M. Lawson Finch Collection

A wider panorama taken on the same day but showing the extensive sidings which could become choked with vans during the fruit season.   *M. Lawson Finch Collection*

carters had to leave their loaded carts in the station yard overnight awaiting the arrival of further empty wagons and vans from Shepherdswell on the early morning train.

Besides its commercial importance Staple also became the operational headquarters of the line between Eastry and Wingham. This honour seems to have been first held by Wingham Canterbury Road but came to Staple as a result of a series of EKR staff changes. The first of these began when the station agent at Staple found himself in trouble as recounted in the *Dover Express* for 9th January, 1925: 'James Ellis Hambrook (70) station master of the East Kent Railway at Staple, was again unfit to appear at the East Kent Quarter Sessions on Tuesday on a charge of embezzlement'. This was one of a number of cuttings collected by PDL for a dossier on the Colonel Stephens' railways which they planned to use in opposing the EKR at local enquiries. They had found out that Hambrook had appeared, ostensibly as an impartial agricultural witness, at one of the hearings for the 1923 Extension of Time Orders. Hambrook had then got himself into trouble with the station accounts but, perhaps mercifully, passed away before the case against him could be heard. He had become ill with worry caused by this affair and in all probability his misfortunes stemmed from the weaknesses of old age rather than from any criminal intent.

At this time the traffic superintendent for the Wingham to Eastry section was Mr A.W. 'Smudger' Smith who was based at Canterbury Road where he was station agent and was assisted by Dick Harffey who had joined the EKR in 1923. Upon Hambrook's suspension Dick Harffey was posted to Staple, being officially appointed station agent there in February 1926. In 1927 'Smudger' Smith left the EKR to work for one of Stephens' other lines, the Selsey Tramway. Dick Harffey was then posted back to Canterbury Road as station agent while the role of station agent at Staple and traffic superintendent for the Eastry-Wingham section was taken by Mr F. Carnell. Fred Carnell was very much an entrepreneur and did much to develop the traffic at Staple.

For many years Staple was known locally as a minor outpost of the Irish domain. This was due to the nationality of the porters employed there. There are many local recollections of passengers watching the cause of Free Ireland being upheld with fisticuffs at no extra charge and of trains delaying their departure until the striking of the decisive blow. These impromptu entertainments, woven together with the eccentric operations of the EKR, are believed to have been the inspiration for the story and film 'Oh, Mr Porter!'. It was therefore particularly appropriate that Gainsborough Pictures hired Kent & East Sussex 2-4-0T *Northiam*, used for many years on the EKR, to star in the film and that its fireman during the making of the film was EKR fireman Colin Abbott.

The Irish dimension also led to another characteristic of Staple station. This was the use of old carriage bodies for accommodation there. In 1926 an Irishman, Mr Egan, was recruited to work at Staple but found it impossible to obtain accommodation in the locality. As a result the railway moved an old carriage from Shepherdswell to Staple for Egan to live in. There is some mystery about the identity of this carriage as EKR staff variously described it as of Midland Railway or Great Northern Railway origin, but photographs suggest it was a London Chatham & Dover Railway vehicle. Egan lived in the carriage for

Staple in August 1950. The windpump has gone and the replacement water tank now takes its supply from the mains. The body of carriage No. 6 has replaced the LCDR body and can just be made out to the rear of the water tank.   *A.F. Pike*

Len Lawrence with a fine floral display stands outside his summer house in Staple goods yard - originally carriage No. 3.   *M. Lawson Finch Collection*

some 18 months while the EKR carpenter, Jim Smith, worked between his other duties on constructing a more permanent wooden bungalow. Egan moved into the bungalow in 1928 and the carriage body was installed at the Wingham end of the platform as a station office. Hitherto the original wooden station building had been used as an office. A new brick building, similar to that at Eythorne, had been constructed on the platform in 1927 but for some reason the telephone had not been transferred to this new building and the wooden building remained in use until replaced by the carriage body.

Egan later moved out of the bungalow and Carnell moved in instead and lived there until 1937. In about 1930 the carriage body began to deteriorate and Carnell purchased it for use as a chicken shed. For this purpose it was rather too large as it stood and it was sawn, with some difficulty, into two halves. The other half is believed to have been sold to a local mill. About 1937 the body of EKR carriage No. 6, ex-Cheshire Lines Committee, was brought up to Staple and installed at the back of the platform on which its predecessor had stood.

In 1946 a further carriage body was brought up to Staple. This had been purchased by Len Lawrence, the ganger on this section. In 1944 he had rented a section of the yard at Staple as a garden plot and in June 1946 he purchased the body of EKR carriage No. 3, also ex-Cheshire Lines Committee, for use as a summer house. The purchase price was £2 and as the carriage body was still there in 1960 he must have been pleased with his bargain. After the line's closure the carriage body was fitted with an extension constructed from one of the platelayers' huts previously standing near the Wingham Engineering Company's works. This was in turn joined by the platform building from Woodnesborough to create a curiously hybrid structure.

At the rear of the platform stood a large corrugated iron building. This was originally built by the Hampshire Chip Basket Company for the manufacture and distribution of the baskets used in the soft fruit trade. The building was later taken over by C.W.Darley Limited, wholesale vegetable merchants, who proclaimed their presence in large white letters across the end of the building.

Another distinctive feature at Staple was the windpump at the Wingham end of the platform. The station was without a mains water supply and when Fred Carnell took up residence there he suggested to Stephens that a well might be provided. Stephens agreed to pay £5 for digging the well and said that if water was found he would also pay for a windpump and tanks to provide watering facilities for locomotives. Carnell and the current porter set to work one Friday afternoon digging what they later claimed to be 'the only square well in Kent'. The reason for this shape was their use of spare sleepers to shore up the sides. By evening a depth of over six feet had been reached but the hole remained dry. Work was therefore abandoned for the day and both men retired to bed wondering which spot to try instead the next day. They were alarmed to find when they woke the following morning that the well had not only filled with water but that the overflow had submerged the running line and loop! Fortunately the flow soon eased off and the surplus waters were carried away by the adjoining stream. The men later explained their alarm as being due to their knowledge that a concrete post marked 903B was to be found in the gulley through which the stream ran by the station entrance. The height given for the spot so marked is 17 feet below sea level! Whilst Fred Carnell did not then have to worry about the prospect of rising oceans and global warming, he was well enough aware that an unstaunched flow of water could eventually flood the whole station site.

Unfortunately Stephens did not live to see the windpump installed at Staple but his successor, W.H. Austen, honoured the undertaking Stephens had made. The equipment was supplied by Lloyds Aeromotors of Letchworth, Hertfordshire, who had supplied similar machines for use on the other Stephens' railways. Allegedly the kit of parts consisted of 300 separate components. There is no doubt that its eventual assembly and erection considerably enhanced the reputation of the two men concerned. The bore of the well was converted to the more conventional circular form as it was bricked in. Because of its more convenient location and its use of free water the water tank at Staple was used in preference to that at Woodnesborough.

Fred Carnell's initiative went beyond providing a water supply. In 1932 he persuaded Austen and the Board to invest in a parcels collection and delivery service rather than relying on local carriers. A lorry was borrowed on trial from the Southern Railway and when this experiment proved successful the EKR purchased its own 30 cwt Chevrolet lorry, registration number KP 6188, and instituted a regular 'farm to rail' delivery service. It seems that this lorry did not last for very long as Carnell later acquired his own lorry and carried out a collection and delivery service under contract to the railway between his duties as station agent. Carnell and the railway eventually parted company when it was claimed that he was carrying produce directly to London rather than putting it on the train.

Traffic always remained comparatively heavy at Staple. In the early days of World War II a bomb dump was sited near the station and the traffic for this together with the boost in agricultural production created even more business for the railway. Manpower was naturally at a premium at this time and Mr Ted Stock, although already over 70 years old, joined Fred Carnell as porter and stayed on at Staple until the war ended. Between them these two men carried out some herculean tasks in the course of their everyday work and even attracted the unwelcome attentions of the Luftwaffe. The following article in the *Kent Messenger* for 27th October, 1950 paid tribute to the work of these men, albeit with a certain amount of journalistic licence!:

'Ghost Train' railway was vital in war time
HOW FRED CARNELL & OLD TED STOCK 'DELIVERED THE GOODS'

For the first time the inspiring record of Kent's most unique railway, the East Kent line which the Railway Executive intend to close on 30th October has been disclosed.The story of how two men 'ran' this front-line railway throughout the late war was recounted to a *Kent Messenger* reporter by 56-years-old Fred Carnell, of Pajodene, Ash.

Variously described as Kent's 'Lilliput' or 'Ghost Train' line the 11 mile single-track East Kent Railway has operated for 40 years. British Railways state that it does not pay its way, and that all but two stations must be shut. But Mr Carnell, supervisor of the other six stations and 8½ miles of line for 19 years until 1949, declares that the East Kent should never be allowed to become derelict.

OF MILITARY IMPORTANCE

It was of paramount importance as a military line in time of emergency, he said, and he quoted figures to show the amount of goods which he and old Ted Stock , then over 70, handled between them from 1940 onwards. In all, they forwarded 30,547 tons of fruit and vegetables during the war years and received another 15,213 tons of incoming goods. Mr Carnell later told the reporter that every bomb for every RAF station in south-east England was unloaded at Staple Station and hidden away in a gigantic dump in the fields around the quiet country station. Often he and Ted were machine-gunned by roving Nazi fighter planes and forced to dive under trucks to dodge bullets and cannon shells. Yet once they loaded 56 trucks in one day. From early morning until late at night the two were hard at it shifting the goods traffic, shunting, and dealing with a mass of paper work in a 100-years-old railway carriage that served as a booking office. 'We worked ourselves to a standstill', Fred told the reporter.

Along with Mr Carnell, Ted headed the village queue to sign on for the Home Guard. The younger man was commissioned as a lieutenant and placed in command of the Ash platoon of the Wingham battalion.

OVER AGE

Mr Stock, father of 10 children, served as a colour sergeant and company quartermaster-sergeant until the authorities found out he was over age. He then promptly joined the ATC and was promoted warrant officer of the 1859th Eastry Squadron. Mr Stock, who lives at School Cottage, Ash, told the reporter that he served in the Royal Marines for 25 years - he was in Korea in 1894 - and worked in Ash brewery for the next 37 years, retiring on pension when the war began. Inundated with work and with no hope of obtaining replacement porters at any of his stations, Mr Carnell called on Ted and persuaded him to join the railway. Old Ted was never issued with a porter's uniform and the super-human tasks which he and the supervisor performed in keeping the line open and running smoothly during the Battle of Britain and the 'invasion scare' days went unnoticed by the powers-that-be. If two British railway workers ever deserved decoration for the part they played in the national effort these two did.

And the job they did was on the railway which inspired A.P. Herbert with the idea that became the theme for the classic railway comedy film 'Oh Mr Porter.' The famous author and playwright spent many hours sitting in Staple station prior to the war, savouring the unhurried atmosphere of the Kent countryside.

STAFF OF 12

The total staff of the East Kent Railway during the war was 12: Mr Carnell, Mr Stock, two drivers, two firemen and six permanent platelayers. All above military age. Formerly owned by the late Colonel H.F.Stephens of Tonbridge, its rolling stock and permanent way was generally antiquated. Despite these seemingly insurmountable difficulties the two carried on without flinching. Their engines, none of which was less than 50 years old, went on puffing through the orchards and hop gardens and only a direct hit on the line stopped the daily train.

Their favourite locomotive was 'Paddy', 71 years old when he died on Mr Carnell and another was 'Coffee Pot', an old saddleback engine - 'We could name them by their whistles far away.' Few passengers were carried but the first-class coach - Queen Victoria's saloon from the old Royal Train - was always included in the train. 'I loved that old railway,' said Mr Carnell, 'and I loved it best when it was a family concern before the Government, and then British Railways, took over. Colonel Stephens, my old guvnor, had 11 little railways and he once told me "Fred, I don't make a lot of money out of my railways but I do have a lot of fun!"'

DID NOT CLOSE

Just before the war £1 shares in the East Kent Railway were worth only 4*d.*, but Colonel Stephens' first thoughts were for his employees and it never closed. When war came Staple station was for a time entirely taken over by the RAF. Heavy howitzers were mounted on trucks and sighted to fire into Pegwell Bay in the event of invasion. A 15 inch gun was brought alongside the platform and this fired at the German battle cruisers as they escaped through the Dover Straits from Brest.

Mr Carnell and Mr Stock rocked with laughter over memories of the pre-war days on the East Kent of the time a whole train rolled gently into Staple minus passengers, driver, fireman and guard. It stopped of its own accord and sometime later the party turned up. They had sighted a hare in a field en route and had given chase. They forgot about the train.

On another well-remembered occasion, an engine arrived at Shepherdswell junction without its train. 'For devilment the driver left his coaches and trucks behind at Wingham, the terminus at the other end!' Once the driver pulled up at Woodnesborough and along with the guard and fireman went into the 'local' to play darts. The solitary passenger thought it politic to buy the next round in order to proceed on his journey.

Authors' Note: Quite what the other East Kent employees made of this article has gone unrecorded. It would appear that journalistic licence transposed features from Stephens' other lines, the Royal carriage for example, and some of the dramatic claims may owe more to enthusiastic sub-editing than to Fred Carnell or Ted Stock.

It was during the war that the final extension to the layout at Staple took place. This was the laying in of an additional siding at the back of the yard to house a rail-mounted gun. This siding remained in place at the end of the war but might as well have been lifted. It has been suggested that a longer siding was also laid at Staple for the use of the RAF bomb stores but we have found no record of this. Similarly we have found no evidence to support accounts that narrow gauge lines were laid to serve these stores. In the remaining years before closure Staple's traffic declined steadily. Never again would Fred Carnell and Ted Stock have the chance to load 56 wagons in a day.

From Staple to Wingham

Beyond Staple the line ran in a generally south-westerly direction through mostly level ground. After about a mile the line passed Brook Farm on the left and came to the Wingham Colliery loop. The short branch to Wingham Colliery ran off to the left from the start of this loop to serve the colliery site. This branch was not built under the railway's powers and there is some mystery about its ownership. It was a lightly laid surface line dividing into three sidings at the colliery. Both the branch and the loop are believed to have been lifted in 1921 but a 6 ft length of standard gauge track remained in place until at least 1960. This passed into one of the old colliery buildings through two massive iron doors, 9 ft 6 in. wide, and originally ran the length of the building and out of the far end. Between the standard gauge rails was laid a similar length of narrow gauge track to a width of 3 ft 6 in. This was for carrying the familiar side-tipping skips so often used by contractors, and it was claimed locally that this mixed gauge track originally ran all the way to the loop. An early photograph of Wingham Colliery Halt shows narrow gauge wagons lying dismantled on the platform. How and why these came to be here it is difficult to say but they do raise the possibility of some sort of narrow gauge connection with the 'main' line.

Wingham Colliery was abandoned at the outbreak of World War I and two of its boilers transferred to Tilmanstone Colliery. Despite the failure of Schneider to purchase the colliery after the war, there was fresh hope that work would resume when PDL purchased the mineral rights here in the 1920s. Nothing came of this either and the site was eventually purchased by the Wingham Engineering Company on 1st May, 1934. The following year the chimney stack was felled by the well-known firm of steeplejacks, Messrs Larkins. This was an operation that proved far more arduous than had been expected due to the excellent quality of bricks and bricklaying used in its construction. Each brick had to be chipped out of the base piecemeal and when the stack finally fell, about teatime one Sunday afternoon, there were some very mixed feelings amongst the crowds of locals gathered on nearby vantage points.

The winding engines, made by Markhams of Chesterfield, were removed as were the last four Thomson boilers. These were hauled to the Southern Railway station at Adisham by the Wingham Engineering Company's traction engines. The site was again sold on 22nd April, 1947 to Grain Harvesters Ltd who converted the huge winding shed for the purpose of cleaning, drying and storing grain. This firm has since built a considerable complex of new buildings and silos on the site and little evidence remains of the colliery that could have brought so much traffic to the line.

Three hundred yards beyond Wingham Colliery loop stood Wingham Colliery Halt (10 m. 18 ch. 4 l.). This was located on the right-hand side of the line just before it crossed the road connecting Wingham and Staple. At the time of Colonel Pringle's Inspection in 1916 the halt was equipped with a 100 ft platform and a waiting shelter. The shelter was subsequently removed and when Colonel Mount inspected the extension to Canterbury Road in 1925 he called for the halt platform to be set back to provide adequate clearance. Local opinion has it that for a brief period there was a short siding across the road here known as Dambridge siding after the nearby Farm. This may have been built to preserve a right of way for double track at the level crossing. It can have had little practical use as a stream runs close to the road here and there is no evidence of the siding having bridged this stream. It must be added that we have found no documentary or photographic evidence for the existence of this siding, which may have been confused with a similar siding at Wingham Town.

Wingham Colliery Halt was the end of the line for passenger services during the railway's early years and trains had to be propelled back to Wingham Colliery loop before the engine could run round for the return journey.

Upon crossing the road beyond Wingham Colliery Halt the line bridged the stream and a footpath which ran along its bank by means of a sturdy wooden trestle bridge. This was later replaced by an embankment through which the stream passed by means of a culvert. The line then continued on an embankment for a further 400 yards before throwing off a siding to the left into the works of the Wingham Engineering Company.

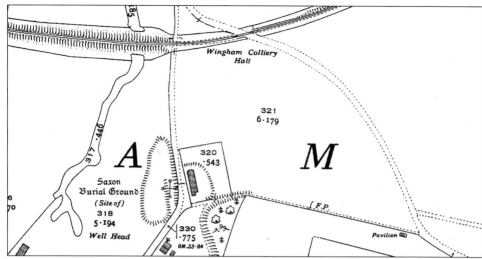

Extract from the 25 in. Ordnance Survey Revision of 1937/38 showing Wingham Colliery Halt.
The colliery itself stood some way to the South and East of the Halt.

Photographs of Wingham Colliery have proved hard to find but this poor view at least gives an
impression of the colliery's substantial chimney.   *Colonel Stephens Railway Museum*

Wingham Colliery Halt seen during its brief period as a passenger terminus. Note the upturned contractor's skip wagon at the back of the platform. Trains terminating here had to reverse some distance before the locomotive could run round the train at Wingham Colliery goods loop.

M. Lawson Finch Collection

Wingham Colliery Halt in 1948 - it has clearly not been inundated with passengers for some time.   *Ralph Gillam Collection*

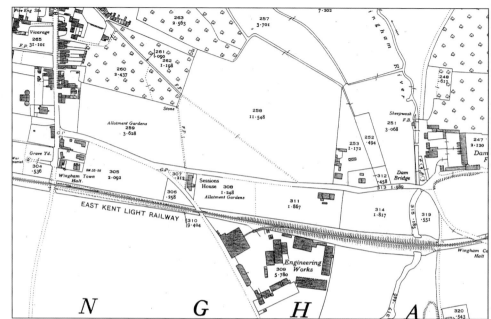

Extract from the 25 in. Ordnance Survey Revision of 1937/38 showing the 'burning' embankment from Dambridge, the Wingham Engineering Co. siding and Wingham Town Halt.

Wingham Town during its own brief stint as a terminus complete with station building, loop and siding. 0-6-0ST *Walton Park* stands with ex-LSWR carriage No. 5.

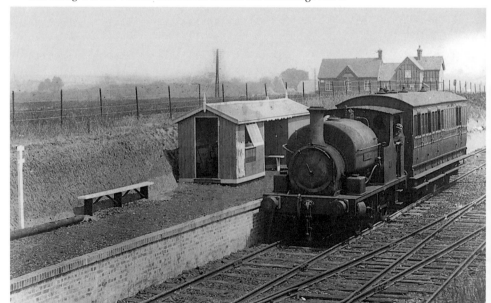

This length of embankment was largely constructed from colliery spoil and was notorious for smouldering internally. For most of its working life, and even after the tracks had been lifted, it was liable to give off smoke and fumes and its periodic subsidences led to the imposition of a 5 mph speed limit. By local account the most persistent fire was at the Dam Bridge end of the embankment. It started in 1938 as a result of someone burning rubbish at the foot of the bank and continued for some seven years. As the coal shale was consumed so the track would subside and the railway's employees claimed that two train loads of chalk were required every week to keep services going. Quite what a 'train load' might be is open to question. The fire would occasionally burst into flames at the surface, consuming the odd sleeper here and there. Whilst this was a problem for the railway before the outbreak of war, with the advent of the blackout it became a real menace. It appears that the embankment had some perverse characteristics in its make up as well as colliery shale. It seldom failed to burst into flames whenever an air raid was in progress, so that the permanent way men would find themselves frantically summoned by the ARP wardens to apply the reserves of chalk kept for such occasions.

The Wingham Engineering Company was founded in June 1889 as the Wingham Agricultural Implement Company and it specialised in the repair and operation of traction engines. Until 1914 the firm had operated from Wingham High Street but moved to new premises, constructed by the engineering firm Lysaghts, alongside the future line of the railway in 1915. Shortly afterwards an agreement was made with the EKR for Wingham Engineering to repair the railway's locomotives and rolling stock for the next five years or until the railway's own workshops could be completed. To facilitate this a railway track was laid from one end of its main workshop to the other.

The EKR Directors instructed Stephens to continue construction of the line to the Wingham Engineering Works in November 1917 and it was the general opinion of the staff of Wingham Engineering that this was completed by 1918. It is known that parts of the 0-6-0 No. 3 were attended to in the Works and that the hired Kent & East Sussex 2-4-0T *Northiam* was re-tubed there in 1921.

The siding received a fairly regular traffic of agricultural machinery, coal and other stores for the engineering company's fleet of traction engines as well as tar for road spraying. There seems to have been little outward traffic from the Works itself, but Wingham Engineering had various clay and gravel pits in the area and are known to have dispatched blue flints from its Stonar pit to the Staffordshire Potteries.

Near to the Wingham Engineering Company's siding stood two crude platelayers' huts. No. 1 hut stood on top of the embankment at the side of the engineering company's buildings whilst No. 2 stood at the foot of the embankment. No. 2 hut was in very much worse condition than No. 1 and leaked prodigiously in wet weather which was why, the unfortunates who had to use it would explain, the company '. . . kep' it hid down below'. Two pump trolleys were permanently parked here for the use of the gangers on this section.

Passing the Wingham Engineering Company on the left and the historic Wingham Sessions House on the right, the running line crossed the road to Goodnestone on the level and entered a shallow cutting. At the end of this

By the 1930s Wingham Town had lost its loop and siding though it retained a building, if not quite as decorative as that with which it was originally supplied.   *M. Lawson Finch Collection*

By Nationalisation Wingham Town had lost everything but its nameboard.
Ralph Gillam Collection

cutting and just before crossing the Adisham Road was Wingham Town Halt
(10 m. 51 ch. 21 l.). The station here was not officially inspected until 1925 but
trains are believed to have run here from about 1920. Originally there was a 125
ft brick-faced platform on the right with a wooden station building similar to
that at Eastry. There was a passing loop on the left and a short siding extended
from the end of the loop across the Adisham Road parallel to the running line.
This siding was probably added to safeguard the double right of way across the
road, but would have formed the starting point of the Wingham & Adisham
Light Railway had it been approved and built.

Wingham Town was quite conveniently situated for the village centre and
with its passing loop made a good terminus for passenger services. Its site was,
however, somewhat limited and, apart from the four wagons that might be held
in the siding across the Adisham Road, it offered little scope for goods services.
It is not clear how long the layout at Wingham Town remained as described.
When Colonel Mount inspected the extension from Wingham Colliery Halt to
Wingham Canterbury Road in 1925 he made no mention of a passing loop or a
siding here. From this date to closure Wingham Town consisted solely of the
single running line, the platform, a smaller waiting shelter than that originally
located here, a plank bench and a nameboard.

Wingham itself was a most unlikely location for a railway terminus. In
Richard Wyndham's South Eastern Survey of 1940 it is stated: 'Had it not three
stations, one would pass Wingham as a village; but town or village, the beauty
of its solitary street and church can never be disputed'. The *Ward Lock Guide* to
Canterbury & North East Kent for 1926 reported: 'A colliery has been
constructed a short distance eastward, and the East Kent Railway runs through
the village'. The Wingham branch of Lloyds Bank is believed to have been built
in anticipation of the colliery coming into operation and the offices above it
were intended for the use of the colliery company but never occupied by them.

With a population of 1,240 in 1935 it must be admitted that Wingham was a
village rather than a town but a village with a respectable pedigree. It boasts the
site of a Roman villa and of a College of Canons founded in 1282. Some of the
collegiate buildings survive in the form of the Inn and 'Canon Row' opposite St
Mary's Church which, itself, has much of interest. Queen Elizabeth I stopped to
dine in Wingham in 1573 on her way to Canterbury.

We have, however, not yet come to the end of the Wingham branch. Beyond
the level crossing by Wingham Town Halt the line crossed fairly level ground
curving gently to the north-west. Passing the site of the Roman villa on the
right, the line encountered the valley of the Wingham River which required the
construction of a substantial embankment through which the river passed by
means of a culvert. Originally there was a wooden bridge here but it could only
take the lighter locomotives in the company's fleet and a culvert proved a better
solution. This embankment was also inclined to smoulder internally. Because
the land on the other side of the river was at a substantially lower level the
embankment sloped downwards at a gradient of 1 in 50. At the end of the
embankment a siding cut off to the right to form the Canterbury Road goods
yard, while the running line ran ahead to the Canterbury Road which it crossed
at an angle. The platform of Canterbury Road Halt (11 m. 5 ch. 94 l.), only 60 ft

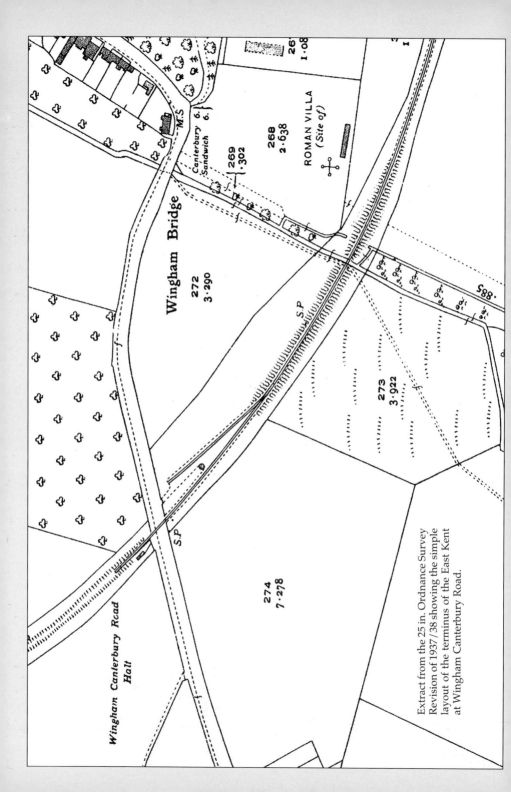

Extract from the 25 in. Ordnance Survey Revision of 1937/38 showing the simple layout of the terminus of the East Kent at Wingham Canterbury Road.

Wingham Bridge

272
3·290

ROMAN VILLA
(Site of)

268
2·638

269
·302

Canterbury 6.
Sandwich 6.

M.S.

273
3·922

274
7·278

Wingham Canterbury Road
Halt

S.P

S.P

S.P

long, stood on the left-hand side of the line almost immediately after crossing the road. Thirty feet beyond the end of this platform the rails ended abruptly, further progress being halted by a sleeper chained to the ends of the rails.

Before looking at the halt in more detail it might be well to recite the circumstances in which the railway came to such an unexpected end in such an unlikely location. Under the Application of 1910 the railway would have continued more or less directly beyond Wingham to Canterbury. But the section beyond the Wingham Parish Boundary, itself still some distance beyond the halt, was deleted because of opposition from the Ecclesiastical Commissioners and the War Department. In 1912 a roundabout extension to Wickhambreux via Stodmarsh was approved and in 1920 an extension from Wickhambreux to Canterbury was also approved. Finally in 1931 the original direct route to Canterbury received approval as well as an extension from Stodmarsh to Chislet if the railway had still wanted it. Apart from some land purchases, minor earthworks and fencing on the Stodmarsh route nothing came of these extensions. But as long as hope for their construction lasted it was necessary for the railway to safeguard its access to the West across the Canterbury Road. Hence the need to construct and open this otherwise redundant final stretch of the Wingham branch.

It is surprising that the railway received approval to open this final section of line to passengers. When Colonel Mount inspected the line in 1925 he seems to have been under a misapprehension, 'The present terminals at Wingham and Sandwich are single line. Upon arrival trains will be drawn forward empty the engine being reversed at loops situated ahead on sections open for goods traffic'. How he missed the fact that the line stopped abruptly beyond the Canterbury Road platform is a mystery that is never likely to be explained.

In the absence of any loop closer than Staple the EKR was obliged to resort to gravity as an essential element in its operations at Canterbury Road. Typically a train arriving there would stop just before the goods siding. The brakes on the carriages and wagons would be applied. The locomotive would then uncouple and take refuge in the siding. The points would then be set for the running line and the carriages would be uncoupled from any wagons they might have in tow. The carriage brakes would be released and the carriage would roll down past the waiting locomotive until clear of the points. The locomotive would then emerge from the siding, couple on to the back of the carriage and propel it across the level crossing into the platform. That was the theory at any rate but it seems to have been easier on many occasions to let the carriage roll all the way to the platform without waiting for the locomotive. A mixture of locomotive power and gravity would then be used to shunt the siding until it was time to retrieve the carriages from the platform, couple up any departing wagons and return to Eastry. It is a miracle that no serious accident ever accompanied these manoeuvres. As road traffic increased it was perhaps as much caution as laziness that led to the practice of loading and unloading passengers in the goods yard and thus avoiding the need to cross the road.

For a terminus Wingham Canterbury Road was not lavishly equipped. A home signal guarded the approach to the single siding and another signal stood on the near side of the level crossing to act as a 'starter' for trains standing at the

The approach to Wingham Canterbury Road showing the solitary siding running off to the right, the round corrugated iron shed in the yard and the Canterbury Road starting signal in the distance.   *M. Lawson Finch Collection*

The opposite view. The bicycle parked against the end of the station building belongs to the station agent, W. 'Smudger' Smith who left to manage the Selsey Tramway in 1927. The next train to arrive will have to remove the wagons from the running line before it can access the station.   *M. Lawson Finch Collection*

platform on the other side of the road. A circular corrugated iron hut, a twin of the one at Shepherdswell, stood in the space between the running line and the siding to serve as a goods shed. Between it and the road stood a rough heap of spoil which may have been intended as a loading dock or may simply have been left behind from some excavation or other. In 1946 the circular hut collapsed and was replaced by a van body mounted on the spoil heap which was levelled up into something that at least resembled a loading dock. The only other regular feature of the goods yard was the seasonal presence there of haystacks composed of hay culled from the lineside, a common feature on Stephens' railways.

The short platform had a sleeper-built face. The station building was that which had originally stood at Wingham Town, except that the three sections were re-assembled in a different order with the open-fronted waiting shelter at the far end rather than separating the two office sections. The first station agent at Canterbury Road was apparently a Miss Hampshire who was succeeded by 'Smudger' Smith and then by Dick Harffey. This succession of appointments suggests that Wingham Canterbury Road was open, at least for goods traffic, well before it was inspected by Colonel Mount in 1925. Dick Harffey remained station agent here until the line closed. He had lost his right leg duringWorld War I but remained extremely nimble despite this loss. He was a popular character both on the line and in the locality and was known for his cheerful and obliging nature. Dick, too, had his moment of glory when the *Star* newspaper published the following article on Tuesday 27th February, 1951:

Two-Trains-A-Day Line To Close
LITTLE BUSINESS
Twenty-eight years of work on the two-trains-a-day East Kent Light Railway come to an end tomorrow for Dick Harffey, aged 55, at Wingham - terminating point of the 11-mile single-track line.

He will watch the 5.56 pm safely on its way back to Shepherd's Well, then lock up his office, a small shed by the Canterbury road, for good.

March 1 has been fixed by British Railways as the closing date for the line that has been a place of pilgrimage for students of Britain's 'joke' railways since 1912.

In future only a three-mile stretch of the line near Dover will be used for coal-hauling from Tilmanstone Colliery.

The line, which was formed to serve the Kent collieries, stopped taking passengers two years ago and has been used since then for freight services by local farmers.

'There has been hardly any business these last few weeks,' said Mr Harffey. 'Just a few parcels to take off and deliver in the village - but we've kept to the time-table.'

'I can remember busier times, especially during the War, but I always managed affairs at this end of the line by myself.'

Former chief clerk of the line, Mr Charles Sampson, who has worked in a converted railway truck in the tiny station of Staple since 1946, said, 'Sometimes the takings from passenger tickets only came to ten shillings a month.'

'One woman caught the morning train from Shepherd's Well for the 11-mile journey to Wingham and was in the train for three-and-a-half hours. 'The driver had to take some trucks to Richborough and do some shunting in the sidings at Staple.'

During World War II the running line was extended beyond the station by the Royal Engineers for a distance of 150 yards. The purpose of this extension is not

A 1930 view of Dick Harffey, station agent from 1927 until closure, stands outside the station building moved here from Wingham Town but re-assembled with the open waiting room at the end.   *M. Lawson Finch Collection*

0-6-0 No. 2 (ex-No. 100) has run into the siding while carriage No. 5 and attached brakevan begin their descent under gravity towards the level crossing in June 1948.   *Ralph Gillam Collection*

clear except that it gave more clearance on this side of the road should the Army have wanted to manoeuvre or store guns or supplies here. This new section of line was equipped with a catch point to prevent unauthorised movements towards the platform.

Following the end of passenger services in 1948 the track was cut short of the level crossing and the track across the road and alongside the platform was lifted. Buffer stops were erected to prevent wagons running away onto the road. The offices on the platform were retained until complete closure of the Eastry-Canterbury Road section when they were purchased by Dick Harffey for £1 and re-erected in his garden.

Today the goods yard is occupied by a Garden Centre but it is not impossible to visualise that a railway once existed here and much of the approach embankment is still intact. On the platform side of the road it is another matter entirely. No dip or alteration is visible in the field there that would suggest that it had ever been anything but one uninterrupted expanse of agricultural property. The pivot upon which the future expansion of the East Kent depended has vanished entirely.

The Branches

The Richborough Port Branch

The branch in general

This branch was always something of an enigma and from the start possessed an almost unreal quality. It may be thought that to express such feelings about a piece of railway line is taking things a little too far, but far from it. Its history concerns us with trains which apparently nobody saw and which seemingly trundled through grassy meadows to a port nobody used. Surely such happenings are far from commonplace?

As will be seen from the description of the branch, the civil engineering works, apart from the bridges at Richborough Castle and their approaches, were slight and the line was mostly a surface one. During 1913 work was carried out by several gangs in a piecemeal fashion all around Eastry and it seems that Poison Cross was reached the same year. The pace of work then slackened and with the outbreak of war became increasingly intermittent. However, it is known that by the spring of 1914 rails had reached Sandwich Road and for a distance beyond as far as Gosshall Sluice on the banks of the Stour. At this point all work ceased due as much to shortage of labour as to shortage of cash.

According to Mr Bob Gardner of Woodnesborough, who worked on this branch from the start, the line rapidly became overgrown and derelict and nothing much further was done to it until 1925 when the track was smartened up as far as Sandwich Road for the passenger services that began that year. There is reason to believe that some goods traffic braved this stretch of line prior to 1925 and goods facilities were clearly indicated as existing at least as far as Sandwich Road in the Railway Clearing House Maps and Handbooks from 1920 onwards.

Richborough Port in 1921 showing Pearson's Wharf, also known as Lord Greville's Wharf, which was to be the ultimate destination of the East Kent. The barges moored along the wharf are returning salvage from the Western Front. The lake at the rear is the flooded gravel pit from which S. Pearson & Son extracted the materials to make the concrete blocks for Dover harbour improvements. The East Kent's Richborough Port station was yet to be built to the right of this picture on the other side of the main road.

Simmons Aerofilms

Preparatory work seems to have begun on the bridge across the Stour in 1923 and in 1926 William Rigby was recalled to construct the bridges over the road, railway and river. About 20 men are believed to have been employed on this work and on track laying. The ganger in charge was a Mr Routledge or Routley, an ex-Shropshire & Montgomeryshire Railway employee. He lived in a van supplied by the EKR which was hauled to the site by locomotive and stationed there for this purpose.

As originally authorised the Stour bridge should have been an opening bridge. In 1927 the EKR applied for authority to erect a fixed bridge instead. Although authority for this was not granted until 1931, it appears that agreement to a fixed bridge was reached with the river authorities and the Board of Trade in the meantime. It is believed that the first train to cross the bridge did so in 1927 or 1928 but freight traffic did not begin until 1929.

Although the branch was usually referred to as the Richboro' Port Line or the Sandwich branch it was actually the second half of Railway No. 1 and should have been the East Kent's 'main line'. The fact that Railway No. 1 to Eastry and Railway No. 2 from Eastry to Wingham were in use first led to this second half of Railway No. 1 being thought of as a branch rather than as a piece of delayed construction. How different the history of the East Kent and the pattern of its services might have been had Railway No. 1 been completed before the outbreak of World War I.

Traffic on the branch

Passenger services on the branch were only run from 1925 to 1928 and at their most prolific consisted of no more than two return workings on two days of the week. One of the more generous timetables, that for July 1928, shows a service operating between Eastry and Sandwich Road on Wednesdays and Saturdays only as follows:

	am	*pm*		*am*	*pm*
Eastry	10.02	3.52	Sandwich Road	10.21	4.10
Poison Cross	10.05	3.55	Roman Road	10.28	4.20
Roman Road	10.08	3.58	Poison Cross	10.32	4.23
Sandwich Road	10.16	4.06	Eastry	10.35	4.25

By all accounts these trains usually ran empty and often failed to run at all. The only other passenger-carrying trains to use the branch would be those for the annual inspections. Inexplicably one of these managed to get itself into the Southern Railway Timetable for 12th July, 1925!

Although a passenger platform was erected at Richborough Port no public passenger trains ever made use of it nor was authority to do so ever sought. If the Port had developed as a centre of industry it is probable that the EKR would have revived passenger services on the branch and extended them to Richborough. This would have depended on Ministry of Transport approval and would certainly have required substantial improvements to the Stour bridge. As Richborough Port saw only piecemeal development there was never any real incentive to develop passenger traffic on the branch. A pathetic reminder of the brief passenger service to Sandwich Road could still be seen in the High Level booking hall at London Bridge in 1939. The fares list there described Poison Cross, Roman Road and Sandwich Road as stations to which through bookings could be had for the asking!

As regards goods traffic the tale is a happier one as the branch provided a modest volume of fruit and vegetables, mostly plums, apples, pears and broccoli. The freight was usually picked up nightly during the week by the engine on the evening run from Shepherdswell to Wingham. As no extra time allowance was made for this the frequent late running of this train became a major bone of contention with station staff. Locally there were strong recollections of the engine on the Sandwich Road passenger turn sometimes leaving its carriages at Sandwich Road and running on to Richborough, presumably Richborough Castle sidings, to pick up freight. Since there was rarely more than a five minute turn round allowed at Sandwich Road it is difficult to see how this could be accomplished, but our informants seem to have been convinced that such trips did occur. Latterly the only train to pick up goods along the branch was the 4.45 pm from Shepherdswell but if the Shepherdswell Office was telephoned early enough a special locomotive could be dispatched.

With the opening to Richborough Port special trains began to operate carrying coal from Snowdown Colliery to the Port for onward shipment by sea. The Southern was responsible for bringing these trains as far as Shepherdswell. In the opposite direction the main source of traffic was pit props for Tilmanstone or Snowdown. These might be carried in the empty wagons returning to Snowdown but more usually required special trains to be summoned as and when ships called.

There is some dispute as to whether any traffic was carried to or from Richborough Port after 1939. The tracks over the Stour bridge are known to have been severed at an unknown date during the war and orders were issued for the demolition of the bridge as a precaution against invasion. The demolition was not actually carried out and local opinion suggested that some traffic was carried into the Port area but we have found no real evidence for this.

It must be added that very few photographs appear to have been taken of the line between Sandwich Road and Richborough Port and there are almost no contemporary accounts of operations on this section. As at Tilmanstone we have had to rely on anecdotal recollections, often made many years after the events recalled, to flesh out the few documented facts that do exist.

The route described

Leaving the junction at Eastry the branch ran straight ahead carried at first on a substantial embankment. The surrounding countryside in this area is extremely flat and bare, made up for the most part of marshy meadows.

The embankment continued for about a quarter of a mile before the line reached ground level. Passing Drove Farm on the left the line then crossed Drainless Road and divided in two to form a passing loop whose two tracks crossed a second level crossing to enter Poison Cross Halt (6 m. 1 ch. 82 l.). The curious name for the halt, certainly the most colourful on the EKR, commemorated the site of a medieval religious foundation whose entire membership is said to have perished by poisoning. Until the commencement of the passenger service this stopping place was known as Eastry (Goods). A nursery situated next to the station provided a fair amount of traffic and there appears to have been intermittent coal traffic for local use.

To the left of the passing loop was a short siding, 168 ft long, which trailed into the further end of the loop. It is believed that this track layout dated from the public opening of the EKR in 1916 and it is likely that mixed trains terminating at Eastry continued empty to Eastry (Goods) to drop off any wagons or vans and to enable the locomotive to run round its train. When opened to passengers the halt consisted of a platform 50 ft long faced with corrugated iron. This was equipped with a nameboard, a seat and two lamps but no covered accommodation was provided. The back of the platform was fitted with a sturdy wooden fence to which were attached two lockable wooden boxes, one above the other. The lower box had at one time had some sort of nameplate or description screwed to its front. The upper box was alarmingly painted 'POISON SANDWICH'. We presume the lower box's description would have been 'EASTRY' or 'EASTRY POISON' as the boxes are believed to have held tokens or staffs for the two sections of line between Eastry and Sandwich Road. There is no reference to such an arrangement in Colonel Mount's inspection of the branch which was meant to be operated on the 'one engine in steam' system. The safeguard represented by keeping the two boxes locked was somewhat nullified by the fact that the contents of the boxes could be obtained by simply lifting the boxes from their bases.

Beyond Poison Cross the line continued its dead straight progress until curving near Grove Manor Farm to face due north. Just before crossing the Woodnesborough to Sandwich road the platform of Roman Road Halt (7 m. 16 ch. 34 l.) was reached. The EKR had some difficulty in naming this halt. At the time of Colonel Mount's Inspection it was designated as Woodnesborough Road Halt but to avoid confusion with Woodnesborough station on the Wingham Line it was opened as Roman Road Halt. In the timetables it was shown as Roman Road, Woodnesborough until 1938 when the 'Woodnesborough' was dropped. As passenger trains had ceased 10 years earlier this can have made little difference to the intending traveller! The title 'Roman Road' was not very much more helpful to the unwary traveller as the locality abounds in Roman Roads.

Roman Road Halt was even less imposing than Poison Cross and consisted simply of a platform 50 ft long. During the early years there was a proposal to install a coal siding here but this was never done. As at Poison Cross and Sandwich Road the platform was on the right-hand side of the line.

Crossing the road immediately beyond Roman Road Halt the line continued due north on a low embankment and in just under a mile came to Sandwich Road (7 m. 79 ch. 90 l.). Here there was another short platform faced with timber uprights and corrugated iron sheeting. There was a 'Whistle' board just before the platform was reached. A small hut at the further end of the platform housed a company telephone and it was from here that calls for special collections could be made to the Shepherdswell Office. On the left-hand side of the track was a large double-faced advertisement hoarding which must have brought in more revenue than was ever earned from passengers at this remote

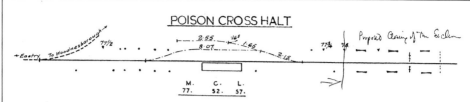

British Railways diagram of track details at Poison Cross. Note the message 'Proposed Closing of the Extension' written in to the right of the station.

Poison Cross Halt showing the passing loop and, just to the left of the wagon, the goods siding.
M. Lawson Finch Collection

The infamous 'Poison Sandwich' box containing the token for the Sandwich Road, later Richborough, branch.
David Kevan

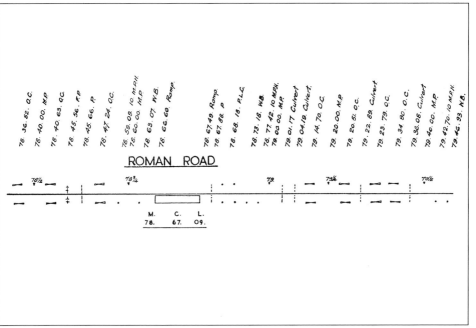

British Railways diagram of track details at Roman Road Halt.

Roman Road Halt offered little to entertain passengers intending to use its eight trains a week.

M. Lawson Finch Collection

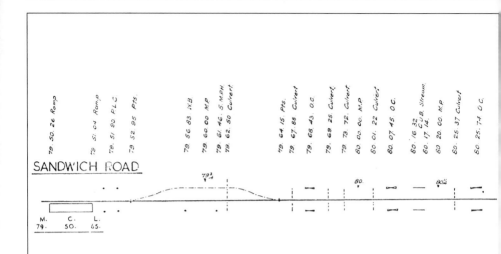

British Railways diagram of track details at Sandwich Road Halt.

Sandwich Road boasted a small cabin with a telephone from which regular customers equipped with a key to the padlock could summon a train to collect farm produce.

Almost as infamous as the 'Poison Sandwich' box was the 'No Gates' warning at Sandwich Road
. . .   *David Kevan*

. . . because here were the only crossing gates on the East Kent.   *David Kevan*

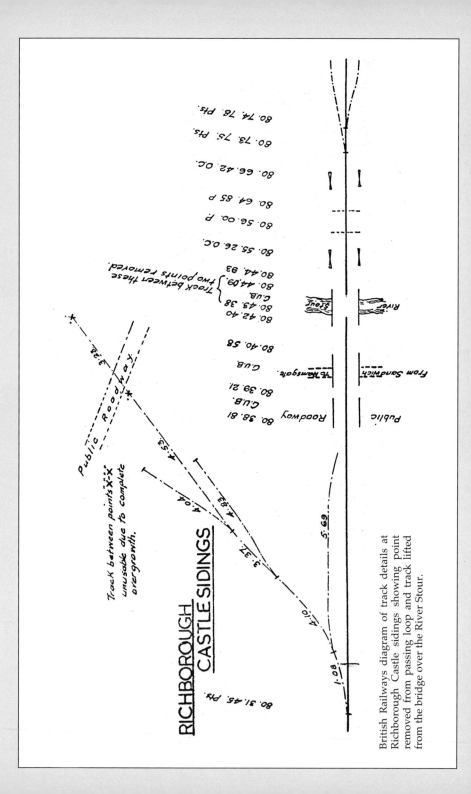

British Railways diagram of track details at Richborough Castle sidings showing point removed from passing loop and track lifted from the bridge over the River Stour.

spot. A water tank had originally stood here to supply locomotives employed on construction work before watering facilities were established at Richborough Castle sidings.

The level crossing beyond the platform was unique on the East Kent in being fitted with gates. Colonel Mount asked for these to be fitted with red warning discs for daytime use and red lamps for use at night. There is no evidence that either of these requirements was fulfilled. Colonel Mount does not appear to have noticed that the gates were both hinged on the left-hand side of the line so that when closed across the road they blocked the road on the Ash side of the line but gave no protection at all on the Sandwich side. We have earlier mentioned that warning notices along the road in both directions announced 'LEVEL CROSSING NO GATES', perhaps 'LEVEL CROSSING SOME GATES' would have been more accurate. On the further side of the level crossing the line divided into a passing loop, 462 ft long. This loop served as a siding for coal deliveries and the collection of local fruit and vegetables.

The line continued ahead on a fairly straight course through marshy grazing land for just under half a mile until it came to the Gosshall stream. The stream was crossed by a 28 ft-span bridge of typically Stephens construction. The plans for this bridge show that it consisted of two girders, 38 ft 8 in. long, supported at their ends on timber piles and intermediately on cast concrete abutments. Shortly beyond the bridge the line began an almost 90 degree turn to the east. This took the line up a steadily rising embankment onto the flanks of some higher ground. This high ground dominates the surrounding marshes and meadows and was the site of a Roman fort and of Richborough Castle. Spoil to build the embankment seems to have been cut from the hillside here thus creating an open area in which the EKR laid out a passing loop and a fan of three sidings (8 m. 61 ch. 70 l.).

The central siding was EKR Railway No. 9 authorised in 1911 to form a junction with the SECR Deal-Minster branch. It cut across the flank of the hill, crossed the narrow road from Sandwich which brings visitors to Richborough Castle and so came to the SECR boundary. Unfortunately for any serious hope of a junction ever being made it was at a considerably higher level than the tracks of the Deal-Minster branch. Stephens referred to Railway 9 on a number of occasions as being completed and only needing to be connected up to the SECR tracks. He was being less than candid. Railway 40, proposed in 1927, would have extended from the end of Railway 9 and run parallel to the Deal-Minster branch as far as the banks of the River Stour. It was a 'spoiling line' intended to prevent anyone developing land here from obtaining their own direct connection to the Southern. It was withdrawn from the 1927 Application on the advice of Sir Herbert Walker of the Southern. If it had been built it would have required a considerable length of embankment to bring the EKR tracks down to ground level.

During the lengthy gestation of the 1913 application for the Light Railway Order, eventually granted in 1920, it was frequently suggested that the EKR should abandon its plans for a line of its own to Richborough Port and to settle for a straightforward junction with the main line at Richborough Castle. This was always resisted by the EKR on the grounds that it needed its own

Aerial view of Richborough Castle sidings with the adjoining bridges and Roman ghosts for company. *Simmons Aerofilms*

The approach to Richborough Castle sidings was somewhat forbidding - not a place to linger on a wet or windy day. Note the water tower and the bridge over the Southern Railway.

M. Lawson Finch Collection

By 1947 the points at the eastern end of the Richborough Castle loop had been disconnected. Since trains could go no further by this date either some gravity shunting or a reversal to Sandwich Road loop would be needed to run round.   *G.A. Cookham*

Road, rail and river bridges at Richborough Castle.   *M. Lawson Finch Collection*

Bridge over the Stour - a far less elegant structure than the road and rail bridge.
M. Lawson Finch Collection

independent access to Lord Greville's wharf. In retrospect a junction at Richborough Castle would have been much easier to construct than the Richborough Port extension. It could have attracted traffic from Tilmanstone and could even have given the EKR a share of World War I traffic to Richborough Port. By insisting on its own line all the way to the Port the EKR delayed the opening of the full Richborough branch until 1929, by which date the usefulness of the branch had all but disappeared.

At the time of the opening of the passenger service to Sandwich Road there was some local publicity to the effect that services would soon be extended to 'Sandwich Castle'. This was to have been for both passenger and goods services but nothing came of this proposal. A Richborough Military Halt was opened on the SECR Deal-Minster branch in 1918 but only for the use of personnel at the Port and was soon closed. On 19th June, 1933 a Richborough Castle Halt was opened by the Southern Railway at the same spot but this too was short-lived. It closed with the outbreak of war in September 1939 and never re-opened.

It seems that the EKR passing loop at Richborough Castle was installed in connection with the construction work and it was equipped with a water tank on a timber trestle to replenish locomotive tanks. The loop and the sidings seem mainly to have been used for loading fruit and vegetables for onward dispatch to London. This was a particularly remote location and few enthusiasts penetrated this far to note the railway's business here. When British Railways took over in 1948 they found that the loop had been converted into a siding by the removal of the further set of points and that the Railway No. 9 siding was completely overgrown and unusable beyond the point where it crossed the road from Sandwich. The rails in the road had been tarred over. This and the invisibility of the track beyond the road led a number of visitors to this spot to believe that the siding stopped short of the road.

Immediately beyond the loop stood the first of two bridges. This bridge carried the EKR across both the road from Sandwich and the tracks of the Southern's Deal-Minster branch. As originally built it was supported on eight crude but substantial wooden trestles. Brick and concrete abutments were then installed beneath the temporary bridge and back-filled with spoil to link up with the embankments on either side, while the three remaining trestles were replaced by brick piers of a more reassuring appearance. One suspects that the substantial construction of the finished bridge was as much due to the Southern Railway's wish not to have EKR trains falling onto its tracks as to any desire for perfection on the part of the EKR.

A comparison with the next bridge, that over the River Stour, seems to confirm this. Here were no sturdy abutments; instead the embankments on either side simply sloped away to the ground and were much affected by erosion and slipping over the years. The centre span of the bridge was supported on two wooden trestles which stood in the river bed some feet out from the banks. Between the centre span and the embankments the tracks were supported by timber bracings as and where circumstances warranted. The whole affair gave the impression of the railway track having been laid through thin air and then propped up by whatever came to hand. The centre span had narrow walkways with handrails on either side, but the sections between the

Definitely not for the nervous - a view from the tracks above the Stour. Garrison buildings from World War I can be seen in the distance.   *M. Lawson Finch Collection*

The three-track exchange sidings. Richborough Port Halt is on the skyline to the right.
                                                                        M. Lawson Finch Collection

centre span and the embankments had neither walkways nor handrails so that anyone crossing the bridge on foot had to rely upon keeping their footing on the sleepers.

Footplate staff were distrustful of the bridge and willingly admitted that sometimes the fireman would be sent ahead across the bridge on foot to wait on the far side. The driver would then set the locomotive slowly in motion and dismount. The train would slowly cross unattended to be halted on the far side by the waiting fireman. The driver would then follow on foot and once safely re-united on the further side the train could proceed on its way.

Two buckets were thoughtfully provided on a post beside the bridge in the event of the timber catching fire following the passage of locomotives. On one visit one of the buckets had a hole in it and the other was empty. There is no evidence that any harm ever befell anyone using the bridge but it must be admitted that the level of traffic over it was rarely likely to test its strength to the limit.

On the Richborough side of the River Stour the branch and its embankment curved round to head north-east and ran through even more desolate marshy land than it had encountered hitherto. Hereabouts the surface geology consists of alluvial deposit and blown sand with patches of larger ballast and the land surface varies between just above and just below sea level. An uninterrupted view was obtained of Richborough Port and its oddly assorted buildings, and the sea. The limits of vision on the horizon are now dominated by Richborough power station and the Sandwich by-pass but during the life of the railway were occupied by tall and isolated trees, the occasional water tower or mast and, in the far distance, some large and intriguing buildings

About 600 yards beyond the Stour bridge the line divided into three parallel tracks. Effectively there was a long parallel loop on either side of the running line. These were used to store loaded coal wagons awaiting the arrival of ships for loading or collection by one of the PDL locomotives. Each loop was capable of holding about twenty-five 10 ton wagons. At this point the line ran alongside an ancient man-made embankment known as the Monks' Wall and these sidings were known as Monks' Wall sidings or Richborough Port sidings. Beyond the end of these loops there was a connecting line to the PDL rail system. The EKR curved to the east and ran parallel to the original alignment of Lord Greville's Tramway. Here there was a slightly shorter loop on the right-hand side of the running line and just beyond this, on the left-hand side, the short platform of Richborough Port Halt (9 m. 62 ch. 82 l.) was reached. About this forlorn and frequently windswept station there is not very much to be said. Its greatest impact was one of loneliness 'twixt marsh and sea' with an added dash of desolation. The chance visitor more than half expected that Will Hay and 'Gladstone' might suddenly appear at any moment and one tended to hang around the place just in case they did. As far as is known no passenger ticket ever bore the magic words 'Richborough Port' or even 'Richboro' Port' as they appeared on the platform nameboard. Whilst Richborough Port may never have had any passengers it did at least have the distinction of being the only East Kent station not located on either Railway 1 or Railway 2, for at this point Railway 1 had ceased and the rails here belonged to Railway 28.

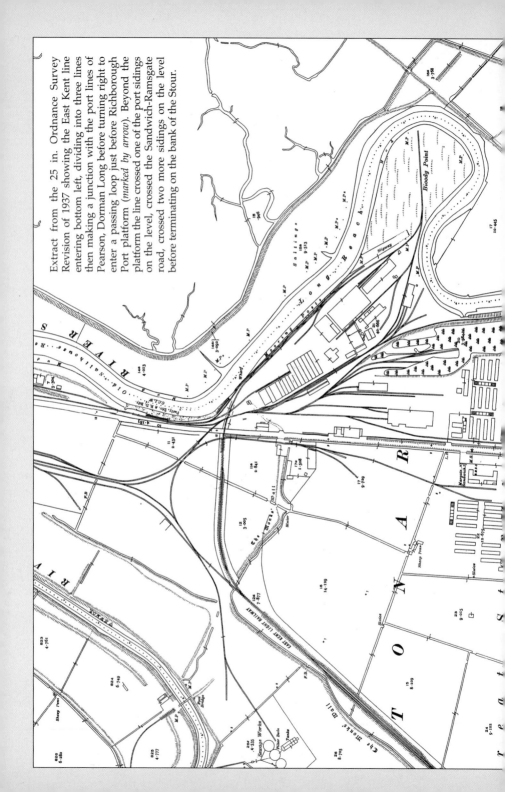

Extract from the 25 in. Ordnance Survey Revision of 1937 showing the East Kent line entering bottom left, dividing into three lines then making a junction with the port lines of Pearson, Dorman Long before turning right to enter a passing loop just before Richborough Port platform (*marked by arrow*). Beyond the platform the line crossed one of the port sidings on the level, crossed the Sandwich-Ramsgate road, crossed two more sidings on the level before terminating on the bank of the Stour.

Port platform looking towards Pearson's Wharf.

Port platform looking towards Richborough Castle ruins on the skyline. The line crossed on the level in the foreground is one of Pearson, Dorman Long's sidings.

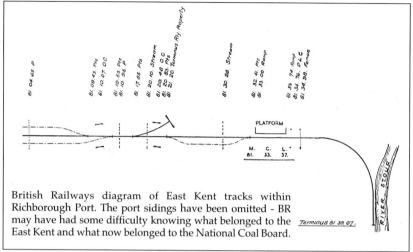

British Railways diagram of East Kent tracks within Richborough Port. The port sidings have been omitted - BR may have had some difficulty knowing what belonged to the East Kent and what now belonged to the National Coal Board.

The short platform was composed of cinders with a wooden sleeper face and a wooden kerb which was originally painted white. On the platform was a plank seat, a name board, two lamp posts and a fence along the back constructed of wooden posts and, allegedly, old locomotive tubes. One wonders if the fence was considered necessary for intending passengers to cling to in the prevailing high winds? Some shelter from the same winds was afforded by the erection of a large vee-shaped advertisement hoarding behind the platform. Immediately beyond the end of the platform the EKR crossed one of the PDL lines at right angles. This line originally ran to the premises of the Cast Stone Company which had occupied the premises of the fire station built by the War Department during World War I. The Cast Stone Company had gone out of business in about 1925 and there seems to have been little danger of collision at this crossing of two railways which was unprotected by any sort of signalling.

Immediately beyond the rail crossing the line crossed the road from Sandwich to Margate, which suffered from a number of level crossings in this vicinity. On the opposite side of the road the line passed the premises originally occupied by Messrs Pearsons for the manufacture of the concrete blocks used in their Dover Harbour Contract, and for which Lord Greville's Tramway had originally been built. Beyond this two more lines belonging to PDL were crossed on the level until at last the EKR drew up alongside the Stonar wharf and stopped. Much of the work on the stretch of line from Richborough Port Halt to the wharf was carried out by a man, known to the railway's platelayers as 'Slim', who lived in Dover and came out to the site each day.

When British Railways took over in 1948 they found that the track across the Stour bridge had been lifted but nevertheless measured the line to its end beside the wharf. The end of the line was 81 miles 39 chains and 7 links from Charing Cross or 9 miles 68 chains and 32 links from Shepherdswell. It is sobering to reflect that it took the best part of 18 years to get this far and that the final section was effectively open for little more than 10 years.

The Tilmanstone Branch

The casual observer standing on Eythorne station platform and looking north could have been forgiven for believing that it was the branch to Tilmanstone Colliery that constituted the EKR main line. This was because the passing loop at Eythorne clearly served the Colliery branch rather than the line to Eastry, which merely led off the loop on the other side of the level crossing while the loop continued a short distance along the branch. This is not really surprising in view of the fact that the traffic to Tilmanstone was considerably greater and more profitable than the traffic to Eastry, Wingham or Richborough.

Beyond the loop the branch climbed gently for about 600 yards so that by the time it had reached the road from Eythorne to Tilmanstone it was necessary to cross the road by a bridge, whereas the main line crossed the same road on the level. This bridge was similar to that at Eastry and consisted of a girder structure on brick abutments. Almost immediately   beyond the bridge the branch entered the property of Tilmanstone Colliery. The ownership of the line beyond this point was a matter of dispute between the colliery and the railway for many years but for operational purposes can be considered to have been part of the branch. The layout obviously altered from time to time in detail but followed the same basic pattern for much of its life. Essentially it had four main features. A line curved off the branch to the right and served sidings supplying the power station, landsales wharf and various other installations. The branch itself split into seven parallel lines, four of which passed under the colliery screens. Beyond the screens the tracks came together again and curved northwards to serve various sidings from which spoil was dumped. The final feature was that the branch ran back alongside the EKR 'main line' and for a period there was a northern junction between these lines here. By the 1930s this junction had been lifted but the end of the branch ran parallel to the 'main line' for some distance and was used for storing colliery wagons.

The Deal Branch

Although this was never built there are various references to work being carried out in preparation for its construction. In March 1917 John Ashworth wrote from the Tonbridge office to Harry Springgay to arrange for John Brenchley '. . . to go on with me to Morrice's land on the Mongeham branch to set out the land in field No. 4 where the earth works have been commenced'. It is known that a parcel of land was obtained in Willow Wood, half a mile north of East Studdal, in 1913 and that trees were felled and a shallow cutting begun. A summary of works completed by 1928 recorded that one mile and 70 chains of the four miles required for Railway 11 had been purchased, together with 16 chains and the eight acre Sholden Lodge estate on the course of Railway 19. A Board of Trade arbitration was awaited regarding the valuation of a further one mile and 73 chains for Railway 11, but it is unlikely that this was actually purchased. Some of the land acquired was sold off in the 1930s and 1940s, but British Railways inherited a number of unsold sites when it took over the EKR assets. There is no surviving physical evidence to identify these today.

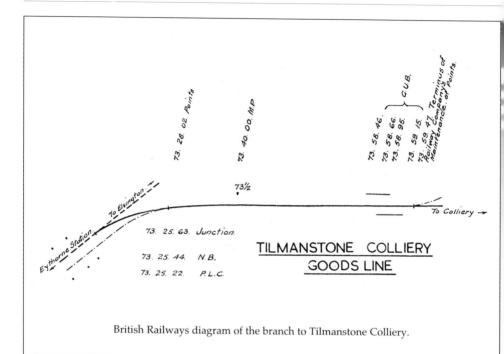

British Railways diagram of the branch to Tilmanstone Colliery.

Tilmanstone Colliery screens looking towards Eythorne, March 1937.

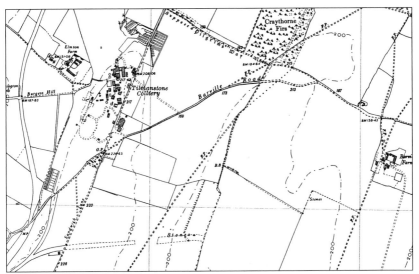

Extract from the 6 in. Ordnance Survey 1949 Revision (track details still missing) showing fenced land purchased for the Deal branch curving away from the Tilmanstone branch (*lower left*) with two unfenced portions beyond Sandwich Lane.

The Guilford Branch

Apart from the removal of tubbing and other equipment from Guilford Colliery there is no evidence that this branch saw any traffic after work on the colliery ceased in 1922 until it was lifted in 1937. We have been unable to find any descriptions of this line while it was open. This account is therefore largely based on an inspection of the course of this line long after it had closed. Two inspections were carried out on foot, the first on Sunday 9th February, 1958 and the second on Saturday 25th July, 1959.

Standing on Eythorne station platform and facing back towards Shepherdswell, the Guilford branch turned off to the left or south on a slight embankment just before the end of the passing loop which it joined. After the lifting of most of the branch a length of line was left in place here as a siding. During World War II the War Department relaid this with bull head rail for about 600 yards and also laid in a siding, about 130 yards long, alongside this in flat bottom rail. These sidings were still in place in 1948.

In 1958 the trackbed of the branch ran almost immediately into an impenetrable thicket before crossing a track between Eythorne Court and Brimsdale Farm on the level. Curving slightly to the left, the trackbed ran out into open pasture across which were to be seen the remains of a number of rotting sleepers. There were also two lengths of flat bottom rail, one of 10 feet and the other of 14 ft 6 in., lying on the course of the railway and two other lengths were lying half buried in the ground a little way off in the field to the right. Remains of sleepers were to be found along the whole course of the line but they were much more in evidence for the first mile.

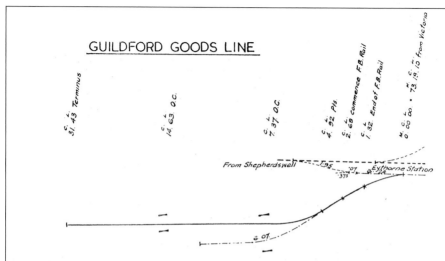

British Railways diagram of what remained of the Guilford branch in April 1948. The short siding alongside the branch was laid in by the War Department.

Embankment and close boarded timber bridge over the bridleway on the Guilford branch in 1935.
Dr J.R. Hollick

The cutting and bridge under Coldred Road in 1935 looking towards Eythorne.
Dr J.R. Hollick

Reaching the meadow boundary the track ran in a shallow cutting and became thickly overgrown with brambles and bushes, before disappearing into dense scrub from which a low embankment emerged on the western side. This was the start of the course of Railway 8 which was intended to create a direct connection towards Shepherdswell from the Guilford branch to Railway 1.

The course of the Guilford branch emerged from the scrub and climbed onto a lengthy embankment which was crossed about half-way along its length by a farm track. Beyond this point the ground rose to meet the level of the line and what appeared to be a small cutting curved in from the left or east. This seems to have been a natural formation. The line then continued on the surface and was crossed on the level, first by a footpath and then by a farm way, before passing through another shallow cutting, from which it emerged to cross the road from Golgotha Hill to Waldershare Park by means of a level crossing.

Beyond the level crossing the Guilford branch ran through a long shaw of trees flanked on the left by a vee-shaped ditch some 15 feet deep. It then ran south-west some 250 yards from the road from Eythorne to Coldred with which it ran parallel. The road at this point formed the boundary of Waldershare Park and ran through a beautiful avenue of tall copper beech trees. The trackbed then entered a wide cutting about 10 feet deep and, swerving south-west around Coldred Church and some ancient earthworks, emerged on the level to cross the lane running from Hazling Dane to Coldred Camp. The branch then continued in a sweeping curve on a narrow embankment some 20 ft high which was broken by a bridle path running from the Coldred earthworks to Shepherdswell. This gap had been spanned by a timber bridge but only the vertical baulks for this remained.

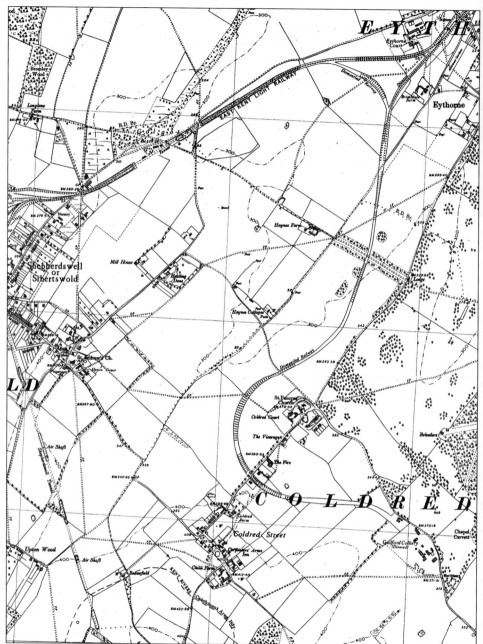

Extract from the 6 in. Ordnance Survey of 1938 showing the course of the Guilford Colliery branch and of Railway No. 8 linking the branch westwards to the East Kent 'main line' to Shepherdswell.

The curve continued round to the south-east and formed an excellent vantage point; smoke from Tilmanstone Colliery could be seen away to the north-east. At this point the branch crossed a steeply sloping arable field and entered a very deep cutting taking it beneath the main road from Eythorne to Coldred and Lydden. The road was carried over the cutting by a girder bridge on brick abutments. This bridge was wide enough to have accommodated double track beneath it. This cutting was too overgrown to be passable and a little way beyond the bridge had been recently filled in. On a visit in 1990 the deep cutting leading to the bridge was also found to have been filled, but a short section of cutting filled with trees and undergrowth could still be observed on the southern side of the road.

The cutting ran out several hundred feet beyond the bridge and the branch once again became a surface line running along a broad grassy depression some 18 paces wide. From its proximity to the road this may have been intended as a possible station site. The trackbed then climbed gently onward before turning to the south to meander through very open land where it was crossed by a wide farm way with gates on either side. It then entered a shallow depression at the top of a rise, from which it emerged on rough ground sloping gently down to the derelict remains of Guilford Colliery where it terminated. A number of colliery buildings remain here.

Considerable work was carried out on the branch by the Guilford & Waldershare Colliery Company at the end of World War I. The nature of this work is only very vaguely described but it is probable that all the heavier earthworks and cuttings date from this period and that the branch was originally built predominantly as a surface line. This work was carried out by under the supervision of a Mr Stupples who had previously worked for William Rigby.

Guilford Colliery in 1935.   Dr J.R. Hollick

The Eythorne Curve

For many years it was possible to trace the course of this projected line (Railway 8) quite clearly and the following description is based on an inspection on foot on Saturday 25th July, 1959.

This line, planned purely as a connecting curve between Railway 1, the EKR main line, and Railway 4, the Guilford branch, was only about two furlongs long. It joined with No. 4 in the thicket mentioned in the preceding description of that line some 200 yards south-west of Brimsdale Farm. From this point, and looking back to Eythorne, it left the thicket on a slight bank and curved away to the north and was soon crossed by a wire strand fence marking the boundary of a field. It then followed the left-hand side of this fence still curving back towards Shepherdswell and ran into a cutting some six feet deep. The left bank was unfenced and formed the boundary of an arable field. The cutting itself was overgrown with grass and wild plants but was free from bushes or scrub along the whole of its length. At the mid-point of the curve the gradient changed from rising to falling and a wire fence and a farm way connected the two banks of the cutting which was now running out. The fence continued along the right-hand bank, while the left-hand one remained unfenced from the pasture which accompanied it right down to the EKR main line. Two lengths of flat bottom rail were lying in the cutting just before it ran out on to the surface and met the main line at the point where a platelayers' hut stood. This was about 50 yards north-west of the occupation crossing at the Eythorne end of the cutting leading to Golgotha tunnel and at a point where the main line has just entered another slight cutting which continued as far as Eythorne loop.

From the inspection of the Guilford end of this curve it seemed clear that rails had been laid here at some time; but apart from the two lengths of flat bottom rail there was no conclusive evidence as to the gauge of this track. These rails may have been discarded during the re-laying of the main line and were of too heavy section to have been used for narrow gauge running. On the other hand the formation appeared very narrow in some places and the older employees of the EKR believed that the only track to have been laid round this curve was a temporary narrow gauge line put down during the construction of Railway 4.

In favour of the line having been built to standard gauge is the fact that some early photographs of locomotive No. 1 show it facing Shepherdswell while others show it facing Wingham; the only logical explanation for this would be that it had made use of the triangular junction created by Railway 8 linking Railways 1 and 4.

The Stodmarsh Branch

This would have been Railway 15 and curved northwards beyond Wingham to take the EKR around the lands of the Ecclesiastical Commissioners before curving south through Stodmarsh to Wickhambreux. Its first part ran more or less along the boundary between the land of Viscount Conyngham and the land of the Ecclesiastical Commissioners. Two miles and 20 chains of the three miles and 53 chains required for this section had been purchased by 1915 and negotiations were proceeding for the purchase of a further half-mile in 1928. Much of this section was fenced off and various minor earthworks were carried out before 1915. These works gradually became derelict and there is no evidence of any significant work being done on the branch after World War I, even though the branch would have played an important part in the various schemes to reach Canterbury, Birchington and Chislet. It is known that an extensive photographic survey was made by Pearson & Dorman Long of the dilapidated works on this line in connection with opposition to the railway's 1927 Extensions Application, but we have found no trace of any of these photographs.

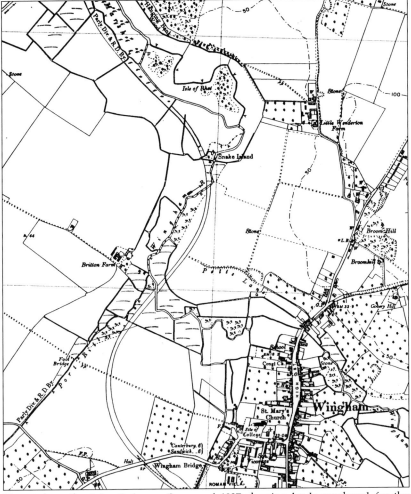

Extract from the 6 in. Ordnance Survey of 1937 showing lands purchased for the Stodmarsh extension curving away beyond Canterbury Road Halt.

William Rigby's 0-4-0ST *Wye* built by Hunslet in 1887 working on the construction of the East Kent. *M. Lawson Finch Collection*

William Rigby's 'Morrison & Mason' Andrew Barclay 0-4-0ST on a construction train near Ash. *M. Lawson Finch Collection*

Chapter Fifteen

Locomotives used on the East Kent Railways

The Contractors' Locomotives

During the early construction of the EKR at least three, possibly four, contractors' locomotives were in use in addition to the line's own 0-6-0STs, Nos. 1 and 2, and hired Kent & East Sussex 2-4-0T *Northiam*.

The first clue as to the existence of these locomotives came when interviewing a veteran member of the EKR staff who recalled: 'In about 1915 one of Rigby's locomotives was left standing on the main line at Eastry. Mr Brenchley and his men moved the engine off the rails and onto the bank. It remained there for quite a while and was then collected and taken to London by road'. He added that the engine concerned was a small saddle tank. Some years later a sepia snapshot turned up showing a small saddle tank at work on the line. This was able to be identified as a Hunslet locomotive named *Wye*. Coupled with the earlier information that this was one of 'Rigby's locomotives' the way was now open to discovering more.

William Rigby carried out a number of contracts for Holman Stephens. In Kent these included the Sheppey Light Railway and the Headcorn Extension of the Kent & East Sussex Railway. Rigby had also carried out a number of contracts for the South Eastern Railway and was therefore no stranger to this corner of England. Moreover he owned a Hunslet 0-4-0ST named *Wye*.

Wye had been built in 1887, Works No. 420. It had outside cylinders, 10 inch bore by 15 inch stroke, and wheels of 2 ft 9 in. diameter. It was a small engine with just a curved backplate instead of a cab and carried Hunslet's vertical sided saddle tank of that period. Large square blocks served as buffers and no vacuum brake was fitted. The couplings were three link chains with large hooks on the ends. It would have been useful for shunting about with the odd wagon or two of chalk or such, but of little use for heavy traffic.

Wye had originally been delivered to another contractor, T.A. Walker, for the Barry Dock contract in 1887. By 1895 it was working for the Mitchell New Colliery Company at Grimethorpe Colliery but in November 1901 was repurchased by Hunslet who sold it to William Rigby in February 1902. It was dispatched a week later to Hither Green sidings where Rigby was carrying out a contract for the SECR. By 1912 it was clearly at work on the EKR, as spares were sent by Hunslet for this engine to 'Rigby's East Kent Railway' in December of that year and again in August 1913. Spares were also sent to Shepherdswell in January and March 1913. *Wye* had left the EKR by December 1915 as Hunslet was then sending spare parts for it to Plumstead. By May 1916 it was at Woolwich Arsenal. Rigby is also known to have used another Hunslet 0-6-0ST (187/1877) named *Sutton* somewhere 'in Kent' but there is no evidence that this was used on the EKR contract.

Evidence regarding the second contractors' engine on the EKR is entirely based on an indistinct photograph published in the local press and now unfortunately lost. This was another 0-4-0ST and differed from *Wye* in possessing a distinctive tall front spectacle plate. This was reduced in width in lieu of spectacles and then flared outwards and backwards to provide some limited shelter from the elements. Not much more is distinguishable but the engine has a Manning, Wardle look about it. William Rigby is known to have had at least one Manning, Wardle 0-4-0ST, No. 602 of 1876 *Royal Engineer*, originally delivered to the Secretary of State for War at Chatham and later known to have been on the Lodge Hill & Upnor Railway. There is, however, no way of telling whether this locomotive was the one pictured on the EKR.

The third contractors' engine has a slightly better photographic pedigree. It was photographed on what was described as the first train along the 'Overland Route' passing through meadows near Ash on 18th April, 1913 and hauling 11 three-plank wagons, five of which are lettered East Kent Railway. The track is light flat bottom rail spiked to sleepers and is not only decidedly undulating but also appears to have been laid without ballast. A second and much less clear photograph shows the same engine in Pedding cutting between Ash and Hammill. This photograph was taken in 1912 and shows Mr J.E. Hougham who was the ganger on this section at the time and clearly recalled that the track was laid through the cutting whilst it was completely under water!

The locomotive in both these photographs is a standard Andrew Barclay 0-4-0ST and, although presumably the property of William Rigby, actually carries the name of Morrison and Mason Ltd, Glasgow. This was a firm of contractors who had four Andrew Barclay 0-4-0ST, Works Nos. 950/1902, 957/1902, 963/1903 and 967/1903, of which three were employed on work at Portsmouth Dockyard between 1908 and 1916. Rigby's locomotive may have been one of these.

This was a more substantial engine than *Wye* and boasted the luxury of a full cab. At the front it carried two substantial wooden dumb buffers, fully two feet square. In the 1912 photograph the locomotive is in apparently good condition as regards paintwork. This is thought to have been light green, lined by a band of black edged both sides in white.

The possibility of there having been a fourth contractors' locomotive was first raised during a conversation in the office at Shepherdswell station when one of the staff asked, 'Don't you want to know about the other little engine?' Unfortunately further enquiries only elicited the information that it was of narrow gauge and had been used in the construction of the line from Eythorne to Guilford. No real information was forthcoming as to the nature of the engine, although there was some discussion as to whether it might have been a petrol locomotive. The only other information obtained was that it was thought to have been of 3 ft or 3 ft 6 in. gauge.

There the matter rested for some time until a reference was traced in one of the local papers to the effect that '. . . the Contractor's narrow gauge line has now been laid right up to the colliery'. If there actually was a narrow gauge line to Guilford Colliery has never been ascertained, newspapers have often confused 'narrow gauge' with 'single track'. When work at Guilford was at a standstill in 1912 because of the difficulties and expense of road transport it would have made sense to push ahead with a temporary narrow gauge line in order to get construction started on the colliery again. Whilst it is strange that such a thing should have gone unreported except in the uncertain terms reported above, there is some evidence that Railway 8, the Shepherdswell-facing link from Railway 4 to Railway 1 near Eythorne, may have been laid with narrow gauge track. The EKR staff claimed that a line was briefly laid here and that, '. . . it had only ever been laid with a light track used for taking sacks of cement up to the colliery site'. If memories are to be trusted, at what was then already a considerable distance in time from the building of the line, then it is reasonable to believe that there was a temporary line to Guilford. It might have been narrow gauge and it might have had a locomotive. Beyond that we cannot safely go.

It is unlikely that there would have been any contractors' engines on the EKR after the railway company took control in 1916. The company would presumably have used whichever locomotives of their own that they had available. It is possible that the work carried out by the Guilford & Waldershare Colliery Co. on improving the Guilford branch might have required additional motive power but there is no record of this. Nor is there any evidence as to what locomotives, if any, were used on the construction of the Richborough Port branch, before the completion of the Stour bridge allowed the company's own locomotives to reach the works in progress. Locomotives could have been hired from PDL for this work.

East Kent Light Railways Locomotives

No. 1

Of all the 'Shepherdswell Sisters' little EKR No. 1 lays a claim as the most interesting one of the lot. It certainly possessed some claim to fame having had the honour of hauling the first official goods train on the line in October 1911. A further honour was the appearance of an engraving of this train on the company's share certificates.

No. 1, an 0-6-0 saddle tank with outside cylinders, was built in 1875 by Messrs Fox, Walker & Company of Bristol to its class 'B' design as Works No. 271. It was built for the Whitland & Taf Vale Railway (W&TVR) and, in view of the financial strictures under which the EKR was to operate, there was something prophetic in the circumstances of its acquisition.

This engine was due to be delivered as W&TVR No. 2 in January 1875 but Fox, Walker seem to have had doubts about the security offered by the company. Unfortunately the company's only other locomotive, another Fox, Walker of the same type and named *John Owen* after the railway's Chairman, chose this moment to break down. The company therefore claimed compensation for its loss and inconvenience. Fox, Walker, who had already agreed to accept payment by instalments, now agreed to pay £125 in compensation and to sell the locomotive outright to the company after five years from 1st January, 1875 for an additional payment of £5. It was agreed to make delivery on 1st March but even this date could not be kept and delivery did not take place until 10th March. For good measure a further £50 compensation was paid.

Right: No. 1 as illustrated in the *Railway Magazine* in December 1911 freshly painted and polished but with an open cab.

Below: No. 1 at Tilmanstone with a special train for shareholders in November 1912. Note the temporary wooden cab fitting.
Colonel Stephens Railway Museum

Bottom: No. 1 with rebuilt cab and still, just about, displaying original style of number.
M. Lawson Finch Collection

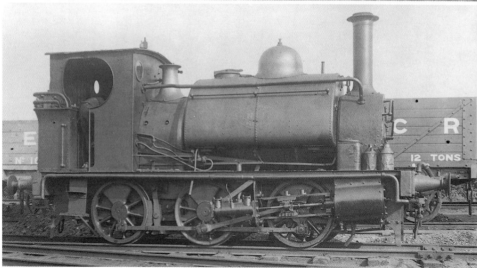

In 1877 the Whitland & Taf Vale Railway became the Whitland & Cardigan Railway and in 1886 its working was taken over by the Great Western Railway (GWR). The latter took the line's three locomotives into its own stock and numbered them 1385 to 1387. The GWR purchased the entire concern in 1890.

No. 2 became GWR No. 1386 and in June 1887 was rebuilt at Swindon with a new boiler having the dome on the front ring and safety valve cover over the firebox. A shorter saddle tank was fitted, but it must be presumed to have been of larger diameter as the capacity remained the same at 500 gallons. The new boiler was of greater diameter being 8 ft 0 in. by 3 ft 7½ in. with 197 one inch tubes. On GWR Diagram A6 the weight was shown as 24 tons 13 cwt though this diagram also gives the number of tubes as 200. No. 1386 spent most of its time on the Great Western after 1887 in the West Country, and is known to have operated at St Blazey and at Weymouth Docks.

According to the EKR Locomotive Register a further new boiler and a new copper firebox were fitted by the GWR in December 1907, together with new cylinders, pistons and valves.

The Register records a general overhaul in November 1909, the fitting of a new driving axle in May 1910 and new tyres in August 1911. In September 1911 it was sold to the Bute Works Supply Company, Cardiff, for £375. It seems that the company was acting for the EKR in this purchase as the Locomotive Register records the locomotive as 'Purchased, ex-Bute Works Supply Co. Ltd, Sept 1911'. Since the GWR dated its sale to Bute Works Supply as 27th September, 1911, this does not leave much time for No. 1386 to have made the journey to Cardiff and then to Shepherdswell before the end of the month. The question would be academic, were it not generally believed that No. 1386 arrived at Shepherdswell in a new coat of paint. Since there are considerable doubts about the exact colour used, it would have some bearing on this question to know whether the painting was done by the GWR or by Bute Works Supply.

Whatever the locomotive's movements prior to purchase might be, it was certainly credited with having hauled the first 'official' goods train between Shepherdswell and Tilmanstone Colliery in October 1911. From then on No. 1, as it had become, took a full part in construction work as well as hauling materials to Tilmanstone Colliery. On several occasions No. 1 was also employed on special passenger workings for the benefit of shareholders.

In August 1912 the Locomotive Register records that No. 1 was fitted with a new right-hand injector. Unfortunately this is the only mechanical attention to No. 1 that is recorded in the Register and relatively few other details are to be found in the other surviving archive sources. This is a pity as photographs of the locomotive over the years reveal a number of alterations that deserve a fuller explanation. The first of these is that the locomotive was fitted with a crosshead feed pump when delivered. This had been removed by 1913 and was still absent in 1919 but had been reinstated by 1923 and was still in place in 1933.

Another early alteration to take place was the enclosing of the locomotive's original open cab in 1912. This was achieved by constructing a rather ungainly back half to the cab out of wood. The 'home-made' effect was emphasised by the fact that the roof line of the extension failed to match the roof line of the

No. 1 displaying the short-lived Hawthorn, Leslie-style chimney at Shepherdswell, 23rd January, 1919.   *Ken Nunn Collection/LCGB*

No. 1 with final GWR-style chimney and cabside identification in September 1934.
                    Ron Jarvis/Midland Railway Trust

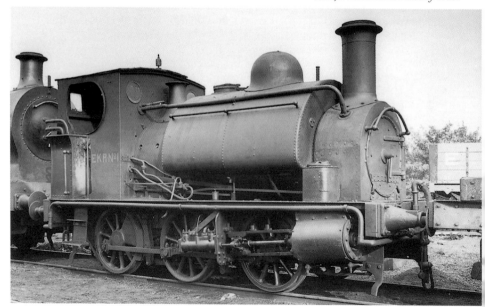

original half-cab. By 1914 this had been replaced by a much better looking steel extension. This could have passed as being part of the original design had it not been for the retention of the original coal rails, which curved decoratively though ineffectually around the rear sides of the new cab.

There is little further evidence of No. 1's early career but in view of the line's limited locomotive resources at this time it is probable that it was used on any duty for which a locomotive was needed. It is most likely to have been employed on the lighter duties on mixed trains to Wingham, shunting at Shepherdswell and Tilmanstone or assisting with the various continuing construction works.

In January 1919 No. 1 was photographed standing in Shepherdswell Yard with its dome cover removed. It is carrying a 'new' chimney remarkably similar to those originally fitted to the Kent & East Sussex Hawthorn, Leslie 2-4-0Ts subsequently replaced by stovepipe chimneys. It is possible that No. 1's chimney came from this source. A fairly heavy overhaul was in progress in 1920 when it is believed that some work was done on the boiler.

No. 1 was out of service again in 1925 giving rise to rumours at the time that it had been withdrawn. A memo survives reporting that 'No. 1 returned to service on 14th April', indicating that it was having another overhaul at this time.

There is some mystery surrounding No. 1's duties after 1920 as it only ever seems to have been photographed standing in Shepherdswell Yard. It is unlikely that it can have been used much on traffic duties to Wingham or Sandwich Road without being photographed and with several locomotives available capable of handling the coal traffic from Tilmanstone it is unlikely that it would have been employed on this. The likeliest use would be shunting at Tilmanstone. Here there was not only a need to assemble trains of loaded wagons and distribute empty wagons for loading, but there was also internal traffic to the bunkers and landsales wharf. There could also have been suitable, and equally unrecorded, employment for No. 1 on the Guilford branch improvements and the intermittent construction of the Richborough line.

In December 1932 No. 1 received a new chimney. The chimney carried in 1919 does not appear to have been satisfactory and its taller Whitland & Cardigan chimney had been refitted at some time in the 1920s on a newly fabricated base. The new chimney fitted in 1932 had a distinctly Great Western appearance but was shorter and thicker than its predecessors and its heavier appearance never really suited No. 1.

No. 1's last recorded run was on 22nd September, 1934. In 1935 the Directors decided to see whether a second-hand boiler could be obtained for locomotive No. 8. If this proved possible it was agreed to dispose of No. 1. In the event it was decided to purchase locomotive No. 100 and to dispose of both No. 1 and No. 8. On 17th July, 1935 it was reported to the Directors that both locomotives had been sold to George Cohen & Sons for £95. Cutting up took place at Shepherdswell but for some reason various parts of both locomotives were left lying around the yard for several years afterwards. One part that was salvaged from No. 1 was the new chimney which was fitted to locomotive No. 7 and suited that locomotive almost as little as it had suited No. 1.

Livery

Prior to arrival on the EKR No. 1 bore the standard livery of the Great Western Railway. It is possible that it was painted in 'middle green' just before delivery. Certainly the photographs of the first official goods train in October 1911 show the engine in a new and gleaming livery but opinions differ as to whether the chosen colour was blue or green. Mr E. Hougham of Ash, who was on the line when No. 1 was delivered, said in 1956 that he had always been under the impression that this engine arrived painted dark green. However, Mr A.G. Crawshaw, who had studied EKR locomotive liveries very thoroughly, suggested that as the engine was purchased in the middle of what might be termed Stephens' 'blue period', the likely livery for No. 1 would have been blue. Certain older members of the EKR staff who were interviewed prior to World War II favoured the view that No. 1 arrived painted blue but would not have sworn to it. In the absence of either documentary or photographic evidence the matter is unlikely ever to be settled satisfactorily.

With all the foregoing in mind the painting can be described in detail. The rear half of the cab side and the back of the cab, footplate edging and wheels were in plain unlined blue or green. The cylinders, tank sides and front, cab sides and front, sandboxes, steps and bunker sides and back were blue or green lined out with a single red line. The smokebox, toolboxes and the remainder of the locomotive were black. The chimney cap was polished copper and the dome, safety valves, both whistles, cab front window frames and firebox front ring were polished brass with the connecting rods, handrails and smokebox handles of polished steel. On the middle of the tank sides was inscribed in unshaded yellow the words EAST KENT RAILWAY between two concentric ellipses surrounding the figure 1 in the centre. This was a fairly standard totem on Stephens' railways and is similar to that of the Metropolitan Railway where he had served his apprenticeship.

The paintwork gradually deteriorated so that a full re-paint was called for at the 1920 overhaul. No. 1's new appearance was an austere unlined black with EKR No. 1 in a single line on the cab sides in unshaded yellow. The chimney cap, safety valves, handrails and coupling rods were still polished from time to time. Around 1925 the rear cab windows were altered from circular to square. By the 1930s a further re-paint was due but never materialised and even with its new chimney the locomotive gave a general impression of neglect. Although not specifically recorded it is probable that its buffer beams were always the regulation vermilion.

No. 2 Walton Park

EKR No. 2 was another outside-cylinder 0-6-0 saddle tank locomotive. It was built in May 1908 by Hudswell, Clarke & Company, Works No. 823, for the Weston, Clevedon & Portishead Light Railway (WC&PR) in Somerset at a cost of £1,200. It was delivered at Clevedon on 4th July painted in Hudswell, Clarke's standard Midland Red livery. It was named *Walton Park* after a station on the WC&PR.

Walton Park was a standard industrial engine adapted for passenger service by the fitting of vacuum brakes, screw couplings and a copper-capped chimney.

Possibly to create clearance for the vacuum pipes, large packing blocks were fixed behind the front buffers.

Walton Park worked on the WC&PR for four years but proved too heavy for the lightly-laid track on that line. When Holman Stephens took over the management of the WC&PR in 1911 one of his early decisions was to find employment elsewhere for this engine which was shortly transferred to the Shropshire & Montgomeryshire Railway, another line under his management. Its stay here was brief as on Saturday 26th April, 1913 Stephens' trusted lieutenant, W.H. Austen, penned the following letter to his employer:

Dear Sir,

Loco Walton Park Salop to Shepherdswell

It is being arranged for the above to be transferred at Meole Brace Junction on Monday next the 28th and at 10.30 am en route to Shepherdswell, pending the above loco runs cool, after the trial trip this afternoon, the result which I was unable to get at the time of leaving our Salop station this afternoon at 4.30 pm although I tried to get Kinnerley several times before leaving. Mr Stanton has promised to wire me result at Euston station which I shall get on arrival and will enclose herewith. I have seen the correspondence which has passed with reference to the transit of this loco and would like to make a suggestion.

I certainly think that one of our men should travel with the loco to see it has every attention. I suggest you let Driver King travel with it. I am sure he will give every attention to it. This can be arranged if you agree to the following. Let Driver Taylor work main-line trains with Fitter Leaker as relief, Night Cleaner-Fireman Jones do the branch driving, this man is quite capable of doing this having been loco driving several years for Mr Rigby before he came with us and myself should not hesitate to put him in charge of a locomotive.

I have arranged this course in the event of you agreeing. If you do will you wire to Mr White or Stanton first thing tomorrow morning (Sunday) so that wire reaches Salop before Office closes at 10.00 am similar to following - 'Driver King accompany *Walton Park* Salop to Shepherdswell, Taylor drive main line, Jones branch line, Leaker arrange.'

This matter can then be arranged in time for Monday morning providing you agree.

Yours faithfully

W.H. Austen

This letter not only conveys the intricacies of staffing Britain's light railways, but is a salutary comment on the ease of communications in an age when it was possible to write a letter on Saturday with every confidence that it would be received and acted upon by Sunday morning! Since the EKR Locomotive Register records the purchase of *Walton Park* as taking place on 28th April, 1913 it must be presumed that it ran cool in the tests referred to by Austen.

On the EKR *Walton Park* was numbered 2 but retained its nameplates. Apart from the contractors' locomotives and the two locomotives hired from the Kent & East Sussex this was the only named locomotive to work for the railway. It is likely that No. 2, being both sturdier and younger than No. 1, was set to the heavier work of hauling coal from Tilmanstone as soon as the pit began to produce coal. The arrival of *Hecate* from the Kent & East Sussex in 1916 may have freed No. 2 for general duties once the line was open for passenger traffic.

By February 1917 *Walton Park* was ready for re-tubing with a new set of steel tubes being fitted. According to Donald Bradley it was dispatched in April to

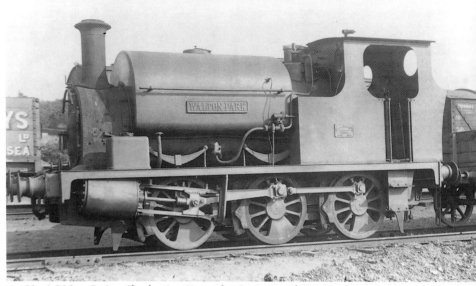

No. 2 *Walton Park* at Shepherdswell on 7th July, 1923 with Hudswell, Clarke plates fitted on forward cab side.   *A.W. Croughton*

No. 2 at Shepherdswell on 6th August, 1927. The Hudswell, Clarke plates are now on the rear cab side. 'E K R' is clearly lettered on the forward cabside but no numeral is shown on the sides.
                                                                                H.C. Casserley

help out on the Plymouth, Devonport & South Western Junction Railway, a line on which Stephens had done much engineering work and with which, although no longer employed there, he maintained good relations. *Walton Park* returned to Shepherdswell in May or June 1917. This has given rise to some accounts giving 1917 as the date on which *Walton Park* was acquired by the EKR. How the EKR managed in *Walton Park's* absence is unclear.

The locomotive situation had sufficiently eased by February 1920 for No. 2 to be withdrawn for a general overhaul. This involved re-tyring all wheels, new chimney, new smokebox front and new axlebrasses, coupling rod brasses, big end brasses, right-hand eccentric strap, motion bar slippers and motion pins. The firebox also required attention with copper patches being fitted to the tube plate and both the right- and left-side sheets.

During the 1920s *Walton Park* was more often seen on the mixed trains to Wingham. In October 1924 it passed a hydraulic boiler test to 210 lb. per square inch. In October 1926 its boiler was sent to Avonside Engineering at Bristol where it was retubed and tested to 250 lb. per square inch. A contemporary note lists a range of other repairs: new smokebox tubeplate, new copper firebox, welding defective firebox wrapper, overhauling safety valves and boiler mountings. Photographic evidence suggests that the maker's plate was moved from the cab side plate to the side of the bunker when reassembly took place.

In 1936 *Walton Park* was standing in the locomotive siding alongside the shed road with its boiler removed but it is not clear whether the boiler was sent away for repairs again at this time. During 1937 the engine was raised on blocks in Shepherdswell Yard and a general overhaul carried out before the boiler was reinstated. The engine was completely repainted in a new lined green livery and its nameplates were removed. *Walton Park* seems to have been turned around during this overhaul – all earlier photos show it facing Wingham, in subsequent photos it is facing Shepherdswell.

In 1941 No. 2 was inspected by the manager of the Hastings & Saint Leonards Gasworks. Although the Gasworks subsequently decided against purchase, there were a number of incorrect reports at the time that No. 2 had been sold. Instead it continued to work intermittently on the EKR. Unfortunately only the last volume of the railway's locomotive mileage register, dating from August 1942, has survived. This shows No. 2 as working in August and September 1942 and in January, February, April, May and August 1943. No subsequent movements are reported and the Directors' Minutes for 22nd July, 1943 recorded a decision to sell both No. 2 and No. 5. On 25th November, 1943 the Directors were informed that No. 2 had been sold for £575.

The purchaser was T.W. Ward & Co. of Titan Works, Grays, Essex who had completely overhauled their acquisition by 1945. In December 1945 the engine was sold to the Purfleet Deep Water Wharf & Storage Company, Essex, where it was named *Churchill* and continued to work until sold for scrap in 1957. At some time during this period it was fitted with the boiler and saddle tank from a Thornewill & Warham engine originally built for Bass Brewery at Burton in 1876 as an 0-4-0 well tank, No. 8, but converted by Hunslet into a 0-4-0 saddle tank in 1898. As can be imagined the combination of parts from such different sources produced an appearance totally unlike the original *Walton Park*,

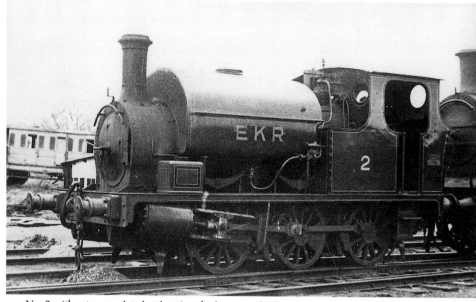

No. 2 without nameplate but bearing the later standard green livery in 1938.

No. 2 running as *Churchill* at Purfleet wharf.

G. Alliez

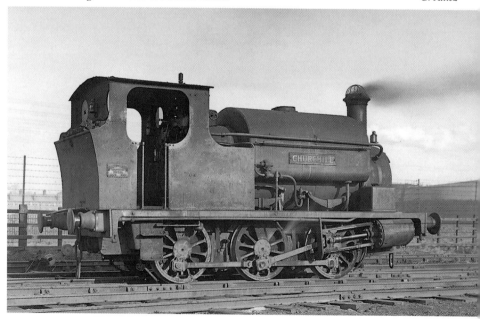

particularly as the conversion also included the fitting of Salter safety valves and a new chimney with a hemispherical spark catcher.

As a final observation on *Walton Park's* career on the EKR it should be noted that several of the staff said that this engine was referred to as 'The Coffee Pot'. This nickname is usually used to describe either vertical-boilered or very antiquated locomotives. *Walton Park* may not have been new but was one of the younger locomotives on the EKR and certainly of more modern appearance than No. 1. Perhaps some unrecorded incident or peculiarity of the engine's operation earned it the title, but this seems to be yet another piece of EKR folklore that will never be explained.

Livery

Walton Park is known to have been delivered to the Weston, Clevedon & Portishead painted in 'Midland Red', a standard colour applied to many of Hudswell, Clarke's industrial locomotives. It must have been made up of particularly enduring ingredients as it lasted until the 1930s. The exact livery as delivered to Shepherdswell was as follows:

Footplate edging and steps: red with a thin yellow line.
Cab sides, front and back, bunker sides and back, tank sides and front, cylinders and sand boxes: red lined with a thick dark line (various descriptions give this as black, brown or green) edged both sides with a thin yellow line.
Wheels: unlined red.
Buffer beams: vermilion lined in white and edged in black with No. lettered one side of the coupling hook and 2 on the other side in unshaded yellow. By about 1924 the lining had disappeared.
Coupling rods, handrails, smokebox handles and the copper chimney cap were all polished when time and inclination allowed.
Nameplates: background variously reported as black or crimson.
Lettering: none at first but by 1927 it sported the letters E K R well spaced and without stops placed centrally across the cab sides in yellow shaded black or green; there was no number on the locomotive side at this stage.
Worksplates: distinctive square plates fixed in the centre of the cab sides at first but moved to the bunker sides when the lettering was applied.

After the 1937 overhaul No. 2 was repainted by the EKR painter, Jim Smith, in Southern-style mid-green. Lining was not unlike the earlier scheme with a thick dark band of black or brown edged on either side with a thin yellow line. This was applied to the front, sides and rear of the sandboxes, around the edges of the saddle tank, around both cab and bunker side sheets as a continuous line and not divided in two as with the original livery. The cylinders were lined on the ends of the wrappings with the thick dark line with one thin yellow line on the inside and the green footplate edging was also lined in black with a thin yellow line on the top. The wheels were green and the hubs bore a circle of black lined on both sides with thin yellow lines. The nameplates were removed and replaced by large unshaded yellow letters E K R. A plain unshaded yellow '2' appeared on the cab sides. The front buffer beam was unlined vermilion with 'No' and '2' appearing as before but in yellow-shaded black. The smokebox, chimney and smokebox door were black but the coupling rods and handrails

No. 2 at Purfleet in September 1954 as rebuilt with Thornewill & Wareham boiler and saddle tank.   *G. Bartlet*

No. 3 as LSWR No. 0394 at Waterloo on 8th March, 1902.   *Ken Nunn Collection/LCGB*

remained bright. At this time the background to the worksplates was painted red but it is not known if this was true of the earlier livery. In some photographs the front cab spectacles appear to have been edged by thin yellow or white lines.

No. 3

This was the first locomotive to be withdrawn by the EKR, as early as 1928. As a result it is better remembered in the forlorn state in which it lingered on in Shepherdswell Yard after withdrawal than in its working condition.

No. 3 was a light 0-6-0 tender locomotive with two inside cylinders and had been built in 1880 by Beyer, Peacock & Company of Gorton, Manchester for the London & South Western Railway (LSWR). It was numerically the last of a class of eight locomotives. The first members of the class had been ordered in 1872 for service on the Barnstaple to Ilfracombe line which was due to open in 1873. In the event opening was delayed until 1874 but this did not prevent the class from becoming known as the 'Ilfracombe Goods'. Six of the class were eventually to be purchased by Holman Stephens for operation on three of the lines under his management.

The Ilfracombe branch was to be a heavily graded line and various special designs were proposed and rejected until, with time pressing, Beattie selected a standard Beyer, Peacock model. Although known as 'Ilfracombe Goods' they were used on both passenger and goods. The final pair, Nos. 393 and 394 (Works Nos. 2041 and 2042), were delivered in 1880. The EKR engine was No. 394. This last pair were of slightly more substantial appearance with thicker tyres, stovepipe chimneys, larger sandboxes, metal brakeshoes and weighed in at 25 tons 4 cwt instead of the 24 tons 7½ cwt of the earlier model.

Between 1888 and 1890 the earlier members of the class were rebuilt with new boilers and other improvements including six-wheeled tenders. Nos. 393 and 394, followed suit at a later date. Otherwise this pair remained substantially as delivered, except that No. 394 exchanged its original dome surmounted by Salter valves for one fitted with Drummond self-loading valves when a new firebox was fitted at some time after 1902. Gradually the class was relegated to lighter duties and placed on the duplicate list; No. 394 became 0394 in 1902 and carried the underlined style of duplicate numbering as 394.

Nos. 0301 and 0393 were withdrawn in 1905 and broken up although their boilers were retained for stationary use elsewhere. Between 1909 and 1916 Stephens bought five of the six remaining 'Ilfracombes' for his Kent & East Sussex and Shropshire & Montgomeryshire lines. No. 0394 was put into store in late 1913 but in 1916 was put back into service shunting at Eastleigh. As the last member of its class it would not have been expected to last long on the LSWR but in 1918 the EKR came to its rescue. The Minutes of the LSWR Locomotive and Carriage and Wagon Committee for 10th October, 1918 record its transfer to the EKR as follows:

The General Manager reported an arrangement made with the East Kent Railway Company for the hire to them of one of this company's 6-wheel coupled type locomotive

No. 3 at Shepherdswell on 23rd January, 1919 still carrying LSWR livery.

Ken Nunn Collection/LCGB

No. 3 at Wingham Town in the early 1920s carrying its EKR number on the buffer beam but not much else in the way of identification.

engines for a term of 5 years from the 1st August, 1918 at a rent of £200 for each year by monthly payments of £16 13s. 4d. The hirers have to keep the engine in good working order and may purchase it at any time upon payment of all instalments then unpaid plus one shilling. The agreement setting forth the arrangement was sealed by the Chairman of the company on 11th September.

The EKR Locomotive Register records delivery as having taken place in November 1918 so it may well have been spruced up before going to Shepherdswell.

It is interesting to note that this locomotive was originally entered in the EKR Locomotive Register as No. 0394 and that No. 3 was added to the entry at a later date. It is likely that the railway was not entirely sure of its ability to keep up payments on the engine and therefore it retained its LSWR livery and identity for some considerable time after delivery. Despite a story that No. 3's period of hire was shortly brought to an end by an outright purchase with money provided by the Government, EKR records confirm that purchase was actually completed in 1926.

There is relatively little photographic evidence of this engine's duties on the EKR. That which has survived suggests that it was primarily used on the passenger and mixed train duties to Wingham rather than on the Tilmanstone coal traffic. Its better water capacity would have suited it well for the Wingham traffic where the loads were rarely taxing.

According to the Locomotive Register No. 3 required its left cylinder to be bored out and bushed with a cast-iron bush of 14½ in. diameter in 1921. This work and the fitting of a new piston and rings were done by the Wingham Engineering Company. On completion of this work the engine was coupled up by the EKR and returned to service on 11th November, 1921.

In 1925 a general overhaul took place. The valves and pistons were examined and new rings fitted; port faces and valves were faced up and new tail rod bushes fitted to the valve spindles. The injectors were overhauled and new injector valve spindles were fitted, together with the big and little end and coupling rod brasses. The motion bars were 'closed', presumably this meant tightening up to prevent loose play. A new firehole ring patch was fitted and stays and tubes renewed as necessary. The engine and tender steam brakes were overhauled with new spring and brake pins being fitted where necessary. Finally a new chimney was fitted. This was of the same pattern as before but appears to have been attached at the base by means of a riveted collar. On completion of these works the boiler was given a hydraulic test and No. 3 returned to service on the 23rd December.

Although the list of items attended to in the 1925 overhaul is extensive it falls considerably short of the sort of renewal which No. 3 might be judged as needing by this date. No. 3 continued in service until 1927 but was out of use in 1928. A photograph taken in May 1929 shows it standing in Shepherdswell Yard with a sheet of metal weighted down on top of the chimney to keep out the elements. It may have been intended to give No. 3 a further overhaul but instead it was left to decay slowly. The Directors' Minutes for 15th October, 1931 record their consent to the disposal of No. 3, which was photographed that month standing at the end of the locomotive siding up against a pile of old sleepers. All its buffers had been removed, its chimney was missing and its dome cover was sitting in the tender.

Later in the 1920s and that LSWR lettering is starting to appear through the worn paintwork. The rear coupling rod has been removed but it is not known if it ever actually ran as an 0-4-2.

Awaiting the end - No. 3 in forlorn condition in the carriage siding at Shepherdswell in 1932.

The rear portion of the left-hand coupling rod was off as were the boiler bands with the boiler cladding slowly lifting out of place.

The Minutes for 21st January, 1932 record that £50 had been offered for No. 3 but Austen was instructed to try to obtain £60. There is no further reference to No. 3 in the Minutes but a note survives recording its sale for scrap in 1934.

Livery

No. 3 was delivered to Shepherdswell in LSWR livery and numbered 394. The LSWR livery would have been the goods locomotive livery of holly green which darkened in service and could be mistaken for black after a time. The normal interval for repainting was four years and in view of No. 3's period out of use, its use on shunting duties between 1916 and 1918 and the problems of wartime shortages, it would have been some considerable time since No. 3 had been last painted when it was delivered to Shepherdswell. Photographs taken by Ken Nunn in 1919 indicate that No. 3 had not been repainted before delivery. It is therefore likely that it arrived in a very dark, almost black, green livery. The green would have been edged in black with a thin separating line of pea green or white, depending on the date of painting, or no lining at all if repainted after 1917. Buffer beams would have been vermilion and lettering and numbering would have been in gilt shaded in black. Looking at the engine from the front the number 394 appeared on the left-hand of the buffer beam between the buffer and the coupling hook. '394' was displayed on the cab sides and 'L S W R' appeared in large letters along the tender sides. It is not clear whether any number appeared on the tender buffer beam but this was the normal practice.

No. 3 was repainted at some time before 1925 and the general opinion appears to have been that black was the chosen colour. The front buffer beam was embellished with 'No.' to one side of the coupling hook and '3' to the other. It seems that the previous cabside number was simply painted over and no number applied in its place, but the locomotive is so dirty in the available photographs that it is not possible to say this with absolute certainty. On the tender sides the 'L' was adapted to make an 'E', the 'S' and 'W' were painted out and a new 'K' inserted in the gap between them and the 'R' was retained. There is no record of the colour used for lettering and numbering. Yellow or white would seem the most likely.

The paint used in the above repaint seems to have been of very inferior quality or was applied sparingly as No. 3's previous identity had begun to re-emerge by the end of the 1920s. This led to the initials on the tender appearing as 'E SKW R' and the re-appearance of '394' on the cabsides. When the well-known railway photographer H.C. Casserley visited the line in 1931 he filled in the original number on the cabside in chalk and most photographs taken subsequently show this number very clearly. This has led to a mistaken belief that No. 3 never lost its LSWR identity while on the railway.

THIS LOCOMOTIVE IS THE JOINT PROPERTY

OF THE EAST KENT COLLIERY CO LTD &

THE GUILFORD & WALDERSHARE COLY CO LTD

Plate fixed to No. 4 and now held in the Colonel Stephens Railway Museum at Tenterden.

Kerr, Stuart's publicity photograph of one of No. 4's classmates.   *M. Lawson Finch Collection*

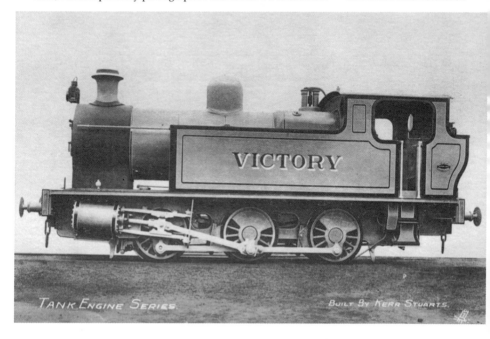

No. 4

No. 4, a solidly built and ruggedly handsome engine, was the one that enthusiasts were most likely to glimpse from the cool cover of the woods that in later years encroached upon the engine shed. There it stood, basking in the sun, a lazy plume of steam wafting from its safety valves from which emanated a peculiar high-pitched buzzing sound. The scene was sylvan and friendly and not easily forgotten.

No. 4 was an outside-cylinder 0-6-0 side tank locomotive built in May 1917 by Kerr, Stuart & Company of Stoke-on-Trent as their Works No. 3067. It was one of that manufacturer's 'Victory' class. The company used a publicity photograph of the next member of the class, Works No. 3068, with the name *Victory* painted in large letters along the tank side. The engine was built for the War Department and was initially allocated to the Railway Operating Division (ROD) as ROD No. 602 but was delivered to the Inland Waterways & Docks Department (IWDD) in June 1917 as IWDD No. 11. Nine other members of the class were delivered to the IWDD between June and September 1917. There are different versions of the initial locations of these locomotives and No. 11 is credited with delivery to both Southampton and Richborough. By October 1919 No. 11 was definitely at Richborough, where it was sold into the joint ownership of the East Kent Colliery Company and the Guilford & Waldershare Colliery Company. The new owners bought the engine for use on the EKR where it seems to have gone into service soon after purchase by them, although it was not until 3rd November, 1920 that a contract was sealed between the three parties for the hire purchase of the engine by the railway. The price was to be £71 12s. 7d. per month for four years, making a total of £3,438 4s. 0d. of which £1,310 2s. 3d. was owed to the Guilford & Waldershare Colliery Company. The debt to this company was paid off in 1925, but the payments to the East Kent Colliery Company became embroiled in a complicated dispute over traffic rates, debts left over from the Concessions period and the ownership of a parcel of land at Tilmanstone. It was not until 1932 that agreement was reached with the Tilmanstone (Kent) Colliery Company to consider any obligations outstanding from the hire purchase of the engine to be discharged.

Part of the hire purchase agreement included an obligation not to alter the appearance of the engine, so it was some time before it was officially described as No. 4 but to avoid confusion that is how we shall refer to it. One final point relating to the hire purchase agreement was that it required the engine to carry a plate reading 'This locomotive is the joint property of the East Kent Colliery Co. Ltd & the Guilford & Waldershare Coly Co. Ltd'. Shortage of space on the plate required the unusual abbreviation of Colliery to Coly. It is believed that this plate was fitted inside the cab. The plate has survived and may be seen in the Colonel Stephens Museum at Tenterden.

The motive of the two colliery companies in purchasing this engine for the EKR was obviously their dependence on the line for the delivery of materials and empty wagons to their premises and the transport of loaded wagons away. The Guilford & Waldershare Colliery was not yet producing coal but hoped

No. 4 in original condition on the East Kent. Traces of IWDD lining remain but no other identification is apparent.

No. 4 with new smokebox and new corporate livery in June 1934. The part of the engine shed in which it is standing has been demolished in preparation for building the new shed.

H.C. Casserley

soon to do so. The co-operation between the two collieries may be explained by the fact that the manager at Guilford had previously been the manager at Tilmanstone. When the IWDD locomotives were put up for auction on 28th October, 1919 it must have seemed an ideal opportunity for the two companies to guarantee adequate motive power for the EKR to meet their needs.

No. 4 was hauled dead one Sunday from Richborough to Shepherdswell via Deal and was put to work straight away. It was used exclusively on the Tilmanstone coal traffic as its weight precluded its operation on the lightly laid 'main line'. Its power would in any event have been greatly in excess of the needs of most of the other traffic that ever developed on the line. Its dedication to coal traffic would explain why it was the only EKR locomotive never to be equipped with vacuum brake equipment.

Mention has already been made of the continuing dispute between the EKR and the East Kent Colliery over payments for the engine. One hazard that was faced by No. 4 in its visits to Tilmanstone appears to have been occasional attempts by the colliery to take possession of the locomotive. According to one account there was once an attempt to cut off No. 4 at Tilmanstone by blocking the line behind it with old colliery trucks. No. 4 was a powerful engine and its driver had little relish for walking back to Shepherdswell to report the loss of his charge. He therefore opened the regulator as far as he dared and knocked the offending trucks out of the way in what was probably the finest turn of speed ever witnessed at Tilmanstone. A less credible story claims that at one time when relations between the railway and the colliery were particularly bad, No. 4 was jacked up on sleepers and its wheels removed to prevent a possible kidnapping. It is more likely that No. 4 was under overhaul at the time.

Tilmanstone Colliery was frequently in financial difficulties itself. On such occasions it was the railway's policy to hold outgoing coal wagons in Shepherdswell Yard until the colliery's cheque had been received. On one occasion the man in charge at Shepherdswell let a coal train onto the Southern without first securing the colliery's cheque. When this was discovered by the authorities at Salford Terrace the man was promptly dismissed. This was, however, done during one of Stephens' absences from Tonbridge. Upon his return he sought out the man and reinstated him with the remark, 'I'm the only one allowed to sack around here', at the same time pushing £20 into his hand. This story was related by the son of the man concerned.

There are no details in the Locomotive Register of overhauls carried out on No. 4, but a memo survives from Shepherdswell Locomotive Department to Stephens at Tonbridge on 9th May, 1925 apologising for failing to notify Stephens of No. 4's return to service on 19th March, 1925. This would suggest that it had been undergoing mechanical attention in that year sufficiently major for its return to service to be worthy of note. A note in the *Railway Magazine* in 1925 corroborates the fact that No. 4 had been out of use for some time although inaccurate in other respects: 'Engine No. 4 of the EKR has also been in steam for the first time since its arrival about a year ago!' A clue to the possible nature of the work carried out at this time is the appearance in photographs after this date of a riveted patch on the lower right-hand side of the smokebox.

By July 1932 No. 4 was feeling the effects of constant shuttling to and fro between Shepherdswell and Tilmanstone as it was reported at the Directors'

No. 4 from the other side and still looking smart in June 1936.

Ron Jarvis/Midland Railway Trust

No. 4 at Ashford works in 1949. Cutting up has begun.

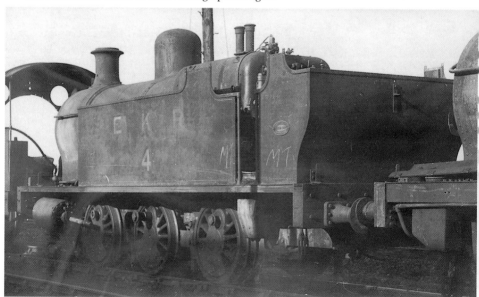

Meeting on the 21st of that month that it needed firebox and tyre repairs. On the 20th October, 1932 it was further reported to the Directors that the repairs needed by No. 4 would cost £476, or might be done more cheaply by buying a copper firebox for £178 10s. 0d. and tyres for £72 10s. 0d. and getting the Southern to fit these. Thus No. 4 set off to Ashford on the 7th December, 1932 for the fitting of a Hunslet firebox. The journey to Ashford was made at the rear of a coal train possibly in light steam as an EKR driver was in attendance on the footplate.

This work proved more extensive than had been anticipated as No. 4 did not return to Shepherdswell until 1st September, 1933, and even then did not go back into service until 14th October. This latter delay may have been due to repainting as No. 4 returned to service in a smart coat of mid-green with yellow lettering. An article in the *Railway Magazine* for September 1934 refers to No. 4 having been overhauled at Ashford where it had acquired a new smokebox and chimney. The new smokebox and chimney did not significantly alter No. 4's appearance, though the new smokebox door was smaller than that previously fitted and was surmounted by a curved handrail in place of the original straight pattern. The chimney was a standard Wainwright pattern.

No. 4 returned to its familiar duties between Shepherdswell and Tilmanstone and, apart from an overhaul in the yard at Shepherdswell between June and September 1939, continued to be so employed until April 1943. The Mileage Register then indicates that it was out of use until January 1945 when it returned to traffic for one day. This may have been to test its condition as the Directors' Minutes for 22nd February report that after two years out of service No. 4 was to be repaired at Shepherdswell. No. 4 returned to service in January 1946 and continued to work regularly until the Mileage Register closed on 1st May, 1948. No. 4's mileage from 23rd June, 1933 to 1st May, 1948 was recorded as 38,562 miles.

Nationalisation had little immediate impact on No. 4 or the other surviving EKR locomotives. A report in the *Railway Observer* of a visit to the line on 18th September, 1948 reported No. 4 as being under repair in Shepherdswell Shed. On 9th January, 1949 it was observed, partially dismantled, in Dover Shed. By now it had been allocated British Railways No. 30948 but the new number was never applied and it was withdrawn from British Railways stock the same month. On 21st February, 1949 it arrived at Ashford and according to the Erecting Shop records was cut up the next day. One curious aspect of its acquisition by British Railways was that its new owners considered it to be 'out of gauge' but this does not appear to have prevented its movement to Ashford in 1932.

As a postscript No. 4 was the first of the 10 Kerr Stuart IWDD locomotives to be scrapped. In 1949 the remainder of the class were distributed as follows:

Works No.	IWDD No.	Details
3066	10	Powell Duffryn No. 18 at the Aberaman Colliery.
3068	12	Manchester Collieries, named *Francis*.
3069	13	Alexandra (Newport & South Wales) Docks & Railway and later became GWR No. 666.
3070	14	Brecon & Merthyr Railway and became GWR No. 2161 before being sold to Ashington Colliery in 1929.

Works No.	IWDD No.	Details
3071	15	Powell Duffryn No. 19 at Aberaman Colliery.
3072	16	Tirpentwys Black Vein Steam Coal & Coke Company.
3073	17	As 3069 but GWR No. 667.
3074	18	Lambton Hetton & Joicey Collieries No. 41.
3075	19	United Steel Company No. 8 at Orgreave Colliery.

As can be seen, it was entirely appropriate that No. 4 should have spent most of its working life in the coal business.

Livery

No. 4 was delivered to Shepherdswell in IWDD livery as follows: The general colour was a medium grey but as time passed this became progressively coated in oil and dirt to present an appearance best described as brownish yellow! The cab sides, tank sides and coal bunker had a wide black border with a thin white line on the inner side. Separated from this border by a strip of grey of equal width was a black band edged on both sides by thin white lines. This secondary lining produced four panels within the black border - one on the tank sides, one on the bunker sides, one on the rear of the bunker, and a small vertical panel on the forward cab sides above the side tanks. 'I W & D D' was carried in large unshaded black letters on the tank sides. The buffer beam does not seem to have had any distinctive paintwork but shortly after arrival 'No.' and '4' were added in yellow shaded black. The IWDD identifications were not removed but were frequently obscured by dirt. No. 4 continued to carry this livery until 1933. It was a condition of the hire purchase agreement not to alter the engine's appearance and it was not until 1932 that the Tilmanstone authorities ceased to contest its ownership.

The livery applied after the 1933 overhaul has been described as Southern medium green with black chimney and smokebox. An unusual feature of these colours was the relatively high gloss. The cab, side tanks and bunker sides bore a continuous single black edging all the way round with a thin white line on the inside. A similar panel was carried on the rear of the bunker but the back and front of the cab were unlined. Two panels with the black border and inside white line were to be found on the step backplates, one above each step. Boiler bands were black lined in white on either side. Cylinder wrappers had front and back edgings in black with thin white lines on the inside edges. Wheels and dome were plain green. Buffer beams were vermilion with 'No'. to the left and '4' to the right in yellow shaded in black. At long last the Railway's initials appeared as large unshaded yellow letters E K R on the tank sides with a large '4' in unshaded yellow beneath the 'K'.

The livery applied to No. 4 became the standard model for subsequent repaints of other locomotives. Thus was turned out the first of the 'Smart Engines' which, once the pride of the little company, are not often recalled today as having been such a glorious sight. Weathering and the rigours of the coal traffic soon took their toll on No. 4's appearance but it was never reduced to the drab anonymity of its pre-1933 existence.

No. 5

EKR No. 5 was originally one of the '415' class of 4-4-2 tank locomotives built by various firms between 1882 and 1885 for the London & South Western Railway's suburban passenger traffic. These were popularly known as the 'Radials' from the trailing radial axle with which they were fitted. No. 5, originally LSWR No. 488, was one of a batch of 11 engines built by Neilson & Co. in March 1885 as Works No. 3209. It appears to have been based at Windsor initially, but the delivery of 'T1' 0-4-4 tank locomotives from 1888 onwards led to the early displacement of the class from suburban work. By 1895 No. 488 was at Exeter, moving subsequently to Bournemouth and then to Eastleigh.

The '415' class were designed by William Adams and were unusual in having relatively small side tanks with a larger well tank below the bunker and footplate. This reduced the weight carried by the coupled wheels and at first gave a better ride than was usual with a four-coupled outside cylinder type. Unfortunately their riding qualities tended to deteriorate significantly between overhauls and this was one of the reasons given by Adams for replacing them on fast commuter duties. They were, nevertheless, extremely attractive engines; even the Adams stovepipe chimneys with which they were fitted managed to look streamlined rather than utilitarian.

In 1903 No. 488's stovepipe chimney was replaced by one of the Drummond lipped pattern. From 1904 onwards the class began to be placed on the Duplicate List and No. 488 was designated 0488 in 1914 although, as with EKR No. 3, this was shown on the locomotive itself by a dash painted under the number. Shortly afterwards it was decided to withdraw the 30 worst specimens of the class and No. 0488 was one of the first eight to be set aside. The outbreak of war led to the repair and reinstatement of seven of these but No. 0488 remained in store until overhauled, painted dark green and sold to the Ministry of Munitions in 1917 for use at the Royal Naval General Salvage Depot at Ridham, near Sittingbourne. It was designated No. 27 here but there is no evidence that this number was actually carried. In late 1919 it moved to the General Stores Depot at Belvedere near Woolwich and was advertised for sale there in August 1920.

By 1920 there was no shortage of second-hand locomotives for sale. Not only did the various military authorities have a wide range of locomotives for disposal, but the main line companies were shedding many of their more elderly locomotives that had been reprieved at the outbreak of war. Under these circumstances there was no great onslaught of prospective purchasers for 'No. 27'. It was an unlikely prospect for the market in many ways. Its axle loading was on the heavy side for light railway work and it hardly fitted the usual specifications for industrial shunting. Unless a major overhaul had been carried out before its sale to the Ministry of Munitions, it is unlikely to have been in particularly good condition after its period of storage at Eastleigh. Nevertheless, something about it must have appealed to Holman Stephens who purchased it from the Disposal & Liquidation Commission in March 1923, delivery to Shepherdswell taking place on 13th April. Here it became No. 5.

Although the date of acquisition is clearly recorded in the Locomotive Register and is supported by other official sources there have been numerous claims that the EKR acquired No. 5 in 1919, 1920 or 1921. These appear to have

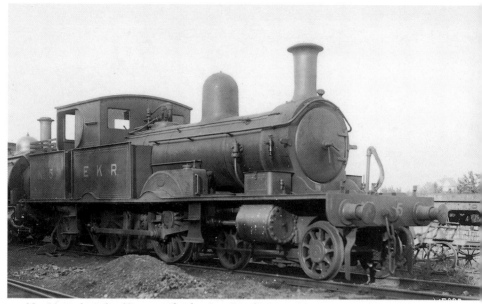

No. 5 in early style of livery at Shepherdswell in the late 1920s.

No. 5 caught in mid-overhaul in May 1935.

Ron Jarvis/Midland Railway Trust

been based on casual replies by Stephens to enquiries concerning the origins of No. 5. Stephens made a number of such misleading statements over the years and it would appear that accuracy in this aspect of the affairs of the railways that he managed was of little importance to him. His enthusiasm for railways did not mean that he was a railway enthusiast in the currently accepted sense. There is some evidence that he found the interest of many contemporary enthusiasts tiresome and that he resented the way in which his lines were represented as living museums, rather than as masterpieces of economy. If approached in the right way, however, he would try to be as helpful as he could, but as a busy man this did not mean that he would necessarily scour through his records before supplying the information sought.

There is no record in the Locomotive Register of the price paid for No. 5 but the company's financial records give a price of £375. This presumably supplies the missing attraction of No. 5 to Stephens. If it was in any sort of reasonable condition it was a bargain, even though its axle loading was heavier than appropriate for the services to Wingham and its design suited rapid acceleration on passenger turns rather than shunting or coal haulage. If the EKR was looking for a sturdy workhorse it seems to have found a retired racehorse instead.

Upon delivery No. 5 was patch painted to show 'E K R' and '5'. Photographs taken in 1927 show 'E K R' on the tanks and 'No. 5' on the bunker sides with faint traces of lining. By 1930 both lettering and numbers had become almost invisible and this continued until the locomotive was laid aside at Shepherdswell in 1934 and subjected to the removal of various vital organs. In a photograph taken by Dr Hollick on 10th March, 1934, No. 5 is missing its chimney, cab, coupling rods, firebox cladding and lagging, front cylinder covers and sand boxes. A visitor to the line in October 1935 was told that No. 5 was 'under repair' but since there was no sign of the engine at Shepherdswell it must be assumed that it had been sent to Ashford for overhaul. In 1936 it was back on the EKR and undergoing a complete repaint in SR green at the hands of Jim Smith. It was said at the time that this was in connection with a proposal to work the engine through to Wingham for which the track beyond Eastry was being strengthened.

It is curious that the only EKR location at which No. 5 appears to have been photographed is Shepherdswell. Although it is obviously in steam in some of these views there are few photographs of it actually attached to a train. This would suggest that it was mainly employed on shunting duties at Tilmanstone or on the infrequently-photographed coal trains between Tilmanstone and Shepherdswell. At least one such trip recalled by George Clements ended in potentially tragic circumstances. Driver Griffin and guard Russell were running a coal train up to Shepherdswell and had '14 on', the maximum load No. 5 was apparently allowed. The normal practice at Shepherdswell was for the train to halt as soon as it had cleared the Eythorne to Shepherdswell road. The brakes would then be applied to enough wagons to hold the train and the engine would be uncoupled and run down into the shed siding. The engine being clear, the points would be reset and the train, with its brakes released, would roll down by gravity into the transfer siding to await delivery to the Southern Railway.

On this occasion No. 5 had run down to the locomotive shed, the brakes on the wagons had been released and the wagons had begun to roll. So far so good until a horrified Russell realised that instead of the wagons entering the transfer siding they were pursuing No. 5 into the shed siding . . . the points had not been reset! Russell tried in vain to apply the brake levers as the wagons passed him. No doubt driver Griffin was not unmoved when he saw what was bearing down on him, but he was even more moved when he and his engine were swept into the shed and clean out of the back to finish up in the orchard beyond. Unfortunately the year of this incident could not be recalled but the Directors' Minutes for October 1930 record that the Shepherdswell Shed had been damaged by driver Griffin on 6th August of that year. This does not, however, appear to have been the first or last such occurrence and it may have been another locomotive that was involved in the 1930 incident.

There are several reports of No. 5 in the *Railway Observer* between 1937 and 1941. A report of a visit on 10th August, 1937 included the information that No. 5 was painted green with yellow lettering and red coupling rods but that it was not in use on that day. On 2nd September, 1938 No. 5 was recorded as being in the shed at Shepherdswell but would be taking over the mixed train duties to Wingham from No. 2 on the following day. On 17th May, 1939 No. 5 was recorded as outside the shed '. . . and has not been used for some time'. A visit in July 1939 did not deal with locomotives individually but recorded them all as in working condition except for No. 4. Finally a visit in November 1940 found No. 5 '. . . outside the shed and looked as if it had been out of use for some time'.

No. 5 continued to see occasional use until 1943. The Locomotive Mileage Register records that it worked once a month from August to November 1942 and worked twice in February 1943, three times in March, four times in April and three times in May. Its very last run on the Railway was on 23rd May, 1943. In July 1943 the Directors agreed to sell No. 5 and No. 2 and at the November 1943 Directors' Meeting it was reported that it was hoped to raise £450 by the sale of No. 5. This proved optimistic as by November 1945 the locomotive had still not been sold although Ward's had offered £61 and Geo. Cohen had offered £80. Under these circumstances the Directors decided to ask the Southern Railway for advice on a fair price for No. 5. Instead of advice the Southern came up with an offer to buy the locomotive themselves. On 28th February, 1946 the Directors' Minutes recorded that the Southern would buy No. 5 for £120. It left Shepherdswell on 14th March and arrived at Ashford the next day for onward dispatch to Eastleigh. According to the late Donald Bradley No. 5 had only run 172,165 miles in Government and EKR service. Even allowing for its years out of service this was a fairly low mileage and confirms the suspicion that its value to the railway was somewhat limited.

For those only interested in No. 5's history as an EKR locomotive this is really the end of its story. However, so unexpected and lengthy has been its career since then that it would be wrong not to include a short reference to it at this point.

No. 5 arrived at Eastleigh on 24th April. It had presented a curious sight on this journey. For some time before its sale it had been stabled in a position where one side was particularly well sheltered. This had left the paintwork on this side well preserved whilst the side exposed to the elements had become severely weathered. As a result the reports of its journey between Ashford and Eastleigh varied enormously depending on which side of the tracks the observant enthusiasts were standing.

On arrival at Eastleigh No. 5 was renumbered 3488 and thoroughly overhauled at a cost of £1,638. This overhaul included the fitting of a spare Drummond boiler in exchange for the Adams boiler it had carried on the EKR. During the overhaul it was discovered that the frames had been crudely but effectively strengthened with patches around the coupled wheel boxes.

The Southern's purpose in buying No. 5 and spending so much on its overhaul was to employ it on the Lyme Regis branch. Adams Radial tanks had proved to be the only locomotives really suitable for this line and the Southern had retained two of the class for it, Nos. 3125 and 3520. As these locomotives aged it became necessary to draft in 'O2' 0-4-4T locomotives to help out when the Radials were not available. Unfortunately the 'O2s' were extremely punishing to the sharply-curved line and the opportunity to acquire a spare Radial must have been a boon to both the motive power and permanent way departments. No. 3488 left Eastleigh for Exmouth Junction in December 1946 and was soon at work on its new territory.

Upon Nationalisation No. 3488 was renumbered 30583 in accordance with a policy of numbering surviving ex-LSWR duplicate list locomotives in a series between 30564 and 30589. The other two Radials became No. 30582, previously No. 3125, and No. 30584, previously No. 3520. No. 30583 did not actually receive its new number until overhauled in October 1949, when it also acquired British Railways lined black livery. Further overhauls took place in 1953 and 1959. At the 1959 overhaul No. 30583 regained its Adams boiler.

In 1958 it was decided to ease the more difficult curves on the line with a view to replacing the Radials with Ivatt class '2' 2-6-2T locomotives. By 1960 this work had been completed and No. 41297 was tried out. These trials were successful and No. 30584 was withdrawn in January 1961. Nos. 30582 and 30583 were retained while remaining doubts about the 2-6-2Ts were considered. By April 1961 these had been resolved and 30583 was sent to Eastleigh in June. Nos. 30584 and 30582 were broken up in 1962 but No. 30583 had meanwhile been bought for preservation on the Bluebell Railway in July 1961. No. 5, in various guises as LSWR No. 488 and BR No. 30583, is still running in the ownership of the Bluebell Railway. Since its story is bound to continue this is not the place to chronicle its deeds in preservation. Our thanks and good wishes go to everyone who has made it possible for at least one EKR locomotive to cheat the cutter's torch.

Livery

As received by the EKR, No. 5 is believed to have borne the London & South Western Railway livery of Dugald Drummond, mainly a medium green. The sides of the cab, bunker sides and back, splashers, sandbox sides and the sides of the toolboxes on the footplate over the cylinders all had a brown border, on the inside of which was a black band edged both sides with a thin white line. This white lining subsequently yellowed and under a layer of grease and dirt eventually acquired an orange hue. It is unclear how complete this livery would have been after its time in military service and then in storage but traces of lining do show up in early photographs.

No. 5 as repainted in the standard green livery.

No. 5 leaves Axminster bound for Lyme Regis as British Railways No. 30583 in August 1956.

Soon after delivery the initials E K R and 'No. 5' were applied in yellow. There is photographic evidence that by 1927 the lettering was shaded to the left and below in black, but early reports refer to the lettering as unshaded. It seems unlikely that the shading would have been added after such a short period but there is no conclusive evidence on this question. The buffer beams were vermilion with 'No. ' and '5' on the left and right sides of the coupling hook respectively, in yellow shaded black to the left and below.

By 1930 it was hard to detect any distinguishing marks on No. 5 at all but in March 1936 a complete repaint was undertaken by Jim Smith. The new livery was the Southern Railway's second shade of green edged in black, the edging lined on the inside with a thin white line. The cab front and rear were plain green but the toolbox had a horizontal black edge top and bottom lined white on the inner edges. The letters E K R without stops or shading were emblazoned on the cab side sheets with a similar '5' on the bunker sides. The buffer beams were repainted as before with shaded markings. The smokebox and chimney remained black. The five boiler bands were also black, the middle three were lined in white on both sides whilst the first and last were lined on the inner side only. The cylinder wrappers had a black border lined white on the inside. Wheel centres had a circular black band lined white on both edges. The remainder of the wheels was painted green. The back plates of the footplate steps were painted green with black edging and white inside lining. Guard irons were vermilion. It is clear that Jim Smith took considerable care and pride with his paintwork.

With engines Nos. 4 and 7, No. 5 formed part of a new look which began to give the EKR locomotive stud a smarter and coherent image. There is little doubt that at this time it would have been a hard task to have found any better turned out locomotives in the South of England. For those who love such railways it is a sad thought that the EKR was never able to develop as it had intended and that its passenger traffic barely developed at all. Had the connections to Canterbury and Deal materialised the railway's passenger services would have had some real purpose, and it is pleasant to contemplate the thought of a regular pattern of cross-country passenger services in the charge of smartly turned out green locomotives.

After leaving the EKR No. 5 ran in Southern Railway plain black livery as No. 3488. British Railways repainted it in lined black livery as No. 30583 in October 1949 using the 'lion and wheel' totem on the centre of the tank sides. This was replaced by the later totem when it received a further repaint in lined black in 1959. On the Bluebell Railway it has carried a variety of liveries but has not yet resumed its EKR finery.

No. 6

No. 6 was originally built as No. 372 for the South Eastern Railway by Sharp, Stewart & Co., Works No. 3714, in August 1891. It was one of 122 'O' class 0-6-0 tender locomotives built between 1878 and 1899 and designed by James Stirling, the South Eastern's locomotive superintendent. The 'O' class were sturdy and versatile locomotives and a number of the class, albeit rebuilt to 'O1' class, lasted

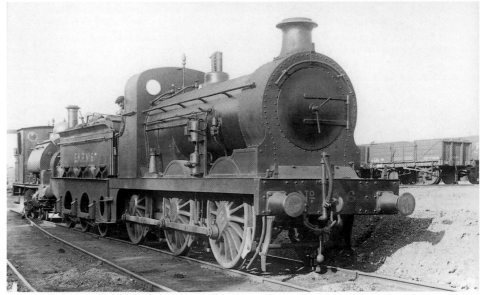

Jim Smith, the Shepherdswell carpenter/painter, seems to have been given a free hand in the matter of lettering. This is No. 6 at Shepherdsell in July 1923 with a style of lettering all of its own. Note the steam reverser fitted to the running plate. *M. Lawson Finch Collection*

Seen from the other side this August 1927 view gives a clear view of the lettering on No. 6's tender - modellers are unlikely to find this script amongst the popular ranges of transfers and will have to work on their freehand skills. *H.C. Casserley*

well into British Railways days. For a successful design it is surprising that only four of the class were sold for service elsewhere and all four came to the EKR.

No. 372 seems to have been allocated to Bricklayers Arms initially and would have seen a variety of goods and passenger duties from there. In September 1901 it was fitted with a new boiler. This was of a pattern designed by Harry Wainwright who had become locomotive carriage & wagon superintendent to the South Eastern & Chatham Railway in 1899. The new boiler was domeless and, being fitted with a deeper firebox and horizontal grate, was pitched 7 in. higher in the frames. This pattern of boiler was not particularly successful and after 1903 most rebuilds of the class used the much more successful boiler designed initially for the 'H' class of 0-4-4 tank locomotives. This was a heavier boiler and locomotives fitted with it were designated 'O1' class. These were also fitted with conventional square cabs. No. 372, however, was still carrying its domeless boiler and rounded cab when the South Eastern & Chatham was incorporated in the Southern Railway in January 1923. At this time it was based at Maidstone West. This is likely to have been its only allocation in Southern ownership as it was withdrawn in May 1923 for sale to the EKR for £800.

Before delivery to the EKR No. 6 was overhauled at Ashford works. This included retubing, moving the steam reverser from the cab to the right-hand running plate and repainting in black. A letter survives from R.E.L. Maunsell, the Southern Railway chief mechanical engineer, to Holman Stephens concerning the work to be carried out as follows:

May 3rd 1923

Dear Stephens,
Old Engine No. 372

Yours of the 2nd inst.

I can do the repairs and alterations to the above engine, charging you with the cost, that you ask for, but think that you should reconsider the question of test. This question was gone into by a Committee of our Association in April 1921 and after a good deal of consideration the following Hydraulic Test was decided upon for New and Repaired Boilers.

'Test Pressure to be not less than 1.25 X working pressure plus 10 lbs, or more than 1.5 of the working pressure'.

The object of having alternative pressure is the undesirability of straining an old Boiler with the maximum pressure that would be applied to a new one. I will apply the 50 per cent pressure if you particularly wish it but I do not recommend it and cannot be responsible for any damage that may be done to the Boiler. If the engine was being repaired for service on this line the test pressure would only be 185 lbs. Please let me know what you wish done in the matter.

Instructions regarding the use of the Steam Reversing Gear are being prepared and will be forwarded to you, and when the alterations to the engine are completed I will hand it over to your men, in steam.

Yours faithfully,
R.E.L. Maunsell

One aspect of the overhaul that has occasioned a certain amount of comment was the fitting of a new chimney of the short pattern used on 'R' and 'R1' class 0-4-4 tank locomotives allocated to the Canterbury & Whitstable branch. These

Lettering was not, of course, always visible on the hard-worked East Kent fleet. No. 6 pauses with a return passenger working to Shepherdswell at Eythorne in May 1927.   *H.C. Casserley*

In this undated view of No. 6 at Shepherdswell the second livery with more conventional lettering can just be made out.

were necessary on the Whitstable branch in order to negotiate the tight clearances of Tyler Hill tunnel. Two 'O' class locomotives had been given short chimneys for working on the branch, but these were of a stunted stovepipe pattern quite different from that fitted to No. 6. Nevertheless the coincidence of No. 6 being fitted with a 'Whitstable' chimney has incorrectly led to the suggestion that this locomotive was one of the 'O' class allocated to the Whitstable branch. The real reason for fitting the shorter pattern of chimney would appear to be that the higher-pitched domeless boiler fitted to No. 6 required a shorter chimney in order to clear the Tilmanstone Colliery screens. Holman Stephens' successor, Mr W.H. Austen, had an alternative explanation when asked about this point. He claimed that Stephens had acquired an aversion to tall chimneys as a result of humorous articles about his railways appearing in the local press, particularly in the case of the Selsey Tramway and Shropshire & Montgomeryshire Light Railway. Remarks concerning both these lines had been published making fun of tall chimneys with slighting references to the *Rocket* and things all harking back to railways long passed. Accepting that Stephens had such an aversion it is unlikely that it would have been sufficient to lead him to spending good money on a new chimney for No. 6, particularly considering the poorer steaming associated with shorter chimneys.

According to the late Donald Bradley No. 6 left the Ashford erecting shop on 8th June and arrived at Shepherdswell five days later. Here it would have presented a markedly different appearance from the other locomotives on the line with its new coat of paint and 'EKR No. 6' marked boldly on its tender sides. It seems to have been used for all types of traffic on the railway and must have been a very welcome addition to the locomotive stud, combining a reasonable standard of power for the coal traffic with adequate water and coal capacity for the longer trips to Wingham.

In 1928 No. 6 required new wheels. This work was carried out in the open in Shepherdswell Yard and required it to be jacked up on two piles of stout timber baulks. One can imagine the enormous effort this must have called for from the staff involved with the very basic tools and materials available. The exercise may explain why the EKR acquired its rail-mounted crane in 1929.

Apart from receiving new wheels No. 6 appears to have required little major attention until 1932. By this date its domeless boiler was well past its prime and a major rebuild of the engine was arranged with the Southern Railway. In September No. 6 arrived at Ashford to be fitted with the larger 'H' class type of boiler. Technically this converted No. 6 into an 'O1' class locomotive but to keep costs down to £1,500 it retained its Stirling round cab , smokebox wing plates and sand boxes above the running plate. This made No. 6 unique amongst 'O1' locomotives. More conventional was the reinstatement of a normal height chimney.

A further overhaul took place at Shepherdswell in September 1935 during which No. 6 seems to have acquired the tender previously attached to sister locomotive No. 8. A report in the *Locomotive Magazine* refers to a new chimney being fitted at this time. This ties in with the purchase of a new chimney from the Southern Railway in June 1935 but quite why a new chimney was required is unexplained. A similar degree of mystery attends a note in the Austen

No. 6 in June 1936 as rebuilt to 'O1' class standards but retaining its rounded cab and side-mounted steam reverser.   *Ron Jarvis/Midland Railway Trust*

In this July 1936 view No. 6 now sports lamp irons fitted to the smokebox. The lower 'O1' boiler means that the boiler handrails are now pitched lower than the cabside handrails. The lower boiler did mean that No. 6 could now sport a taller chimney.   *H.C. Casserley*

Collection at Tenterden, recording a bill dated 6th November, 1936 from the Southern Railway for £1 18s. 11d. for repairs to No. 6 but giving no further details. A report in the *Railway Observer* for September 1937 recorded No. 6 as operating the Wingham afternoon service on the 10th August and to have been painted black with numbering and lettering in yellow. In the November 1938 edition it was recorded that in September 1938 No. 6 had been awaiting repairs with the frames and boiler parked outside the shed at Shepherdswell and its cab a little way off. A further report in the January 1941 edition recorded that in November 1940 No. 6 appeared to have been recently repainted and was in excellent condition. Appearances can be deceptive as in 1942 the Locomotive Mileage Register only records it as working during August.

The Directors' Minutes for 22nd July, 1943 record that No. 6 had been damaged as a result of driver's carelessness on 19th July. The Mileage Register records No. 6 as leaving for Ashford on 27th July and returning to Shepherdswell on 7th October, after which it continued to work until December. No. 6 appears to have had an excursion before returning to Shepherdswell as it was observed on 6th October piloting an ex-Great Western War Department Dean Goods locomotive on a special from Ashford towards Hastings. This was not the only occasion on which No. 6 piloted War Department Dean Goods locomotives. A report in the August 1944 *Railway Observer* recorded an extraordinary expedition on the 21st July that year. No. 6 had set out from Shepherdswell with the 5.00 pm Wingham mixed train which consisted of 22 empty wagons and one of the LCDR six-wheel carriages. At Eythorne two Dean Goods, Nos. WD93 and WD95, were waiting in steam whilst another two, unfortunately unidentified, were parked on the remaining section of the Guilford branch. After some complicated shunting No. 6 detached 19 of its wagons and propelled them up to Tilmanstone. Upon returning to Eythorne No. 6 backed on to the three remaining wagons and carriage. The two WD locomotives then coupled on to No. 6 and the train proceeded triple-headed to Staple where the WD locomotives uncoupled. No. 6 finally arrived at Canterbury Road about 20 minutes late. From Woodnesborough onwards there was only one passenger aboard the triple-headed train.

The Directors' Minutes for 9th November, 1944 record that No. 6 needed new wheels. A set was reported to be available for the engine, probably retained since the scrapping of No. 8, but new wheels would be needed for the tender. Whether these were found or whether the spare wheels were fitted has gone unrecorded but it is known that a new boiler was fitted at Ashford between 19th January, 1945 and 15th March. From May 1945 No. 6 worked every month until April 1948. The Mileage Register records a total mileage from 9th November, 1932 to 20th January, 1948 of 94,765 miles. By now No. 6 was the property of British Railways who renumbered it 31372; no attempt was made to apply the new number or any other change in identity with the result that it could be seen shunting at Dover in EKR livery. British Railways withdrew No. 6 in February 1949. On 24th February it arrived in the erecting shop at Ashford and was cut up the following day. Its tender is believed not to have been cut up until May of that year.

No. 6 under overhaul outside Shepherdswell Shed in August 1938 - overhauls under such circumstances could be protracted affairs.   *A.G. Wells*

No. 6 in British Railways ownership, somewhat the worse for wear but still carrying its East Kent livery.

Livery

No. 6 was first seen at Shepherdswell in July 1923 in unlined black with 'EKR No. 6' along the sides of the outside-framed tender a little lower than the mid-point between the top of the springs and the horizontal handrail. This lettering in unshaded yellow and an unorthodox script extended approximately from the centre of the leading wheels to the centre of the trailing ones, about 11 feet. The buffer beams on both engine and tender were unlined vermilion with the usual 'No. ' on the left of the coupling hook and '6' on the right. This livery was still in place in 1927 but shortly after this No. 6 acquired a new coat of black paint with the letters 'E K R' without stops painted in yellow along the tender and the numeral '6' on its cabside.

Following the 1932 rebuild No. 6 was repainted black with the same style of yellow lettering. The buffer beams were marked as before except that the lettering was now shaded to the left and below in black.

By 1939 No. 6 was painted in Southern Railway dark olive green passenger livery. Lining in black and white was applied as follows: cab front and sides and tender sides and back edged in black with a thin white line on the inside, footplate valence green with a black band along the bottom edge separated from the green by a thin white line, boiler bands black with white lines on either side, tender frames green with a black band following the outline with a white line on the inside. Both these colours similarly ran round the three cut-outs in the frame and also around the front of the cab where it met the boiler. The buffer beams on both engine and tender were vermilion but the only marking carried was a yellow '6' to the right of the coupling hook shaded below and to the left in black. Motion and coupling rods were red. A larger than usual 'E K R' without stops was placed centrally in unshaded yellow on the tender sides with a smaller '6' on the cab sides. By 1946 much of the lining had vanished and no significant alterations to livery took place before scrapping in 1949.

No. 7

EKR No. 7 was an 0-6-0 saddle tank locomotive delivered as No. 127 to the London & South Western Railway by Beyer, Peacock & Company in 1882, Works No. 2125. It was to a fairly standard Beyer, Peacock design of which the LSWR bought six examples for shunting in 1876, a further two in 1877 and a final 12 in 1882. The first batches were quite ornate with polished domes and copper-capped chimneys but the last batch, including No. 127, was delivered with stovepipe chimneys and painted domes. All three batches were designated the '330' class but were more popularly known as 'Saddlebacks'.

In its early days No. 127 was allocated to Nine Elms where this class worked very long hours, month in and month out. In so doing they acquired a reputation for their strength and general reliability. They came to be referred to as the 'Nine Elms Shunters' and, of all the classes and types that shunted the yards there, they were the only ones to which this description was immediately understood to refer.

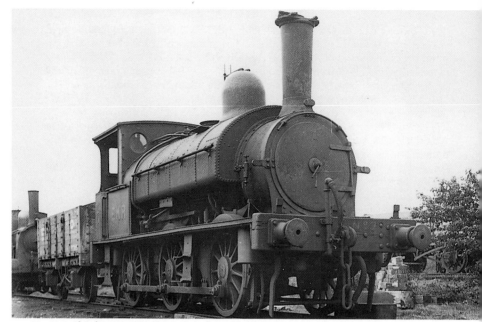

No. 7 at Shepherdswell in May 1927. Note the lettering on buffer beam and cabside with the number on the side of the bunker.   *H.C. Casserley*

No. 7 in May 1935. Note repair to the top of chimney, no number on the cab side but Beyer, Peacock plate visible on the splasher over the centre wheels.

Ron Jarvis/Midland Railway Trust

Shortly after the turn of the century No. 127 and seven other members of the class were fitted with vacuum ejectors and pipes so that they could be used for marshalling and piloting passenger stock. In October 1911 it was transferred to the Duplicate Stock List as No. 0127 and in 1912 was based at Eastleigh. In 1917 No. 0127 was transferred to Dorchester with No. 0334 to assist with shunting at Weymouth, but returned to Eastleigh in 1918 as one of the carriage & locomotive works pilots.

In 1923 No. 0127 passed into the hands of the Southern Railway and was designated No. E0127. This may not have been applied to the locomotive before it was withdrawn in May 1925 and sent to await disposal at Eastleigh. It was common for locomotives to linger here for some time before cutting up, but in August No. E0127 was retrieved from the disposal line and taken in for overhaul having been sold to the EKR for £380 to become its No. 7. Whether this sum included the cost of overhaul is not clear nor is the extent of the work performed. Certainly it was not until 9th January, 1926 that No. 7 left Eastleigh works; even then it did not travel straight to Shepherdswell but went instead via Brighton and Hastings to spend several days at Rolvenden works on the Kent & East Sussex Railway. The purpose of this visit to Rolvenden remains a mystery. Whatever its purpose it had been accomplished in time for No. 7 to arrive at Shepherdswell on 15th January.

No. 7 passed a hydraulic test to 190 lb. per square inch on 30th July, 1926 and performed satisfactorily on both coal and passenger traffic. It was not in the peak of condition, however, and besides requiring a new buffer beam within 18 months of arrival also acquired a variety of patches to its smokebox door over the following years. Its chimney was decidedly moth-eaten by 1934 despite a report in the *Railway Observer* for March 1934 describing No. 7 as '. . . in good repair but apparently out of service'. A report in the same journal for May 1935 described No. 7 as '. . . in deplorable condition', though to be fair the same was also said of locomotives Nos. 1 and 2.

In November 1935 an overhaul was started at Shepherdswell which included riveting a brass wrapper around the top section of the chimney. It is not clear how long such a repair was expected to last, but by the following year it was found that the smokebox had also worn out. Mr W.H. Austen therefore designed a new smokebox. The drawings for this were prepared at the offices at Salford Terrace, Tonbridge, Kent where Austen had presided since Holman Stephens' death. The smokebox was then fabricated by the Southern Railway at Ashford works and fitted at Shepherdswell after the old one had been cut away with oxy-acetylene torches. This work was in full swing at Easter 1936 and was completed by fitting a new chimney of Great Western Railway pattern. This is almost certainly the one previously fitted as a replacement on locomotive No. 1 and has led to the widespread belief that No. 7 was also fitted with No. 1's smokebox. In December 1936 No. 7 was completely repainted in the railway's now standard version of Southern Railway livery. It presented a strikingly different appearance from its former self and must have been a fascinating sight to visiting enthusiasts.

No. 7 seems to have worked hard until 1942 but is only recorded as working during January in 1943. In 1944 it worked in April, May and September but did not work again after 28th September. The Directors' Minutes for 8th November, 1945

No. 7 in March 1937 displaying its new chimney, smokebox and smart green livery. Note the clear view of the crank fitted to smokebox side to operate the sanding mechanism.   *Jim Jarvis*

No. 7 awaiting cutting up at Ashford in March 1946.

H.C. Casserley

record offers for No. 7 together with No. 5 from Ward's and Cohen's of £61 and £80 respectively for scrap. When the Directors approached the Southern Railway to ascertain a reasonable price for No. 5 they also asked for advice on a price for No. 7. The Southern's offer of £90 was accepted and No. 7 was dispatched to Ashford on 14th March, 1946 and cut up on 23rd March. One of the Ashford staff saved No. 7's whistle as a memento but whether it still survives is not known.

Livery

As received No. 7 was painted in unlined black with 'E K R' without stops on the cab side sheets and a matching '7' on the bunker sides. These markings were applied in yellow shaded red. Its original wooden front buffer beam carried a small 'No. 7' on the right-hand side of the coupling hook and above the centre line of the buffer beam. This, in plain yellow, was almost exactly similar in size, position and type to that carried by the Kent & East Sussex Railway's 'Saddleback' No. 4. This raises the possibility that No. 7 may have made its mystery stop at Rolvenden in order to be painted or at least lettered. By 1928 a new buffer beam had been fitted; this carried the larger and more usual 'No.' to the left of the coupling hook with '7' on the right.

After the Shepherdswell rebuild in 1936 No. 7 was a bright and beautiful sight in the fully lined-out Southern Railway green passenger livery. Black edge bands with an inside white line were applied to the cab front, top and bottom cab side sheets, bunker sides and end, splashers and saddle tank. A black band around the sandboxes was lined in white both on the inside and outside. Unlike the KESR No. 4, the dome on No. 7 remained painted over in green and no attempt was made to polish the copper cap on the Great Western chimney. This and the smokebox were painted black. The number 7 was moved to the cab side sheets and the letters E K R without stops were moved to the lower sides of the saddle tank. Lettering was in yellow and apparently unshaded, although A.G. Crawshaw believes they may have been shaded in red. By 1946 the number 7 is known to have been shaded and the colour used is firmly believed to have been black. This shading was to the right and below the yellow.

The wheels were painted green and the hubs bore circular black bands lined inside and out with thin white lines. The buffer beam faces, buffer shanks, guard irons and, most enjoyably of all, the coupling rods were vermilion. All other sides of the buffer beams were black. On the buffer beam faces 'No.' and '7' appeared on either side of the coupling hooks. This lettering was in yellow shaded black to the left and below. By 1946 the buffer beam markings had ceased to appear in photographs but a photograph taken at Ashford works while No. 7 was awaiting scrapping shows the 'E K R' and '7' standing out sharply. Was this an example of touching in for record purposes or of a valedictory cleaning?

No. 8

No. 8 was a twin in most respects to No. 6. It was built as South Eastern Railway 'O' class No. 376 by Sharp, Stewart in September 1891, Works No. 3718. Like No. 6 it was also fitted with the transitional Wainwright higher-pitched domeless boiler though this did not happen until April 1916.

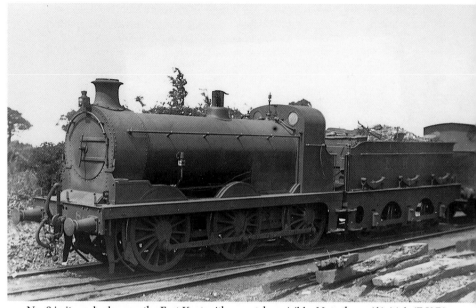

No. 8 in its early days on the East Kent with no patches visible. Note the serif initials 'E K R' on the tender, and lamp irons fitted to the smokebox.

No. 8 in September 1934. Still relatively smart but the smokebox side and door have required patching.   *Ron Jarvis/Midland Railway Trust*

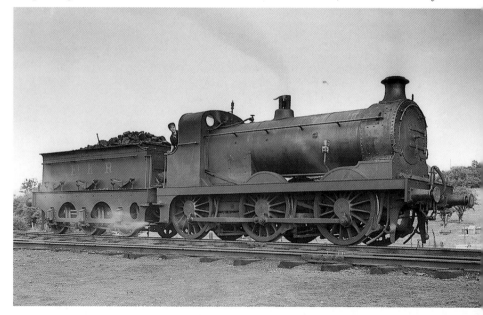

Like No. 6 it was originally allocated to Bricklayers Arms and at Grouping in 1923 was allocated to Maidstone West. Under Southern Railway ownership it became No. A376 and this prefix was added when it was repainted in Southern Railway goods black in July 1924. It was withdrawn by the Southern in 1928 and sold to the EKR for £1,085 in September that year, arriving at Shepherdswell on 22nd September.

No. 8 differed from No. 6 in that its steam reverser remained in the cab. Like No. 6 it was also fitted with a short 'Whitstable' chimney before delivery to the East Kent. Unlike No. 6 it had a relatively short career on the EKR and has usually been dismissed as a bad buy. However, there is plenty of photographic evidence of No. 8 being used on the mixed trains to Wingham and there is no reason to suppose that it did not play a full part with the coal traffic as well. If No. 8 was used with any degree of continuity, its purchase price would have represented a substantial saving on the costs of hiring a locomotive for the same period. In the event its boiler was condemned in March 1935 and it proved cheaper to purchase a new locomotive than to have No. 8 repaired. Its tender was retained as a replacement for that attached to No. 6.

There is some disagreement concerning the disposal of No. 8. The Directors' Minutes for 1935 record that No. 8 had been sold to Cohen's for scrap together with No. 1 for £95. There would be no difficulty in accepting this version but for the belief of the EKR staff that it had been sold to the Southern for scrap. Another version has it that the Southern took No. 8 in part-exchange for the locomotive that replaced it, No. 100, and that it was the Southern who employed contractors to cut No. 8 up at Shepherdswell. In the absence of firm documentary evidence we must be satisfied with the fact that it was cut up in or about 1935 by persons unknown for a sum unspecified.

Livery

Throughout its life on the EKR No. 8 ran in unlined black. The letters E K R were applied by hand to the tender in a unique serif style. The figure 8 was carried on the cab sides but is rarely visible in photographs. These markings are believed to have been in unshaded yellow. The buffer beams were vermilion with 'No. ' and '8' on either side of the coupling hook. Photographic evidence suggests that these markings at least were shaded. Despite the comments about the visibility of its lettering, No. 8 was usually kept in unusually clean condition. Whilst this is a tribute to the attention paid by driver Sedgewick and fireman King, its usual crew, it may well have been that it was their regular cleaning which gradually erased its identification.

Few changes were made to No. 8 on the EKR, but as it neared the end of its life a large patch was riveted to the right hand side of the smokebox and a smaller one between the handrail and the chimney base. It seems that the smokebox as well as the boiler was nearing the end of its useful life.

Some of the EKR staff argued strongly that at one time this engine was painted green. But George Clements had no doubt that No. 8 arrived in plain black livery at Shepherdswell and in black it seems to have remained.

Two more patches on the smokebox door of No. 8. Note the conventional location of the reversing lever compared with No. 6.

Another view of No. 8's smokebox door patches and some evidence of scorching. Note that the cabside handrail had never been raised to match the boiler handrail.

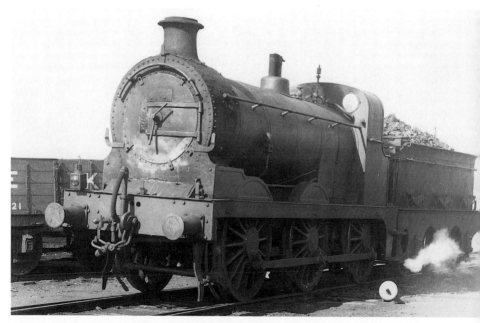

No. 100 (later No. 2)

This was the third representative of the 'O' class to be owned by the EKR and had been built by Sharp, Stewart in September 1893, Works No. 3950. Its South Eastern number was 383 and it had been rebuilt to 'O1' class in August 1908. This rebuilding consisted essentially of the fitting of an 'H' class boiler and a 'C' class cab but various other alterations were carried out at the same time. These included fitting steel buffer beams, moving the sand boxes to beneath the footplate, fitting steam sanding gear and moving the steam reverser from the cab to the right-hand footplate.

No. 383 was initially allocated to Bricklayer's Arms and remained at this shed under the successive management of the South Eastern Railway, South Eastern & Chatham Railway and Southern Railway. The Southern renumbered it A383 in 1923, although the prefix does not seem to have been applied until it was repainted in Southern lined black livery in 1925. In or about 1931 it was renumbered again as 1383. In 1935 it entered Ashford works for a major overhaul which included the fitting of a replacement boiler and a new firebox. No. 1383 left the works on 12th April but had only run 2,086 miles before being withdrawn for sale to the EKR for £850.

It will be recalled that EKR No. 8 had been condemned in March 1935 and that the Directors had decided to purchase a replacement locomotive rather than repairing No. 8. In the event they obtained an absolute bargain in No. 1383 which was not only freshly overhauled but was also of the higher 'O1' specification. When it is considered that it had cost the EKR £1,500 to have No. 6 partially converted to 'O1' condition the £850 paid for No. 1383 is remarkably low. There is some suggestion that the remains of No. 8 and the tender from No. 6 were included in this transaction, thereby bringing the book value of No. 1383 up to £1,200. We have found no documentary evidence for this and it does not fit easily with the Directors' Minute to the effect that No. 8 was sold together with No. 1 for scrap to Cohen's for £95. Even if a true price of £1,200 could be confirmed, No. 1383 would still have been a considerable bargain.

We have continued to refer to this locomotive as No. 1383 in the above account as we have now to tackle the thorny problem of explaining why it arrived at Shepherdswell on 23rd June, 1935 carrying the unlikely designation No. 100! Two suggestions are easily rejected. It was not the hundredth locomotive to be bought by the 'Colonel Stephens Empire', nor is it likely that it was necessary to apply a long number in order to fill the gap on the cab sides left by removing its numberplate! To get any further it is necessary to examine the limited evidence available. This boils down to three issues. Firstly, No. 100 should logically have been No. 9. Secondly, a close examination of the numerals applied to the locomotive and tender bufferbeams show that the last digit is of smaller dimensions than the first two and applied slightly out of alignment. Thirdly the numbers painted on the cabsides are painted as unusually small figures on a surface that appears to have been recently repainted. It is possible that a previously applied number had been painted out and the small numerals applied in its place. We are completely confident that No. 100 was initially painted No. 10 by the Southern and altered to No. 100 on arrival at

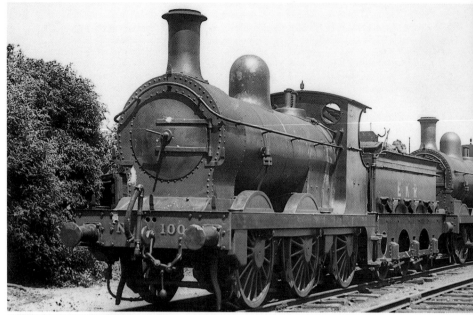

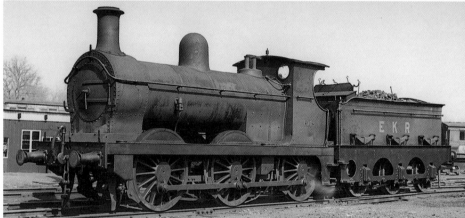

Top: No. 100 at Shepherdswell in July 1936. No. 6 is at the rear.

H.C. Casserley

Above: No. 100 in April 1939 with cabside number visible. For such a high number it is strange that it was applied with such small figures. *Jim Jarvis*

Right: A right-hand view of No. 100 in June 1939 showing the steam reverser fitted to the running plate as on No. 6. *R.F. Roberts*

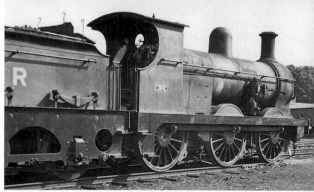

Shepherdswell. We therefore have to ask why the locomotive was numbered 10 instead of 9 and why 10 subsequently became 100?

Donald Bradley has advanced the explanation that the number 100 was applied because the paint foreman at Ashford had received no instructions as to numbering and thought that '100' could safely be applied without risk of duplication. Ashford is not very far away from Shepherdswell nor were EKR locomotives exactly strangers to the works. It seems unlikely that such a high number would have been applied without further enquiry, but it is perfectly feasible that 10 could have been judged to be a reasonable number to apply under such circumstances. An alternative explanation, entirely without supporting evidence, is that the railway contemplated purchasing two locomotives and that the purchase of No. 9 fell through with the resulting jump in numbering from 8 to 10.

As to the decision to increase 10 to 100 one of us was fortunate enough to interview Mr W.H. Austen in the 1950s and to ask him exactly that question. He answered: 'We were thinking about our image at this time and having little or no knowledge about what was going to happen in the future, and a decision was taken to build up a new stock of locomotives on most of the lines and to fight back at the 'Rocket' image with more modern-looking stock and also to renumber all the locomotives all over the country in one continuing sequence starting with No. 100'. It must be remembered that this interview took place a long time after the numbering and that Mr Austen may simply have been trying to rationalise the incident. His explanation cannot be discounted out of hand, however, and points to a conscious decision made for image purposes to take advantage of the incorrect No. 10 by turning it into No. 100. There, until further information comes to light, it seems that the matter must rest.

With locomotives Nos. 4 and 6 recently overhauled and capable of handling the bulk of the coal traffic, supplemented after 1936 by No. 5, it is not surprising that No. 100 seems to have been mainly used on the mixed turns to Wingham during its early years on the line. As the condition of the other locomotives deteriorated No. 100 played a larger part on the coal traffic, but for years it spent the greater part of its time on the twice daily trips to Wingham and associated shunting.

When the surviving Locomotive Mileage Register began in August 1942, No. 100 was clearly one of the more dependable locomotives in the EKR stud as it worked regularly until October 1943. In 1944 it worked steadily from January to October when, on the 20th of that month, it went to Ashford for firebox repairs. It resumed work on the 11th December and continued in service until returning to Ashford for a major overhaul on 21st November, 1945. Accompanying this overhaul came a decision to abandon the fanciful No. 100 in favour of a new identity as No. 2 . Even the choice of this number poses some interesting questions. Why take the number of the most recently departed member of the locomotive stock instead of the long vacant No. 1? Possibly it was intended to allocate No. 1 to the recently acquired 'O1' No. 1371, or was it intended that No. 1371 would take the spurned No. 9? We shall probably never know.

The 1945 overhaul was quite extensive according to a record held in the Austen Collection at Tenterden Railway Museum. The wheels were re-tyred, the firebox was fitted with a new copper tubeplate and new right- and left-hand half sides, the boiler was re-tubed and a new set of stays was fitted. The note concludes with

No. 100 renumbered as No. 2 at Shepherdswell in 1947. It would outlast the condemned carriages in the background for a few years more.

'No. 2' under British Railways' ownership. The wagon in the background carries the legend 'FOR USE ON EAST KENT SECTION ONLY'.   *John-Scott Morgan Collection*

the information '. . . returned from Ashford as No. 2 9th February, 1946'. Some reports suggest that No. 2 was fitted with a replacement boiler during this overhaul but this does not match the reference to re-tubing No. 2's boiler.

On 7th December, 1946 the Directors' Minutes record that No. 2 had been derailed at Woodnesborough along with carriage No. 10 on 13th September of that year. The derailment was apparently due to the gauge spreading but fortunately neither the engine nor the carriage were damaged. The Locomotive Mileage Register records No. 2 as working regularly from its return in February 1946 until April 1948, when records ceased. A mileage total is given from 28th September, 1935 to 20th January, 1948 of 73,447 miles.

With the closure of Shepherdswell Shed No. 2 was transferred to Dover. It frequently returned to its old haunts but was also to be observed shunting at Dover Harbour still bearing its EKR livery, the last reported observation being on 17th July, 1949. On 18th September, 1949 it ran light to Ashford for repairs. It was observed standing in the yard there on 8th October bearing both its EKR number and its new British Railways number 31383 on its cabsides, and its old Southern number 1383 appearing through the worn paintwork on its tender. After repairs it was repainted in unlined black with '31383' on its cabsides but for some reason was not fitted with a cast smokebox numberplate. It returned to Dover on 29th October, 1949, where it continued to work until put into store there in March 1950. Withdrawal came on 7th April that year and it was cut up at Ashford on 24th April, 1951.

This account of No. 100, alias No. 2, also known as 383, A383, 1383 and 31383, can fittingly end with a favourite anecdote of one of the authors. One quiet and sunny morning he was sitting on the seat at Wingham Canterbury Road station watching a small and rather grubby youth hurling large pieces of ballast at any company property in sight. After some time the youth accosted the author and enquired what he was doing there. Upon receiving the reply that the author was interested in the line, the youth vouchsafed the information that he knew everything there was to know about the EKR and intimated that any question could immediately be resolved from his immense store of knowledge. The author pondered for a moment before asking whether the young man could explain why one of the locomotives had once been numbered 100. Hurling another stone at the waiting room he replied,'Oh yes. It was the first engine to reach one hundred miles an hour on the line'! It was with little sense of loss that the author refrained from delving further into the minutiae of EKR lore from that particular source.

Livery

There seems to be some doubt as to whether No. 100 arrived on the line as a green or as a black engine. It had certainly been painted black in 1925 and there would be no reason to suppose that it was painted in any other colour after its 1935 overhaul, were it not for the fact that some members of the EKR staff were sure that No. 100 arrived painted dark green. In the apparent absence of contemporary observations we have been unable to resolve this question. No lining is evident in the photographs taken during this period, which would tend to favour the view that it arrived in the Southern unlined goods black livery of this period. 'E K R' was applied in large yellow letters to its tender and a very small '100' on its cabsides. The locomotive and tender buffer beams were vermilion with 'No. ' to the left of the coupling hook and '100' to the right, the final digit being slightly smaller and not quite in alignment. These were in yellow shaded below and to the right in a dark colour, probably black. This shading was the opposite to that applied to No. 6. No. 100 retained this livery, latterly in a very grimy state, until going to Ashford in 1945. As a result many photographs fail to reveal any identification at all on the locomotive.

Upon returning to the line as No. 2 the engine appears to have remained in plain black with the tender lettering as before but with a plain 9 in. high figure 2 in yellow on the cab sides. The buffer beams were unlined vermilion with a yellow figure 2 on the right-hand side just under the footplate. This figure was a standard Southern Railway transfer shaded black with yellow highlights. When No. 2 returned to Ashford works in September 1949, Mr E.B. Trotter observed that the wheels were lined in green, black and white. This would tend to confirm that the earlier reports of it being painted green on delivery to the EKR were correct. At the same date Mr Trotter observed that the tender carried the letters E K R in 1 ft high yellow letters but that the earlier lettering SOUTHERN and figures 1383 were also visible through the later paintwork.

With a good number of very similar engines operating on the main lines and branches in Kent it is perhaps not surprising that No. 100/2 attracted little attention during its time on the railway. Certainly there are few references to it in the contemporary railway press. Given this scarcity of information it must be emphasised how much the authors owe to the staff of the old EKR for their continued help in the face of a barrage of questions, once for a whole day. Whilst it might be invidious to single out individuals, extra special recollections come to one author's mind of pleasant hours spent in the company of G.W. Rogers, G.H. Clements and driver N. Sedgewick who went to considerable lengths to obtain the answers which they felt they could not supply themselves. Very many people have helped with this book but assistance given so readily at first hand by staff is the stuff of which such histories as this are made.

No. 1371

This was the last locomotive to be purchased by the railway. It did not arrive at Shepherdswell until March 1944 and no attempt was made to allocate an EKR number to it nor to alter its appearance to indicate its new owners.

No. 1371 was a further example of James Stirling's 'O' class and had been built by Sharp, Stewart, Works No. 3713, in 1891. It had been South Eastern Railway No. 371 and had been converted to 'O1' class in June 1909. At Grouping it had become No. A371, although this number was probably not applied until it was repainted in Southern Railway livery in 1926. At some date after 1931 it was numbered No. 1371. In 1933 it was based at Maidstone West where it had also been based at Grouping, when it would have kept company with EKR No. 6 and the now defunct No. 8. By World War II it was based at Tonbridge and played its part in the Dunkirk evacuation piloting ambulance trains up Hildenborough Bank.

The Directors' Minutes for 25th November, 1943 record that locomotives Nos. 2 and 5 were to be disposed of and that a new locomotive would be obtained to replace them. In February 1944 arrangements were made for the purchase of No. 1371 and the Locomotive Mileage Register shows it to have started work on the EKR on 13th April. The late Donald Bradley has recorded the purchase price for No. 1371 as £1,125, although the Directors' Minutes for 16th March, 1944 give a price of £750. It may be that the higher sum included overhaul and delivery expenses in addition to purchase price.

According to the Locomotive Mileage Register No. 1371 worked regularly from April 1944 until records ceased in April 1948. The total mileage from 3rd April, 1944 to 20th January, 1948 is recorded as 12,159 miles.

In 1948 No. 1371 became the property of British Railways and was allocated No. 31371, but was withdrawn on 8th January, 1949 without the new number being applied. It was cut up at Ashford on 19th February, 1949.

Livery

No. 1371 arrived in Southern Railway wartime black livery without lining. The word SOUTHERN in the new style of rather squat lettering ran along the side of the tender just below the handrail and the figures 1371 were carried on the cab sides. These markings would have been in gold shaded with green. On the front buffer beam the figures 1371 were carried on the right-hand side in smaller shaded numerals. No further painting appears to have been carried out by either the EKR or British Railways.

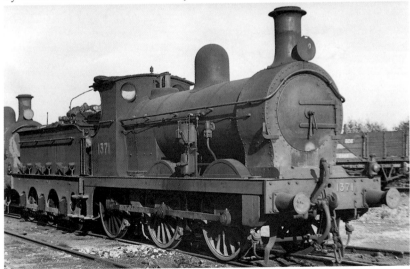

No. 1371 at Shepherdswell in September 1948. British Railways has managed to repaint the wagon in the background but No. 1371 retains full Southern Railway livery. No. 6 at the rear has separate smokebox and side handrails whereas on No. 1371 and No. 100 the handrail ran continuously along the boiler and around the smokebox.

M. Lawson Finch Collection

It has been suggested that No. 1371 would have received the number 3 in due course. Although this number had long been vacant and would logically have followed the re-numbering of No. 100 as No. 2, there is no official or documentary evidence to support this suggestion.

The Hawthorn, Leslie Twins

EKR has always generated mysteries and puzzles. One of the earliest of these concerned an advertisement placed in the *Locomotive Magazine* for 15th April, 1914 by the locomotive manufacturers R. & W. Hawthorn, Leslie of Newcastle-on-Tyne. The advertisement included a picture of an outside-cylindered 0-6-0 sidetank locomotive bearing the inscription EAST KENT RAILWAY and the name *Gabrielle*. The same advertisement appeared in the issues for May, June, July and August and has occasioned considerable speculation over the years.

That the locomotive had some connection with the EKR was obvious when set against the fact that Tilmanstone Colliery not only had a 'Gabrielle' shaft but also had a 'Gabrielle' dynamo in the electricity generating station. Gabrielle was the name of one of Arthur Burr's grand-daughters and Arthur Burr, it will be remembered, was introduced to Holman Stephens by none other than James Mathew of R. & W. Hawthorn, Leslie.

The next clue to the connection between the locomotive and the EKR is a report by Holman Stephens to the Third Annual General Meeting of the railway in May 1915. This was to the effect that the contractors had failed to deliver the two engines mentioned in the previous year's report as being under construction. He went on to add that, 'It is reported that the makers have disposed of them to other purchasers'. When this information is coupled with the fact, supplied by Gordon Green of the Industrial Railway Society, that one copy of the official photograph of *Gabrielle* used in the *Locomotive Magazine* was endorsed on the reverse 'E 3026 and E 3027', then the mystery would seem to be explained as follows: not one but two locomotives were ordered by the East Kent Contract & Financial Company, the order was cancelled when it became apparent that funds would not stretch to the purchase of new locomotives and they were eventually sold to other purchasers.

Both locomotives were built in 1913 and *Gabrielle* was the first of the pair. In the very month that the *Locomotive Magazine* advertisement appeared it was purchased by the Wemyss Coal Company and left Hawthorn, Leslie's works in May 1914 for delivery to the Wellesley Colliery near Methil in Fife as Wemyss Coal Company No. 15, still bearing the *Gabrielle* nameplates. It remained at Wellesley until cut up in July 1972. From January 1947 it was a National Coal Board locomotive and went through various numbers as the coalfields were reorganised; at one time it was running as *National Coal Board No. 29 Fife & Clackmannan Area*, by which stage it had lost its nameplates. It should be emphasised that it was the property of the Wemyss Coal Company rather than the Wemyss Private Railway. As such it was painted in light green rather than the brown used on the private railway.

The second locomotive, Works No. 3027, is believed to have been intended to carry the name *Rowena*, after another of Arthur Burr's grand-daughters. Tilmanstone

Hawthorn, Leslie's advertisement in *The Locomotive Magazine* featuring *Gabrielle*.

Colliery, needless to say, also had a 'Rowena' Shaft and a 'Rowena' dynamo. Nameplates do not appear to have been cast for this engine before the cancellation of the contract and it bore the name *Northumbria* and the number WD1 when sold in November 1914. It was delivered to Sir John Jackson Limited at Porton Camp in Wiltshire but it is not clear whether it was purchased by this firm or by the War Department. It is reported to have subsequently gone to the Kinmel Park Camp Military Railway near Rhyl in North Wales. In 1919 or 1920 it was sold to the Ebbw Vale Steel Iron & Coal Company for use at Ebbw Vale Steelworks as No. 36 but still named *Northumbria*. The steelworks were purchased by Richard Thomas & Company in 1935 and it was transferred to this firm's Redbourn Iron & Steel Works at Scunthorpe in 1936 as *Redbourn No. 4*, again keeping the *Northumbria* nameplates. It remained at Redbourn until dismantled in June 1963, although its frame was retained for service as a scrap wagon carrier until this was cut up in August 1965. We are grateful to Gordon Green and the Industrial Railway Society for their help in supplying most of the details concerning the industrial service of these locomotives.

Details taken from the Hawthorn, Leslie catalogue for 1921 show the hauling capacity of this model of locomotive as:

On the level	1,566 tons
up 1 in 200	866 tons
up 1 in 100	554 tons
up 1 in 50	310 tons
up 1 in 33.3	208 tons

Although not quite as powerful as the Kerr, Stuart engine, No. 4, they would still have been very useful if the money had been available to bring them to Shepherdswell. One wonders if they would have lasted quite as long on the EKR as they did in industrial use.

Right & below: *Northiam* on construction duties in 1913.
M. Lawson Finch Collection

Bottom: Northiam at Shepherdswell *c.* 1923 in its distinctive Kent & East Sussex Railway livery.

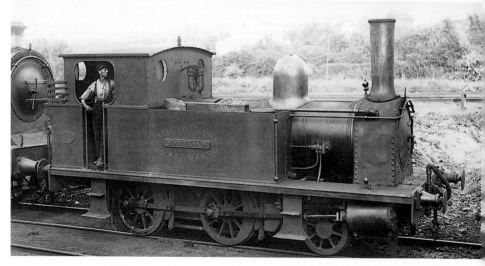

Locomotives hired by the East Kent Railway

KESR No. 2 Northiam

This was one of a pair of 2-4-0 sidetank locomotives built in 1899 by Hawthorn, Leslie, Works No. 2421, for the Rother Valley Railway, upon which it hauled the inaugural passenger train on 2nd April, 1900.

Northiam was delivered with an attractive brass-capped chimney but this was subsequently replaced by a stovepipe chimney. This did little for its appearance but presumably improved its performance. When the Rother Valley Railway became the Kent & East Sussex Railway in 1904 this locomotive retained its original number and its name, *Northiam*, after one of the larger villages served by the line. It was a useful and versatile locomotive on the KESR but was transferred on hire to the EKR in September 1912 and put to use on construction work. There does not appear to be any official record of how long it remained on the EKR, and it appears that *Northiam* returned to the KESR from time to time as the KESR Ledger records 14s. 3d. against the East Kent Railway on 30th June, 1913 for 'Engine to Shepherdswell'. It is known that a new set of steel tubes was fitted to *Northiam* at Shepherdswell in January 1914. It is likely that it returned to the KESR later that year when construction work on the East Kent virtually came to a standstill.

On 14th July, 1918 *Northiam* was dispatched to work on the Weston, Clevedon & Portishead Light Railway. In June 1919 its cylinders were bored out to 12½ inches and new pistons fitted at Clevedon. In 1921 *Northiam* was again retubed, its firebox tube plate patched and it was lifted and painted. On 22nd August, 1921 it returned to the KESR but barely had time to draw breath before going to work on the EKR again on 10th September, 1921.

Northiam may have taken part in construction work on the Richborough branch but its main duties on the EKR seem to have been on the mixed trains to Wingham. According to EKR staff it was also the last locomotive to work on the Wingham Colliery branch.

Life on the EKR seems to have taken its toll on *Northiam* as the KESR Rolling Stock Register records the following entry: 'New leading axle, made and put in by Southern Railway Ashford, whilst engine at Shepherdswell November 1922'. More extensive work was recorded in March 1925: 'New copper firebox, tubeplate and boiler retubed at Shepherdswell'. This was followed by a report in the *Railway Magazine*, '*Northiam*, hitherto idle at Shepherdswell, has recently worked passenger trains'. This suggests that *Northiam* had been out of service for some time prior to this overhaul.

Unfortunately there are no further entries for *Northiam* in the KESR Rolling Stock Register and no records amongst the surviving EKR papers to document its subsequent life at Shepherdswell. The KESR Ledgers continued to record payments by the EKR for engine hire until 1929. The Ledgers for 1930 onwards have not survived but it is believed that *Northiam* remained on the EKR until 1930 and may not have returned to the KESR until 1931. It is known that *Northiam* was repainted at Shepherdswell in KESR livery before leaving the EKR following a thorough overhaul. It is strange that this received no publicity in the railway press at the time, as *Northiam* was repainted in the elaborate royal blue livery with red lining which had long since ceased to be used on its home line.

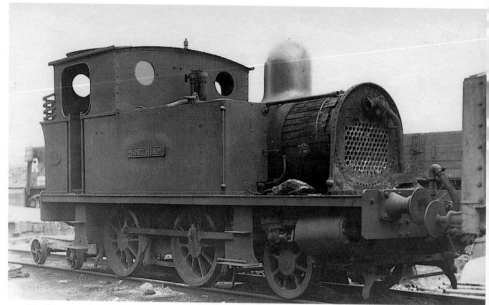

Northiam receiving attention to its smokebox in August 1927.   *H.C. Casserley*

Northiam prepares to depart for Wingham with carriage No. 11 on 16th July, 1930.

A.W. Croughton

Northiam returned to regular service on the KESR but was to have one last connection with the EKR. In 1937 it was hired to star as *Gladstone* in the film 'Oh, Mr Porter!' inspired by life at Staple station. Filming took place on the Basingstoke & Alton Light Railway and *Northiam* was accompanied and fired by EKR fireman Colin Abbott. For the film *Northiam* was fitted with a fancifully elongated chimney and the rear portion of its cab was removed.

Upon returning to Rolvenden *Northiam's* full cab was reinstated but its working days were virtually over. It last ran on 22nd August, 1938 and was cut up at Rolvenden in 1941.

Livery

Northiam was delivered to the Rother Valley Railway painted royal blue and lined out in red. Its chimney cap and dome were brightly polished. Its nameplates were fixed centrally on its sidetanks and its Hawthorn, Leslie plates were fitted to the bunker sides. When the Rother Valley Railway became the Kent & East Sussex the words KENT & EAST SUSSEX RAILWAY were painted in an elliptic garter around its nameplates. This was to remain its livery throughout the rest of its life and, as already recounted, was faithfully renewed by the East Kent.

KESR No. 4 Hecate

Hecate was an 0-8-0 sidetank locomotive built for the KESR in 1904 by Hawthorn, Leslie, Works No. 2587. Locomotives with four coupled wheels were unusual on British light railways and its purchase has never satisfactorily been explained. The favourite versions are that it was intended for through running along the SECR main line to Tonbridge, or for running on the intended extension to Maidstone which would have involved steep gradients. It may simply have been that Stephens thought that such a design would be more suitable for the section of the KESR between Tenterden and Headcorn.

Hecate's name was one of several classical names favoured by Stephens and was also applied by him to two locomotives on the Shropshire & Montgomeryshire Light Railway. It is curious that none of the EKR locomotives was ever named, with the exception of *Walton Park* which was delivered already named by the Weston, Clevedon & Portishead. There was certainly no shortage of historical names associated with East Kent that could have been used. It is true that the EKR was short of money but this was equally true of Stephens' other lines. Perhaps the memories of Arthur Burr's fancy to name almost anything after his family and colleagues prejudiced the EKR Directors against such practices.

Since the axle loading permitted on the Kent & East Sussex between Rolvenden and Robertsbridge was only 10 tons *Hecate*, although by no means a giant of a locomotive, was restricted to working between Rolvenden and Headcorn. Traffic on this section never developed to the extent that had been hoped and *Hecate's* comparative size and power was rarely used effectively on the Kent & East Sussex. By 1914 the line had seven other locomotives and a steam railcar available for services that could be handled comfortably by three

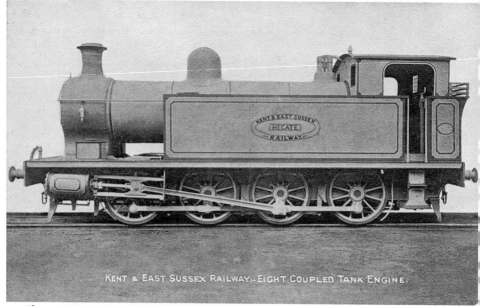

KENT & EAST SUSSEX RAILWAY.-EIGHT COUPLED TANK ENGINE.

This manufacturer's publicity photograph of *Hecate* was used to acknowledge correspondence sent to Stephens' Tonbridge office.

Hecate at Shepherdswell. Construction of the North Bank embankment seems to be proceeding in the background.

locomotives. Judging from the absence of repairs recorded, *Hecate* seems to have been used sparingly.

The opening of the EKR to public services in October 1916 with only two fairly small 0-6-0 saddle tank locomotives created an ideal opportunity to find regular work for *Hecate*, and it was transferred on hire to Shepherdswell on 25th November, 1916. It seems to have been used exclusively on the Tilmanstone coal traffic for which it was the only really suitable locomotive until No. 4, the Kerr, Stuart 0-6-0T, arrived in October 1919.

Hecate remained on the EKR until 5th August, 1921. Its return to the KESR seems to have been prompted by the financial position of the EKR and the falling off of coal traffic from Tilmanstone in that year. Between *Hecate's* departure and the arrival of 0-6-0 No. 6 in 1923 the burden of the Tilmanstone coal traffic must have mostly fallen on EKR No. 4. Before leaving Shepherdswell *Hecate* was treated to a major overhaul. This was recorded in the KESR Rolling Stock Register: 'General Overhaul, New Axle Brasses, Coupling Rod Bushes metalled up, Retubed with secondhand steel tubes, New Cab Roof, Wheels turned up, New Lubricators fitted etc etc Jan 1921 after which run only for one week's trial on East Kent Railway, and returned from East Kent Railway to Kent & East Sussex Railway Friday 5th August, 1921 (Hot Boxes *en route*)'. Although the overhaul is dated as January and *Hecate's* departure did not take place until August, it is quite likely that the overhaul took most of the intervening months to complete. This is not surprising in view of the limited facilities then available at Shepherdswell. The reference to a new cab roof suggests some sort of accident under the screens at Tilmanstone.

Upon returning to the KESR, *Hecate* was set aside pending attention to the damage occasioned by running hot on its return from Shepherdswell. In 1922 it was lifted and work carried out on its axle brasses, springs, big and little ends and eccentric straps. New Furness cylinder lubricators were fitted and it was returned to service on 8th February, 1922. There is, however, little evidence of its receiving more than occasional employment after this date.

Hecate served no real further purpose on the Kent & East Sussex until July 1932 when it and three old carriages were exchanged with the Southern Railway for an 0-6-0ST locomotive, similar to EKR No. 7, together with two bogie carriages and a spare boiler for the newly acquired locomotive. *Hecate* was prepared for movement to Ashford works for overhaul but promptly ran hot and had to be repaired before the journey could be made. *Hecate* eventually left Ashford on 8th September, 1933, painted lined black and bearing Southern Railway No. 949 but retaining its nameplates. In this guise it ran light to Tonbridge on 16th September where it was briefly employed on local freight duties. It then went to Nine Elms but may have spent some time at Guildford *en route*. The bulk of its future career was to be spent shunting at Nine Elms with occasional interludes at Clapham Junction and Guildford. In 1939 it went to Eastleigh for overhaul and was fitted with an LBSCR boiler of the type usually carried by 'D' class tank engines. *Hecate* returned to Nine Elms and continued to serve there until damaged in a collision with 'King Arthur' class No. 30789 *Sir Guy. Hecate* managed to reach Eastleigh under its own steam on 20th March, 1950 but was condemned and broken up the following week.

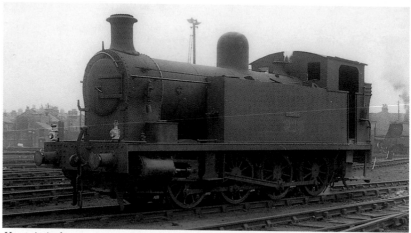

Hecate in its later guise as a Nine Elms shunter, Southern Railway No. 949.

Livery

Hecate's livery whilst running on the EKR was virtually identical to that carried by *Northiam*, i.e. royal blue lined out with narrow red lining, polished chimney cap, dome and safety valve cover and 'KENT & EAST SUSSEX RAILWAY' in an elliptic garter around its nameplates positioned centrally on its sidetanks. The colour of the lettering does not appear to have been recorded. Upon returning to the KESR it retained its blue livery but its lettering seems to have worn away. By 1928 it had been spruced up with the initials K.&.E.S.R. appearing in a straight line above its nameplates. In Southern Railways ownership it ran in standard lined black goods livery with 'SOUTHERN' above its nameplates and '949' below them in yellow.

Locomotives hired from the Southern Railway

The first recorded reference to the EKR hiring locomotives from the Southern Railway is in some papers relating to the Railway's tax returns. These papers are dated 1931 but seem to refer to the previous tax year. One of the items reads 'Temporary loan of SR engine £10 15s. 2d.' There is no further information on the matter and apparently no contemporary reports of Southern locomotives working on the EKR. There may well have been other 'temporary loans' but, if so, they have gone unrecorded.

During World War II it was frequently necessary to hire 'O1' locomotives from the Southern. When the surviving Locomotive Mileage Register was begun on 1st September, 1942, 'O1' No. 1426 was on hire. There is no record of how long it had been on the EKR or whether other locomotives had been on hire before it. It returned to the Southern on 24th September, 1942. Subsequent hirings were as follows:

No. 1430	19th April, 1943 to 7th December, 1943
No. 1066	20th December, 1943 to 7th March, 1944
No. 1437	7th March, 1944 to 27th March, 1944
No. 1373	23rd March, 1945 to 23rd May, 1945 and 3rd December, 1945 to 11th February, 1946.

A rather more surprising hiring was Southern No. 1604 from 28th September, 1944 to 13th January, 1945. This was a 'T' class 0-6-0T originally built by the London, Chatham & Dover Railway in 1891 which seems to have arrived at short notice to cover the withdrawal from service of 0-6-0ST No. 7. Presumably the Southern had no 'O1' locomotives to spare at the time.

War Department Locomotives used on the East Kent

The War Department acquired a wide range of locomotives during World War II but seems to have used only one type of locomotive on the EKR. This was the Great Western Railway 'Dean Goods' class of 0-6-0 tender locomotives of which 260 were built between 1883 and 1889. The class had seen military service during World War I when 62 had been 'conscripted' by the Railway Operating Department. During World War II 108 members of the class were taken over by the War Department and many served overseas. They were also widely used on military lines in Britain and were considered particularly suitable for use with the various rail-mounted guns operating in Kent. A number of the locomotives so used were fitted at Swindon with pannier tanks and condensing equipment to increase their water capacity and to reduce their visibility to prowling enemy aircraft. Other common adaptations to the class were the fitting of water-lifting gear to enable water to be picked up from ponds or streams and the use of Westinghouse brake gear.

It has not proved possible to draw up a definitive list of the 'Dean Goods' locomotives used on the EKR as locomotives were not permanently allocated to particular locations. It is known that some of them were fitted with condensing gear, even though this put them well over the recommended axle loading for the line beyond Eythorne.

We have found no photographs of the Dean Goods locomotives during their period on the East Kent but this photograph of No. 70169 and another member of the class on the Shropshire & Montygomeryshire Railway gives an idea of their general appearance.

The following 'Deans' are known to have been on the EKR but it is likely that other members of the class were also used:

WD No.	GWR	Comments
No.	No.	
93	2433	On EKR 1943-44. Seen at Eythorne 21/7/44. Left EKR 31/8/44 for Longmoor via Redhill.
95	2470	On EKR in 1944. Seen at Eythorne 21/7/44. Left EKR 31/8/44 for Longmoor via Redhill.
96	2425	On EKR in 1944.
97	2442	On EKR in 1944. On Guilford branch stub 21/7/44.
171	2545	On EKR between September 1940 and December 1941 in connection with rail-mounted anti-aircraft guns . Named 'Betty'. On leaving Kent went to WD depot at Burton Dassett.
175	2511	On EKR c.1944.
177	2430	On EKR in 1944. Condensing gear. Parked on Guilford branch 21/7/44. Noted at Eythorne early September 1944 but at Canterbury 13/9/44.
179	2466	On EKR in 1943. Condensing gear.
197	2540	On EKR in 1944. Condensing gear.

The EKR was not the only 'Stephens' Line to be served by this class. Rail-mounted guns and attendant 'Dean Goods' were also based on the Kent & East Sussex and other members of the class were based on the Shropshire & Montgomeryshire during the war. Although none of the 'Dean Goods' purchased by the War Department were returned to the Great Western Railway at the end of the war, a number of the class remained in use with the Great Western and subsequently British Railways. The last was not withdrawn until 1957 and No. 2516 survives in preservation at Swindon.

It has been suggested that one of the diesel-electric locomotives subsequently used with the rail-mounted guns at Martin Mill had previously operated on the East Kent, possibly in connection with the RAF ammunition stores at Staple, but we have found no evidence to confirm this.

Locomotives types used on the East Kent by British Railways

This subject is covered in general in Chapter 13 and in the absence of any sort of regular observation of the line after the withdrawal of the 'O1' class there is little that can be usefully added.

Tilmanstone Colliery Locomotives

Tilmanstone Colliery mainly relied on EKR locomotives until it came under the National Coal Board. It is recorded by the Industrial Railway Society as having owned a Hawthorn, Leslie 0-4-0T, No. 3072 of 1914 named *Shakespeare*, purchased from the Ministry of Munitions and subsequently working for the Broughton & Plaspower Coal Company. However, the location given for this locomotive during the ownership of Tilmanstone (Kent) Collieries Ltd is Shakespeare Cliff Colliery at Dover, long closed by then, and there does seem to be some uncertainty about its connection with Tilmanstone.

More widely accepted is the presence at Tilmanstone of a 3 ft gauge Kerr, Stuart 0-4-2ST *Advance*, Works No. 876 of 1904, purchased from T.W. Ward at Grays in 1929 but little further seems to be known of its work at Tilmanstone or its subsequent disposal.

In NCB days the following 2 ft gauge diesel-mechanical locomotives were reported here: Hudswell, Clarke Works Nos. 686 and 687 of 1948 and Orenstein & Koppel Works No. 20045. Hudswell, Clarke 686 has been preserved at Amberley. Other narrow gauge locomotives worked underground. The NCB also had two standard gauge locomotives at Tilmanstone. Four-wheeled Hunslet diesel-mechanical, Works No. 4679 of 1955, bore the number 10 and was here from new until the late 1960s. In 1964, possibly while No. 10 was absent for overhaul, Peckett 0-4-0ST No. 2156 of 1955, *Cadbury No. 10*, was drafted in from Chislet Colliery but it does not seem to have stayed long.

Hammill Brickworks Locomotives

The Brickworks operated four 4-wheeled internal combustion locomotives on their short 2 ft gauge system from the claypits to the works These were F.C. Hibberd petrol-mechanical No. 1670 of 1930, F.C. Hibberd diesel-mechanicals Nos. 2306 of 1940 and 2586 of 1941, and Ruston & Hornsby diesel-mechanical 223702 of 1944.

A narrow gauge clay train on the Hammill Brickworks line passing the photographer at speed. To our uninitiated eyes it would appear to be one of the two Hibberd diesel-mechanicals. *Ralph Gillam Collection*

Chapter Sixteen

Carriages and Wagons

Carriages

The carriages of the EKR were typical of those operated by light railways in general and of those equipped by Holman Stephens in particular. They were all obtained second-hand, third-hand in several cases. They came from various sources and with no covered accommodation they suffered grievously from the elements. The ratio of brake carriages to non-brake carriages was high and the provision of first-class accommodation limited. It is surprising that first class accommodation was provided at all since the railway's Annual Reports record no instance of the carriage of such passengers. For many years the bulk of passengers were coalminers carried between Shepherdswell and Tilmanstone. Certain of the carriages were reserved solely for this traffic and, although there is no official record as to which carriages these were, we have indicated the likely candidates .

The main sources of information on which this account is based are two East Kent Railway carriage stocklists compiled in the 1920s, the EKR Annual Reports, the Rolling Stock Register of the Kent & East Sussex Railway, a list of carriages for sale in 1946, an inventory made by British Railways at Nationalisation and the recollections of staff and visiting enthusiasts. Inevitably, there are contradictions. These are sometimes due to the relative lack of interest in carriages shown by most enthusiasts until recently, but official sources are not entirely blameless either. One of the oddities is that some of the carriages seem to have grown and shrunk between successive measurements; we have used the East Kent's own measurements but would warn the scrupulous modeller that carriage body lengths may only be accurate within tolerances of plus or minus six inches. We have endeavoured to reconcile or explain the more widely perpetuated discrepancies and confusions surrounding the carriages, but we are well aware that some questions remain unresolved.

The first five carriages known to have been acquired by the EKR came from the Kent & East Sussex Light Railway. This line was also managed by Holman Stephens and, like the EKR, had at one time planned a considerable number of extensions, notably to Maidstone, Cranbrook and Rye. The railway would also have provided the rolling stock for a railway between Robertsbridge and Pevensey and for the Hadlow Railway planned near Tonbridge. None of these plans came to anything and the KESR was left with a fleet of passenger rolling stock far in excess of its requirements. It was therefore only too happy to divest itself of some of this surplus.

The actual dates on which these carriages were acquired, or the sums involved, were not officially recorded by either the KESR or the EKR. There is evidence that the KESR, which had bought, but not paid for, a large quantity of coal from Tilmanstone, set the debt for the carriages and various other materials supplied to East Kent Contract & Financial Company against the amount owed for the coal to the East Kent Colliery Company. It should be remembered that until 1916 the EKR did not actually own any of the rolling stock purchased on its behalf by the East Kent Contract & Financial Company. Circumstantial evidence suggests that all of these carriages were acquired in 1912 and 1913.

One of the KESR carriages was destroyed in an accident in 1917 and the first extant EKR carriage list numbers the remaining KESR carriages as Nos. 1, 2, 3 and 6. Since carriages 4 and 5 were not acquired until 1919 or 1920 it is possible that carriages were not numbered on the railway until then. Since no two of these carriages were the same there would have been no difficulty in telling them apart.

Carriage No. 1

Origin	Built by R.Y. Pickering & Co. Ltd of Wishaw for the KESR in May 1905.
Description	Bogie brake composite vestibule saloon.
Obtained from	KESR in 1912.
Livery	Kentish Brown & Ivory on KESR but dark red at first on EKR, later grey and, in 1946, green.
Features	Bogie coach with duckets either side at brake end, straight sides, large square windows.
Disposal	Scrapped by British Railways 1948.

Carriage No. 1 had been supplied new to the KESR by R.Y. Pickering as bogie brake composite saloon No. 17 in May 1905. Its body was 41 ft by 8 ft and ran on light four-wheel bogies with a 5 ft 6 in. wheelbase and 3 ft 1 in. diameter wheels. A central gangway ran the length of its saloons which accommodated 16 first class and 28 third class passengers. It had been supplied as part of a rake of three carriages but the other two, an all-third and a third brake, had been re-sold to Pickering in 1909 and gone to the Woolmer Instructional Railway at Longmoor. Its livery on the KESR had been Kentish Brown and Ivory but it was dark red during its early years on the EKR. On the KESR the brake end had been repainted red but, as trouble was experienced with this coat of paint lifting, it is not clear if this feature was retained upon delivery to the East Kent.

No. 1 was used to convey Concessions shareholders between Shepherdswell and Tilmanstone on 27th November, 1912 and at the time it was stated that it had been purchased 'a few days ago'. It was used for several subsequent tours of inspection but probably saw little other use until passenger services commenced in October 1916. It was not used on the workmen's trains to Tilmanstone.

In 1920 its accommodation was altered to 20 first class and 32 third class but it is unclear whether this was achieved by fitting additional seats or simply by re-assessing the capacity of the existing seating. Apart from occasional periods out of service for repairs, No. 1 seems to have been used regularly on the Wingham services until the mid-1930s. In 1946 two further bogie carriages were purchased and the opportunity was taken to repaint No. 1 in a shade described by Mr A.G. Wells at the time as Apple Green. At an earlier stage it had been described as dull red and prior to its 1946 repaint was reported as grey. Despite its relatively new coat of paint, No. 1 was promptly condemned by British Railways when they took over the line in 1948. For some reason the carriage's

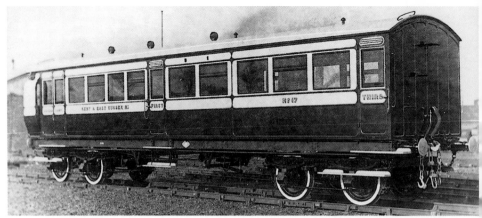

No. 1 at the Wishaw works of R.Y. Pickering prior to delivery to the Kent & East Sussex Railway as their No. 17.   *Historical Model Railway Society*

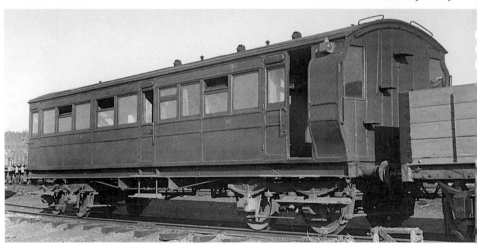

No. 1 in full 'dull red' livery at Shepherdswell.   *M. Lawson Finch Collection*

Traces of the original brown and ivory can be seen in this April 1939 view.

                                                                                                                                   Ron Jarvis/Midland Railway Trust

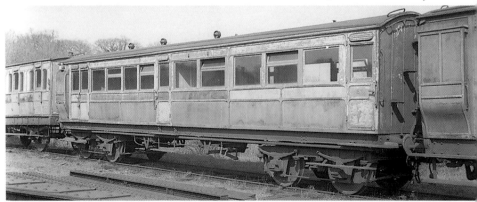

body was removed, presumably at Shepherdswell, and the frame towed to Ashford for cutting up.

There is an early report in the *Locomotive Magazine* that there was a second carriage of the same sort as No. 1 on the East Kent but we have found no evidence to substantiate this.

Carriage No. 2

Origin	North London Railway.
Description	4-wheel passenger brake van.
Obtained from	KESR in 1912 or 1913.
Livery	Brown and ivory when delivered, later grey.
Features	Raised look-out at one end (later removed), two small windows cut in opposite end, small louvred doors to dog compartment in lower side panels at look-out end, sides panelled, single high waist beading, additional footboard.
Disposal	Scrapped by EKR in 1947 or early 1948.

This was one of two North London Railway four-wheeled passenger brakevans purchased by the KESR from William Jones of London in 1904. North London carriages were popular with Britain's light railways and the brakevans, which had originally been built not only to carry luggage but also the gas supplies for carriage lighting, were particularly capacious. These two were numbered 14 and 15 and ran on the KESR in a varnished brown livery. No. 15 was retained by the KESR until 1948. It seems likely that No. 14 was delivered to Shepherdswell in brown and ivory but latterly it appears to have been painted grey. There may possibly have been other colour schemes in the interim. The only firm livery detail to have been recorded is that the inscriptions 'E K R' at one end and 'No. 2' at the other end were to be found in yellow in two round-ended panels below the eaves on each side. Delivery seems to have taken place in 1913 but may have been late 1912.

On the EKR this carriage became No. 2 and saw much use in the early years when it was the only brake carriage apart from No. 1. At some date its original raised end lookout was removed. After 1920 it spent much of its time in the sidings at Shepherdswell but may have been used for workmen's trains or to provide covered accommodation on construction trains. Used or not, it survived until advertised for sale in 1946. As it was still to be seen in a dilapidated state at Shepherdswell on 27th November, 1947 it must have failed to find a purchaser. It was not specifically mentioned in the inventory of stock drawn up by British Railways and might already have been broken up; it may have been mistakenly recorded as a goods brakevan as the figures for these do not match known EKR vehicles. The following dimensions are taken from the 1946 sales list:

Length over body	18 ft 6 in.
Length over buffers	21 ft 11 in.
Width	8 ft 0 in.
Wheelbase	11 ft 0 in.

The body of a very similar vehicle has survived and may be inspected at the North Woolwich Railway Museum.

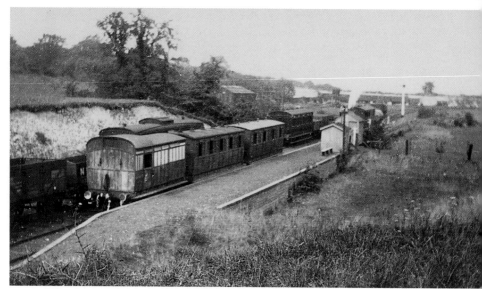

Unfortunately a poor photograph but the only one we know of showing No. 2 with its birdcage lookout intact and sporting a two-tone livery - presumably brown and ivory. It is coupled to the two CLC carriages, Nos. 6 and 3. It would be interesting to know what a SECR centre lookout passenger brake is doing in the siding behind No. 2.   *M. Lawson Finch Collection*

No. 2 as it was usually to be seen on the East Kent with its lookout shorn to roof level and a uniform grey livery.   *M. Lawson Finch Collection*

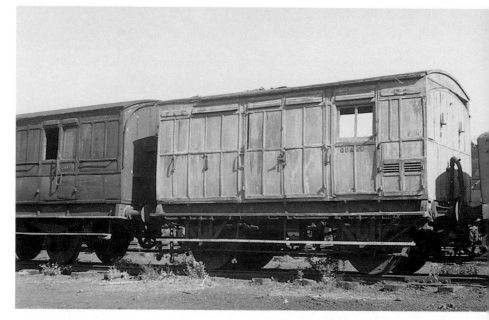

Carriage No. 3

Origin	Cheshire Lines Committee.
Description	Originally four-wheeled, four-compartment composite but later down-rated to all-third.
Obtained from	KESR 1912 or 1913.
Livery	Latterly grey.
Features	Rounded corners to panels and windows, deep waist panels, additional footboard.
Disposal	Body dismounted 1946 and sold for use as bungalow at Staple station.

This was one of a pair of carriages purchased by the KESR, then known as the Rother Valley Railway, in 1902 from R. Frazer & Company of North Shields and came to the EKR in 1913 or late 1912. They had originally been provided for the Cheshire Lines Committee by the Manchester Sheffield & Lincolnshire Railway (MSLR) and therefore fulfilled, by a most circuitous route, Edward Watkins' aim of running carriages from Manchester to Kent referred to in Chapter One. According to Mr G.H. Platt, who has made a study of Cheshire Lines carriages, No. 3 was probably built at Gorton works in 1870. At some time, possibly at Frazer's, a large letter A had been riveted to the solebar on each side. The purpose of this identification is not known. A carriage of similar general design survives in preservation on the Keighley & Worth Valley Railway.

No. 3 had been KESR No. 12 and was delivered to Shepherdswell as a composite carriage seating 12 first class and 20 third class passengers. In 1920 it was down-rated to an all-third carriage seating 40 and seems to have been reserved for workmen's trains at this time. Certainly it was seldom used after the cessation of the workmen's services and spent most of the 1930s resting in the carriage siding at Shepherdswell. In 1946 it was advertised for sale together

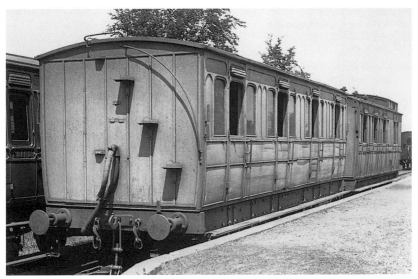

Carriage No. 3, originally a Cheshire Lines Committee vehicle, coupled to ex-LCDR No. 9 at Shepherdswell.

with carriages 2, 7, 8 and 9 and sold to Mr Len Lawrence as a summer house at
Staple station. It is to Mr Lawrence that we are indebted for the sales list which
was attached to his bill of sale. One curious feature of the list is that it gives the
length over body for No. 3 as 27 feet 8 inches whereas the standard length, and
that given by the KESR for this vehicle, was 27 feet 6 inches. The other
dimensions for this carriage were as follows:

Length over buffers	31 ft 6 in.
Width	8 ft 0 in.
Wheelbase	17 ft 2 in.
Height of body	6 ft 9 in.
Height to eaves	6 ft 0 in.

This carriage has often been described as of Great Eastern origin, probably
because of the great similarity in appearance of Great Eastern and MSLR
carriages built in the late 19th century, the only significant difference in style
being the deeper waist panel of the MSLR design. The total absence of
identification on No. 3 during the years that it stood out of use at Shepherdswell
certainly cannot have helped visiting enthusiasts to determine its origins.

The Great Eastern Carriage

Origin	Built for the Great Eastern Railway in 1876 by Brown, Marshall & Co.
Description	Four-wheeled, five-compartment all-third.
Obtained from	KESR in 1912 or 1913.
Livery	Probably brown.
Features	Internal narrow side gangway, additional footboard.
Disposal	Damaged beyond repair in accident in 1917.

This five-compartment four-wheel third class carriage had been built as Great
Eastern Railway No. 274 in 1876 by Brown, Marshall. It was purchased by the
Rother Valley Railway (later the KESR) from the Great Eastern as No. 13 in
October 1903. The KESR subsequently came under pressure from the Board of
Trade to make its carriages more suitable for the collection of fares *en route*,
which had hitherto been achieved by the guard making his way from
compartment to compartment and carriage to carriage along the footboards
outside the train. No. 13 was therefore subjected to the indignity of having one
seat-width removed from each of the intermediate banks of seats to provide a
15 inch internal gangway along one side from end to end. Since the partitions
separating the compartments only came to seat-back height this surgery was
less drastic than it might sound although it did reduce the carriage's seating
capacity from 50 to 42. No attempt was made to provide access between
carriages so the perils of fare collection were only partially diminished. In the
event No. 13 was the only carriage converted by the KESR in this way and the
line reverted to acquiring ordinary compartment carriages as soon as the Board
of Trade appeared to lose interest in the matter.

This carriage was on the EKR by 1913 but in 1917 it was damaged beyond
repair in the collision at Eythorne Court. There is no evidence that this carriage
had ever been allocated a number by the EKR.

The dimensions of this carriage when on the KESR were:

Length over body	26 ft 0 in.
Length over buffers	29 ft 4 in.
Width	8 ft 0 in.
Wheelbase	15 ft 3 in.

Carriage No. 4

Origin	Midland Railway (built 1882).
Description	Six-wheeled, four-compartment composite slip brake.
Obtained from	Midland Railway in 1919.
Livery	Midland Red.
Features	End windows in brake end, additional footboard.
Disposal	Broken up by British Railways 1948

Minute 6007 of the Midland Railway Carriage and Wagon Committee Minutes, dated 16th October, 1919, reads: 'Resolved - Sell old third class carriage unfit for further main line traffic to Mr Stephens of the EKR for £180 (originally built as composite slip)'. The actual date of delivery has gone unrecorded, as has the motivation behind the Railway's nominal restoration of this carriage to its original configuration of two first class and two third class compartments. In appearance it was a typical Midland carriage of its period, though as a slip coach it possessed only a small brake compartment rather than the larger luggage compartments with which the Midland equipped their contemporary three-compartment brake thirds.

Although slipping carriages *en route* was never intentionally practised by the EKR, the absence of run-round loops at the platform at Shepherdswell and anywhere at all at Canterbury Road meant that something very like slipping would take place at these termini as has been described.

The Midland carriage became No. 4 on the EKR and is recorded as carrying a 'dull red' livery at first. This could have been its original Midland livery faded with the passage of time, but as the same description has been given of the livery of other carriages on the line it may have been the standard EKR colour at this time. It had become very decrepit by 1947 but was then belatedly selected for refurbishment. Little was done apart from fitting new roof canvas before work was abandoned in the face of imminent Nationalisation. It has been reported that No. 4 was repainted in dark olive green but this was probably the result of confusion with another six-wheeled carriage that was refurbished at this time. British Railways were not impressed by No. 4 and promptly earmarked it for scrapping when they inspected the line in April 1948.

The dimensions for this carriage in the EKR stocklist were:

Length over body	31 ft 6 in.
Length over buffers	35 ft 2 in.
Width	8 ft 0 in.
Wheelbase	22 ft 0 in.
Brake Compartment	4 ft 6 in. by 7 ft 6 in.

Carriage No. 4 was originally a 6-wheel Midland Railway composite slip brake.

No. 4 running with ex-LSWR 6-wheel third brake No. 5 - these two carriages often ran together.

Carriage No. 5

Origin	London & South Western Railway.
Description	Six-wheeled, three-compartment third brake.
Obtained from	LSWR or War Department.
Livery	Initially dull red, later dark green.
Features	Additional footboard.
Disposal	Broken up by British Railways 1948.

This carriage first appears in the EKR stock returns in 1920. Unfortunately it is not possible to get a clear date for its acquisition or its previous history as the LSWR records of carriage sales had become very vague by this date. It could well have been one of the many carriages sold by the LSWR at this time, but could equally well have been purchased from the War Department who had obtained a number of LSWR carriages during the war. It seated 30 third class passengers and was very similar to two carriages operated by the KESR, except that the guard's side lookout duckets that were a feature of this type of carriage had been removed from the EKR example at some time before delivery. Unlike No. 4 it was equipped with an extremely capacious luggage compartment. The two vehicles often ran coupled together and made a very pretty train indeed. It was still in reasonable condition in 1946 and was in regular use until the arrival of the LSWR bogie carriages, but failed to meet British Railways' approval in 1948 and was promptly condemned.

The East Kent dimensions for this carriage were:

Length over body	34 ft 6 in.
Length over buffers	37 ft 11 in.
Width	8 ft 0 in.
Wheelbase	20 ft 0 in.
Brake Compartment	16 ft 9 in. by 7 ft 6 in.

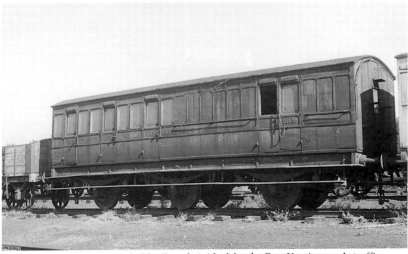

The capacious luggage area in No. 5 made it ideal for the East Kent's parcels traffic.

M. Lawson Finch Collection

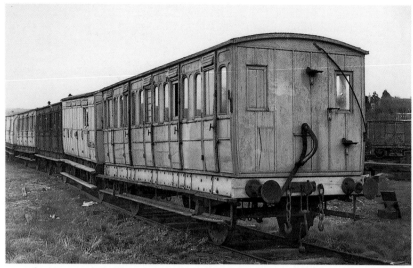

No. 6 had been adapted for workmen's services long before it came to the East Kent and it seems to have been mainly used on the miners' trains to Tilmanstone. *H.C. Casserley*

Carriage No. 6

Origin	Cheshire Lines Committee.
Description	Four-wheeled five-compartment all-third.
Obtained from	KESR in 1912 or 1913.
Livery	Brown when delivered.
Features	Internal gangway along one side, two windows cut in each end, additional footboard.
Disposal	Body dismounted 1937 and used as office at Staple station.

This was the second of the pair of Cheshire Lines Committee carriages purchased by the Rother Valley Railway from Frazer of North Shields. Its Rother Valley and KESR number was 11. It was a five-compartment third class carriage, which had been altered by Frazer by cutting a narrow gangway along one side to connect the compartments in the same way that the KESR subsequently altered its Great Eastern carriage and presumably served as a model for that conversion. This had the effect of reducing its seating from 50 to 42 places. Frazer was a dealer in second-hand carriages and regularly carried out such conversions on the carriages they supplied to collieries and minor railways. Although described in the EKR lists as a 'corridor' vehicle there was no facility for entering adjacent carriages. One further distinctive embellishment was the fitting of two windows in each end of the carriage. The presence of these end windows led some accounts to suggest that this carriage was a brake vehicle.

No. 11 became No. 6 on the EKR and was probably one of the carriages dedicated to workmen's traffic. It appears to have been officially withdrawn from service in 1937. Its body was subsequently removed from its chassis and used as accommodation at Staple station. Its dimensions in the EKR Stocklist were:

Length over body	27 ft 2 in.
Length over buffers	30 ft 10 in.
Width	8 ft 0 in.
Wheelbase	17 ft 2 in.

Comparing these measurements with those taken on the KESR it would appear that the body length had shrunk by 4 inches whilst the wheelbase and length over buffers had increased by 2 inches!

Carriage No. 7

Origin	London Chatham & Dover Railway.
Description	Four-wheeled, four-compartment all-third.
Obtained from	South Eastern & Chatham Railway in 1920.
Livery	Latterly grey.
Features	Sunken ovals in lower door panels, vertical beading in centres of lower body panels and prominent roof ventilators.
Disposal	Broken up in 1947 or 1948.

This was the first of a rake of three carriages purchased from the South Eastern & Chatham in 1920 and had originally been an all-first vehicle with the distinctive oval door panels of its type. It had been demoted to all-third before

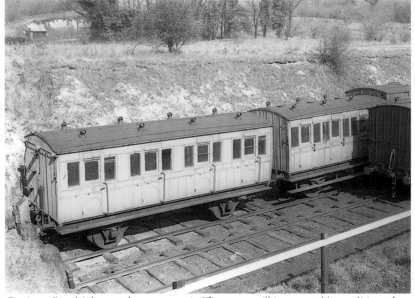

Carriages 7 and 9 frequently ran as a pair. They were still in reasonable condition when photographed in April 1939, long after the miners' trains had ceased. *Jim Jarvis*

its arrival on the EKR and as such seated 40. Its dimensions in the 1946 sale list were given as:

Length over body	25 ft 0 in.
Length over buffers	28 ft 8 in.
Width	8 ft 6 in.
Wheelbase	14 ft

This carriage usually ran with one or both of the other LCDR vehicles with which it came to the EKR and it seems that this set was reserved for workmen's traffic. Its livery on arrival has gone unrecorded but at an early stage was reported as grey and later as dull red. By 1946 it was in very poor condition with most windows broken as a result of the firing of the War Department guns at Shepherdswell.

No. 7 was one of the carriages advertised for sale in 1946 but found no purchaser and was broken up at some date after April 1947. A note in *Model Maker* refers to it still standing at Shepherdswell in March 1949 painted brown and being of LNWR origin. It is unlikely that British Railways would have omitted this carriage from its inventory had it still been at Shepherdswell in April 1948, and it is safer to presume that No. 7 had been broken up by this date.

One other source of confusion surrounding this carriage is that the body of an almost identical vehicle was used as an office on Staple station platform until replaced by that of the Cheshire Lines carriage No. 6 around 1937. This body is dealt with later but for the time being it is sufficient to state that it had no connection with carriage No. 7.

Carriage No. 8

Origin	London Chatham & Dover Railway.
Description	Four-wheeled, four-compartment all-third.
Obtained from	South Eastern & Chatham Railway in 1920.
Livery	Dull red.
Features	Typical LCDR straight panels.
Disposal	Broken up in 1947 or 1948.

Although this carriage came to the EKR, as an all-third, its generous dimensions suggest that it had originally been built as an all-first. The dimensions given in the 1946 sale list were:

Length over body	26 ft 0 in.
Length over buffers	29 ft 8 in.
Width	8 ft 0 in.
Wheelbase	15 ft 0 in.

This carriage seated 40 and was reported as bearing the standard dull red livery in the 1930s but does not otherwise seem to have occasioned much comment. By August 1946 it was standing in poor condition at Shepherdswell and was broken up prior to British Railways making its inventory of rolling stock.

Carriage No. 8 is flanked by two ex-CLC carriages Nos. 6 and 3 when seen in July 1936. No. 8's paintwork seems to have fared rather better than that of its companions.   *H.C. Casserley*

Carriage No. 9

Origin	London Chatham & Dover Railway (*but see text*)
Description	Four-wheeled, three-compartment third brake.
Obtained from	South Eastern & Chatham Railway.
Livery	Dull red, later grey.
Features	Large raised lookout above brake compartment, vertical beading in centres of lower body panels, additional footboard.
Disposal	Broken up by March 1948.

The two early EKR stocklists recorded this carriage as of South Eastern Railway origin but the 1946 sale list gave it as a London Chatham & Dover vehicle and its appearance was much more typical of that line than of the South Eastern. The raised lookout suggests that it was originally built for the through services via Snow Hill tunnel to the Great Northern. The dimensions given in the sale list were:

Length over body	25 ft 0 in.
Length over buffers	29 ft 8 in.
Width	8 ft 6 in.
Wheelbase	14 ft 0 in.

Intriguingly, both the sale list and the stock list attempted to fit a brake compartment 9 feet square into a carriage only 8 feet 6 inches wide. Seating capacity was 30.

This carriage was in regular use well into the 1930s and possibly even into World War II but at the end of the war was standing at Shepherdswell in a sorry state, its windows smashed by gunfire concussion. In one respect it differed from most of the carriage fleet by this date. It had been EKR practice to identify its carriages with raised figures and numerals but over the years these either dropped off or were removed and replaced by painted identification. No. 9 seems to have retained a full set of raised numerals until the end.

In June 1946 No. 9 was recorded as bearing grey paintwork. It was broken up by March 1948.

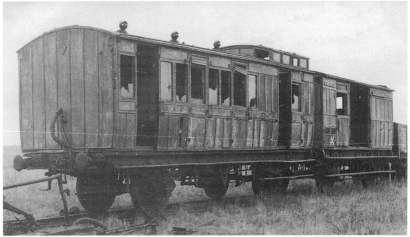

Carriage No. 9 was one of those damaged by gunfire concussion during the war. It awaits its fate with carriage No. 2 on the North Bank siding in December 1947.   *R.W. Kidner*

Carriage No. 10

Origin	London Chatham & Dover Railway.
Description	Six-wheeled three-compartment brake composite.
Obtained from	Southern Railway in 1926.
Livery	Dull red latterly Southern Green.
Features	Typical LCDR duckets at brake end supplemented by narrow end windows in brake end, short additional footboard below guard's compartment.
Disposal	Rumoured to have been transferred by British Railways to one of the London electric train depots for staff use.

This brake composite came to the EKR with one third class compartment and two first class compartments giving seating for 10 third class and 12 first class passengers respectively. Originally the third class would have been second class. David Gould suggests that this was originally LCDR carriage No. 14 built in 1893 and withdrawn by the Southern in September 1926 bearing its SECR number 2663. The provision of further first class accommodation on the EKR at this time seems a little strange, but may have been intended to bolster the line's image in the eyes of potential investors. No. 10 was purchased for £57 5s. 9d.

Dr J.R. Hollick recalls the early livery of this carriage as the standard dull red though this may simply been its SECR livery. It was quite badly damaged in an otherwise unrecorded accident in July 1927, but was considered worth repairing and was returned to traffic in a further coat of red. One curious feature to survive these attentions was the display of emergency instructions in French - presumably a survival from boat train service in the past.

No. 10 continued in regular service throughout the 1930s and the war years. At the end of the war it was overhauled and repainted in Southern green. This refurbishment was apparently carried out so that No. 10 could be used on the morning train which involved shunting sidings that were too sharply curved for the bogie carriages acquired from the Southern. It had by now been demoted to all-third but made up for this loss of status by indicating the class of each compartment with a large gold '3' transfer on every compartment door. In this

Carriage No. 10 had two of its three compartments designated as first class in this June 1934 scene. This seems excessive when it is considered that the only first class passengers on the East Kent were the holders of free passes. *H.C. Casserley*

In this later, but sadly undated, photograph all compartments have become third class.
M. Lawson Finch Collection

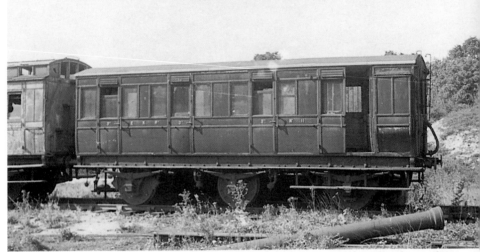

Carriage No. 11 was always designated third class on the East Kent. It was still in fair condition when photographed in September 1947 and must have been away from Shepherdswell when howitzer practice was under way. *G.A. Hookham*

Members of the Norbury & South London Transport Club provide an unusually high payload for carriage No. 5 as it prepares to leave Staple at 7.00 pm on 24th July, 1948. Note 'FOR USE ON EAST KENT SECTION ONLY' branding at the bottom of the lower front panel of No. 5. *John L. Smith*

condition it has been suggested that No. 10 sufficiently impressed British Railways for them to set it aside for further use as departmental accommodation. According to Mr E.B. Trotter in 1949, 'This coach is now used as a stores van in one of the London electrical depots'. It has been suggested that the depot concerned was Selhurst but we have found no evidence for this.

The EKR measurements for No. 10 were:

Length over body	27 ft 10 in.
Length over buffers	31 ft 3 in.
Width	8 ft 0 in.
Wheelbase	18 ft 0 in.
Brake Compartment	7 ft 6 in. by 8 ft

Carriage No. 11

Origin	London Chatham & Dover Railway.
Description	Six-wheeled, three-compartment brake third.
Obtained from	Southern Railway.
Livery	Dull red.
Features	As No. 10 with additional centre window in brake end.
Disposal	Broken up by British Railways 1948.

This carriage was purchased for £56 16s. 8d. in 1927. David Gould has identified it as LCDR No. 43 of 1891 which was withdrawn by the Southern in October 1926 still carrying its SECR number 2691. It was generally similar to No. 10, but had been built as a slip coach which presumably accounted for the additional window in the brake end. There is no evidence that the EKR had actively sought to purchase a slip coach, but it is a strange coincidence that the line should have acquired two such vehicles.

Although built as a first and second class composite it was delivered to the EKR as an all-third seating 30 and performed reliably through the 1930s and the war years. It seems to have retained its moulded figures and numerals and remained in fair condition when compared with much of the earlier stock in 1947. It had not been included in the 1946 sale list and the railway seems to have hoped to obtain more service from it. British Railways were less impressed: their inventory of April 1948 carried the fatal verdict, 'Will be broken up'.

Dimensions were the same as for No. 10.

Bogie Carriages No. 5 and No. 6

Origin	London & South Western Railway.
Description	Bogie corridor four-compartment lavatory brake thirds.
Obtained from	Southern Railway.
Livery	Southern Green.
Disposal	Taken into British Railways stock.

In February 1945 the EKR Directors decided to withdraw some of the older carriages and therefore sought replacements from the Southern Railway. In November they were informed that the Southern was looking out two suitable carriages for them. In February 1946 the Southern offered them two carriages at

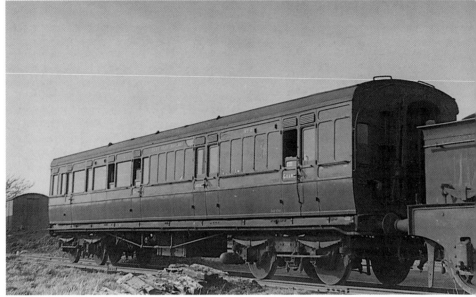

Carriage No. 6 at Canterbury Road 25th April, 1947. Note the grounded van body in the background which had replaced the round corrugated iron shed as a goods store.

H.C. Casserley

Carriage No. 3 in use as a summer house at Staple complete with topiary locomotive.

Len Lawrence

£75 each and their arrival was reported in July 1946. They were both London & South Western Railway 56 ft 0 in. bogie corridor brake thirds of 1911 vintage. These had been Southern Nos. 3126 and 3128 and became EKR Nos. 5 and 6, though not necessarily in the same order. The brake end of No. 5 was towards Wingham and that of No. 6 was towards Shepherdswell.

Since the carriages were rarely, if ever, used in tandem their corridor connections were superfluous but they each had a toilet and 32 upholstered seats. Since such comforts were already taken for granted on the main line and little improvement was possible in the journey times, the arrival of the 'new' carriages did not generate a new rush of custom. Nevertheless, they must have rendered the few remaining fare-paying journeys being made over the line rather more tolerable.

Both carriages arrived in excellent external condition carrying Southern malachite green paintwork and lettered 'EAST KENT RAILWAY' in yellow. British Railways had small inscriptions added in white 'FOR USE ON EAST KENT SECTION ONLY'.

Prior to the British Railways inspection and inventory of April 1948 it is clear that the line's new owners were aware that these two carriages could be of further use as a document dated 24th March, 1948 makes clear: 'Rolling Stock - Passenger: 7 coaches, 5 of which are condemned and 2 similar to Nos. 1 and 6 of the KESR, i.e. Bogie Third Brakes, 32 seats each, which it is suggested be transferred to KESR to replace condemnations if it is decided to discontinue the passenger service on the East Kent Railway.' The wheel really would have come full circle if the EKR's final carriages had taken over the services on the line that had supplied its first carriages, but it was not to be. Other LSWR corridor stock was found for the KESR and the EKR carriages continued in service on their home line until the end of passenger services in October 1948. Both carriages were reinstated to Southern Region stock under their Southern numbers in the *Carriage Working Notice Appendices* in September 1948 but had been deleted by the next issue in May 1949. It is unlikely that their East Kent numbers were actually painted out and their Southern numbers reapplied as it was as 'No. 5' that one of the carriages was reported at Ashford in 1949 as having no lights.

Postscript - A Staple Diet of Coaches

Mention has been made earlier of the use of coach bodies as accommodation at Staple station. According to EKR staff interviewed in 1955, the first coach body used at Staple was of Great Northern Railway origin and had originally stood as a complete vehicle in storage in the sidings at Shepherdswell. In about 1926 it had been hauled very carefully to Staple to provide accommodation for an Irish porter. The latter had been unable to get lodgings in the area in view of the troubles then occurring in Ireland. At a later date it had been dismounted from its chassis and put to use as an office on the platform and was sold at some date before 1936. Two of the staff from Shepherdswell were sent up to Staple to saw it in half with the use of a large cross-cut saw. This was a terrible task as the wood proved to be as hard as iron and was the hardest that the carpenter had ever had to cut. One half was then put to use as a chicken shed at Staple while

Above: Wagons Nos. 9 and 2 at Canterbury Road in 1926. Both are three-plank wagons but No. 9 has dropsides whereas No. 2 has a drop door. *M. Lawson Finch Collection*

Right: Wagon No. 13 was originally an SER 10 ton express goods wagon (Diagram 1327) which has had the high rounded ends removed but still remains its Mansell wheels in this 1939 view. *C.C. Bowker*

Below: Wagon No. 16 was originally built by Cravens in 1875 for the LCDR where it was numbered 431. Like many East Kent wagons its SECR lettering has emerged alongside its EKR lettering. *M. Lawson Finch Collection*

the other half was transported to Barnsole Windmill near Staple. A search was made at the windmill in the 1950s but no trace of the carriage half, nor of footings upon which it might have stood, could be traced.

Photographic evidence suggests that the carriage involved in this story was of London Chatham & Dover Railway origin rather than Great Northern as it appears to have been a twin to EKR No. 7. Nor is there any evidence of the carriage having stood intact in the sidings at Shepherdswell, though that is not to say that it could not have done so. It does seem more likely, though, that the body was purchased as a body rather than as a complete coach and it may indeed have been intended for use at Shepherdswell. The truth of the matter, as with so many anecdotes concerning the railway, is unlikely ever to be known for certain but it makes a nice tale and contains sufficient detail not to be discounted out of hand.

There were, of course, two further bodies at Staple. Both the Cheshire Lines carriages ended their days here. No. 6 was brought here in or about 1937 to replace the 'Great Northern' body but was located behind the platform rather than on it. During the early years of the war it served to control the traffic to and from the adjacent RAF bomb depot. It was still there in 1951 but the date of its eventual demise has gone unrecorded.

No. 3 arrived at Staple in 1946 to serve as a summer house for Mr Len Lawrence, but again details of how long it lasted here are not known except that it is known to have survived the lifting of the line.

Wagons and Miscellaneous rolling stock

Any account of EKR wagon stock in the early years is complicated by the initial confusion between the property of the East Kent Contract & Financial Company and that of the EKR, which did not own any rolling stock until it took over from the Contract company in 1916. A good example of this was the hire purchase by the Contract company of 50 wagons for Snowdown Colliery which were charged, in part at least, to the railways company. When the Contract company subsequently resold these wagons the railways company had some difficulty in recovering the payments it had made for them, but it could be said that for a time these wagons were partly owned by the railway.

There was probably a similar confusion between the railway's own wagons and the various wagons used on the contracts for the construction of the railway and the collieries. This would have been further complicated when Tilmanstone Colliery began to produce coal and obtained its own fleet of wagons as well as loading coal in the wagons of the various main line companies. Loads for destinations away from the railway would be carried in colliery or main line company wagons but internal traffic at the colliery, for example from the screens to the Landsales wharf where coal was stored for local distribution, could be carried in EKR wagons as would the colliery shale used extensively as ballast on the railway. The end result, if we pick a year at random, is that in 1917 the *Railway Year Book* showed the EKR as owning 21 wagons while the *Universal Directory of Railway Officials* showed a total of 140 wagons.

Wagon No. 19 was built to SER Diagram No. 1329 of 1864 as an 8 ton coal wagon. It still has its shallow rounded ends, self-containing buffers and Mansell wheels. It is standing next to the haystack in Canterbury Road yard. *M. Lawson Finch Collection*

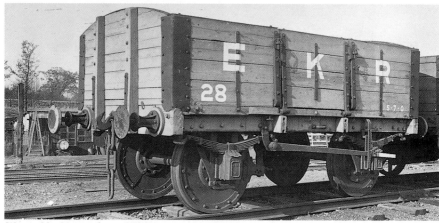

Wagon No. 28 was also to SER Diagram No. 1328 but was an 'express coal wagon' of a type built from 1876 with larger wheels. *M.Lawson Finch Collection*

Wagon No. 29 was one of the last survivors of the Mansell-wheeled SER wagons on the East Kent when photographed in September 1947. Curiously the dimensions for this wagon were omitted from the 1929 wagon list. *G.A. Hookham*

If this were not enough the situation is further complicated by the fact that three manuscript lists of EKR wagons survive covering the years 1920, 1924 and 1929. It is obvious from the lists that a considerable amount of renumbering took place; but it is also obvious from photographs that much of the renumbering only took place on paper and many vehicles continued to carry their old numbers. We shall therefore give a general description of stock used on the railway before considering the wagon stock lists in detail.

Open Wagons

These constituted the bulk of the railway's wagon stock and were extremely varied. By 1929 there had been at least 21 different varieties of open wagon used and more were to come. Four wagons seem to have been obtained new in 1911 and may have been the only new items of rolling stock owned by the railway. Their builder has not been discovered. They were three-plank dropside 8 ton wagons and were described as ballast wagons.

Apart from two five-plank wagons obtained from the LMS the remainder of the open wagons were all of three- or four-plank variety and were of 8 or 10 ton capacity. Length over buffers ranged from 14 ft 0 in. to 16 ft 0 in. and wheelbases from 8 ft 0 in. to 9 ft 6 in. Buffers could be dumb buffers, self-contained, sprung or a combination of dumb buffers at one end and self-contained at the other. Most were braked on one side only. Some had drop sides and some had side doors.

Most wagons were either inherited from the construction contracts or purchased second-hand from dealers or the main line companies. A number of wagons are identifiably of South Eastern Railway origin with shallow curved ends and leather-clad buffers. During the 1920s a number of wagons were rebuilt, though it is not clear how much of the original wagons actually survived this process as the 'rebuilt' wagons cannot easily be matched with the dimensions of earlier stock. Neglect and rough shunting made it a hard life for wagons on the EKR and the distinction between repairing a wagon and rebuilding it is not always clear.

Amongst the authors' notes are various references to particular wagons but the numbers of the wagons concerned do not match any particular stock list. Nos. 16 and 23 are recorded as four-plank wagons 'ex-Harrison & Gamm' [*sic*] of Rotterdam; the firm of Harrison & Camm supplied wagons to the Isle of Wight Central Railway with which Stephens was briefly connected and it is likely that this is the same firm. A No. 9 is recorded as a 12 ton wagon ex-Birmingham Water Supply Co. No. 8, but it is known that from 1920 to 1929 No. 9 was carried by an 8 ton three-plank dropside wagon. Finally a No. 26 was an ex-GWR three-plank wagon. It is possible that these wagons were Tilmanstone Colliery or NCB stock rather than the property of the railway.

Two wagons that were easy to distinguish were the two ex-LMS five-plank wagons Nos. 40 and 41 which were very crudely painted 'EAST KENT RLY' on the top planks only so that the lower half of 'L M S' was still visible. On No. 41 it was also possible to read 'FOR INTERNAL USE ONLY' and '417130'. Other wagons were neatly lettered with large initials E K R though the paintwork often wore away to reveal the original owner's initials thus 'S E E K C R R'. One such wagon was No. 16 whose peeling paintwork also revealed its previous identity as SECR No. 10346, originally LCDR No. 431 built by Cravens in 1875.

A van body in use as a permanent way store at Eastry. This was probably the body from van No. 16 withdrawn around 1922. Note that there is no signal cabin shown in this view and the ground frame is open to the elements.

Van No. 17 of SER origin. The East Kent wagon list of 1924 recorded this van as 'No. 32 ex-No. 17' but the number 17 seems to have been carried until 1948.

In 1945 the Director's Minute Book recorded a decision to scrap 10 wagons and to purchase 10 replacement wagons from the Southern. These replacements appear to have been ex-LBSCR 10 ton five-plank wagons originally built to Diagram 1369 or 1370. These became EKR Nos. 1 to 10. Their Southern numbers were 18855, 25450, 23872, 25336, 23844, 22794, 22834, 23821, 22803 and 23112 respectively. After Nationalisation they reverted to their Southern numbers and were retained for internal traffic.

There may be some connection between these wagons and some open wagons which were recorded as standing on the Guilford Colliery branch. These wagons were lettered 'SIR LINDSAY PARKINSON' and their presence was usually explained by EKR staff as having been left there by the Guilford & Waldershare Colliery. They are known to have been pressed into use by the EKR but it is not clear that they were ever actually purchased by the railway. Correspondence in 1959 with the firm of Sir Lindsay Parkinson & Co. Ltd revealed that it had no record of any of its own wagons going to the EKR, but two suggestions were made as to how such wagons might have got there. Firstly it had disposed of a number of wagons in the South in the 1930s which had been used on the Grimsby Dock and East Lancashire Road contracts. Secondly it had purchased a large batch of wagons from the Southern in 1945 for a contract in Egypt. It was suggested that the wagons on the EKR might have been diverted from wagons prepared for its own order or that the Southern had prepared more wagons than had actually been needed and had diverted the surplus to the EKR. It is therefore possible that the wagons supplied to the EKR in 1945 were delivered in Sir Lindsay Parkinson livery and ran in this guise before acquiring EKR identification. The matter must remain one of conjecture.

Wagons in the livery of private owners or of the main line companies were a common sight on the EKR as its own wagons were purely for internal traffic.

Box Vans

It has to be admitted that the official records make almost no sense when compared with the surviving photographs of these vehicles. When a small dose of misinformation from British Railways is added to the mix one is inclined to despair.

The official story is that one van was purchased in 1920. Two more appeared in 1921 but one of the three was withdrawn in 1923. From 1924 to 1938 the company's returns show two vans and when stock returns were resumed in 1946 the total was still two. However, a list of assets drawn up in 1942 recorded only one van so it might be supposed that one of the pre-war vans had been withdrawn between 1938 and 1942 and another purchased to replace it between 1942 and 1946.

So far so good but the wagon lists complicate the story. The 1920 list recorded one van, No. 16. The 1924 list gives two vans, 'No. 31 ex-No. 16' and 'No. 32 ex-No.17'. The 1929 list gives two vans, again given as Nos. 31 and 32. We then have to add the information from British Railways in 1948 that van No. 17 was to be broken up and that 'LCDR box truck No. 33 used as a tool van will need replacement shortly'.

Now for the photographic evidence. A number of photographs clearly show a van numbered 17. It is of SER origin and received minor alterations over the years but retained the number 17 until withdrawn in 1948. The East Kent also had a SER van body that was used as a permanent way store at Eastry - this might account

Wagon No. 26 and van No. 33 at Shepherdswell at an unknown date but probably *c.* 1945. See text for details of the van.

Pickering carriage No. 1, LCDR carriage No. 10 and Midland Railway van No. 42 at Shepherdswell August 1939. This is probably the same van as No. 33 shown above.

Ron Jarvis/Midland Railway Trust

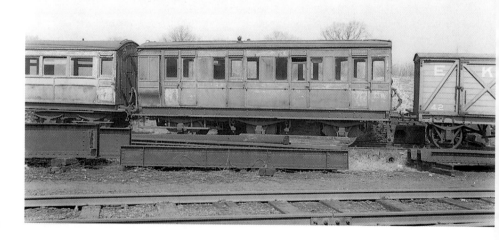

for the van withdrawn in 1923. To these must be added two vans of Midland Railway origin numbered 33 and 42 - though we believe these are actually one van of Midland Railway origin carrying different numbers at different times.

A plausible explanation of the situation, allowing for the fact that vans may have come and gone without being photographed, might go as follows. An SER van was purchased in 1920 and numbered 16. It was withdrawn in 1923 and put to use as a store. Two more vans were purchased in 1923. One of these was of SER origin and numbered 17. It should have been renumbered 31 in 1924 but never was, and nobody saw fit to inform the clerks at Tonbridge so it appeared in the 1929 list as No. 31. The other is likely to have been a Midland Railway van, one such van appears in the background of a photograph we believe to have been taken in 1926, and by the mid-1930s this van was carrying the number 42. This seems to have been the highest number allocated by the East Kent which probably indicates that it had carried another number previously and was renumbered for some reason best known to Jim Smith, the painter/carpenter, but never officially recorded. This van was then withdrawn before the 1942 list of assets was drawn up and then reinstated as Tool Van No. 33. It seems unlikely that the East Kent should have obtained an identical Midland Railway van for this purpose in the middle of the war. We can at least be certain that British Railways were mistaken in believing that van No. 33 was of LCDR origin.

Timber Trucks

The EKR owned three of these and usually described them as rail bogies. They reputedly came from the Highland Railway; it is curious that the Shropshire & Montgomeryshire had very similar vehicles from the Caledonian Railway. Their dimensions are recorded as 12 ft 0 in. long over body and 14 ft 4 in. over buffers, 7 ft 6 in. wide and 7 ft 0 in. wheelbase. They had dumb buffers. They appear to have been much renumbered. They are given as Nos. 17-19 in the 1920 list, as 'Nos. 28-30 ex Nos. 8-10' in the 1924 list, as Nos. 33-35 in the 1929 list and as Nos 30-32 in the list prepared by British Railways in 1948. There is documentary evidence of them carrying Nos. 8-10 in 1923 and photographic evidence of them carrying Nos. 33-35 (though by the late 1930s the number 35 was also being carried by a three-plank dropside wagon). They first appear in the Annual Reports in 1920 and lasted until 1948 when they were promptly condemned by British Railways. They are known to have been used to transport rails but were also useful as runners for the railway's crane.

Crane and Match Truck

These first appear in the Annual Reports in 1929 but are not included in the 1929 stock list. There is some doubt as to whether there ever was a match truck as no such vehicle has been identified in any of the photographs of the crane which is usually shown with one of the timber trucks instead. Curiously, one of the open wagons, No. 27, disappeared from the stock returns at the same time that the crane and match truck are shown as being acquired. The reference to a match truck may therefore have been no more than a book-keeping exercise.

The crane itself was lettered EKR No. 1. It was a six-wheeled 10 ton type and is described in an inventory compiled by British Railways in 1948 as '. . . the old

Two of the East Kent timber wagons, Nos. 33 and 34, with a variety of East Kent open wagons.

The East Kent crane between wagon No. 2 and semi-repainted LMS wagon No. 41 seen from both sides in October 1931. *(Both) H.C. Casserley*

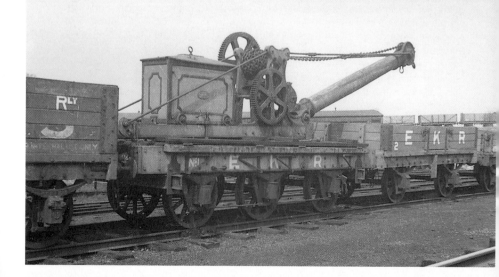

Ashford breakdown crane'. It seems to have been used for heavy lifting work around Shepherdswell Yard rather than for breakdown work which was usually accomplished by the use of screw jacks, elbow grease and free ale in equal quantities! On a single track line with a trackbed of doubtful strength or stability the value of a breakdown crane would have been severely limited. British Railways lost little time in disposing of the crane after they took the line over.

Goods Brakevans

The EKR did not use goods brakevans until World War II. In 1942 the Directors' Minute Book records an agreement to purchase an old 10 ton brakevan from the Southern for £100. The vehicle proved satisfactory but the Directors asked the Southern to reduce the price in view of the vehicle's age and the Southern obligingly reduced the price to £60. The brakevan was probably the LSWR roadvan that was operating on the EKR after Nationalisation as No. 54873 and which had been recorded as withdrawn by the Southern in December 1942. It had originally been built by the LSWR in 1899 to Diagram 1541 as No. 11199 and in 1938 had been allocated for Plumstead & Angerstein wharf traffic.

A second roadvan of the same type appeared later. The two vans were virtually identical except that this one had bars in the windows at the non-veranda end. Both brakevans ran with their veranda ends facing Wingham. One of these vans was allocated No. 34 by the EKR but it is not certain whether this was ever carried. It is possible that the second roadvan did not arrive on the line until 1948 [*see* 'British Railways Inventory' *page 441*].

A third brakevan was running on the East Kent by 1947. This was of the standard Southern Railway design with end platforms. This may have been on loan from the Southern as although there are a number of references to the EKR having three brakevans it seems that this figure included the ex-North London Railway passenger brakevan.

LSWR road van as East Kent No. 34 on 15th August, 1946.   *A.G. Wells*

The Wagon Lists

These lists, preserved in the Austen Collection in the Tenterden Railway Company archives, were hand-written and no attempt seems to have been made to transcribe their details into the rolling stock register. The 1920 and 1929 lists gave dimensions and buffer details for the wagons. To enable comparison of the three lists we have given an identifying letter to each distinctive set of dimensions. The different buffer arrangements are shown as D (dumb), C (self-contained), D/C (dumb at one end and self-contained at the other) and S (sprung). The 1924 list does not give dimensions but included brief descriptive comments as shown on the table.

	1920 List				1924 List			1929 List		
No.	Type	Dims.	Buffer	Type	Tons	Comment	Type	Dims.	Buffer
1	Open	A	D	Open	8	Rebuilt	Open	H	S
2	Open	A	D	Open	8	Ballast	Open	A	?
3	Open	B	S	Open	8	Ballast	Open	B	S
4	Open	A	D	Open	8	Rebuilt	Open	I	S
5	Open	C	D/C	Open	8	Rebuilt	Open	J	S
6	Open	C	D	Open	8	Rebuilt	Open	I	S
7	Open	C	D	Open	10	Rebuilt	Open	I	S
8	Open	C	D	Open	8	Rebuilt	Open	I	S
9	Open	B	S	Open	8	Ballast	Open	B	S
10	Open	D	D/C	Open	8	Ballast	Open	D	D/C
11	Open	D	D	Open	8	Ballast	Open	D	D
12	Open	B	S	Open	8	Ballast	Open	B	S
13	Open	E	D	Open	8	Rebuilt	Open	J	S
14	Open	B	S	Open	8	Rebuilt	Open	I	S
15	Open	F	D/C	Open	8	Rebuilt	Open	K	?
16	Van	G	?	Open	8	Rebuilt	Open	M	S
17	Timber	L	D	Open	8	Rebuilt	Open	N	S
18	Timber	L	D	Open	8	Rebuilt	Open	H	S
19	Timber	L	D	Open	10	Ashford	Open	O	S
20	-	-	-	Open	10	Ashford	Open	J	S
21	-	-	-	Open	10	Ashford	Open	?	?
22	-	-	-	Open	10	Ashford	Open	I	S
23	-	-	-	Open	8	Ashford	Open	O	C
24	-	-	-	Open	10	Ashford	Open	P	C
25	-	-	-	Open	8	Ashford	Open	P	C
26	-	-	-	Open	10	Ashford	Open	I	S
27	-	-	-	Open	8	Ashford	-	-	-
28	-	-	-	Timber	-	ex No. 8	Open	P	C
29	-	-	-	Timber	-	ex No. 9	Open	?	?
30	-	-	-	Timber	-	ex No. 10	Open	J	S
31	-	-	-	Van	-	ex No. 16	Van	Q	?
32	-	-	-	Van	-	ex No. 17	Van	R	S
33	-	-	-	-	-	-	Timber	L	D
34	-	-	-	-	-	-	Timber	L	D
35	-	-	-	-	-	-	Timber	L	D
36	-	-	-	-	-	-	Open	S	C
37	-	-	-	-	-	-	Open	T	C
38	-	-	-	-	-	-	Open	U	C
39	-	-	-	-	-	-	Open	U	C
40	-	-	-	-	-	-	Open	V	S
41	-	-	-	-	-	-	Open	V	S

It will be noted that the only wagons to bear the same numbers in all three lists are Nos. 2, 3, 9, 10, 11, and 12.

Key to dimensions

Letter	Length over body	Length over buffers	Width	Depth	Wheelbase
A	15' 0"	17' 4"	7' 6"	1' 9"	8' 6"
B	15' 0"	17' 10"	7' 6"	1' 9"	9' 2"
C	14' 9"	17' 1"	7' 6"	2' 0"	8' 9"
D	14' 0"	16' 4"	7' 6"	1' 9"	8' 0"
E	14' 9"	15' 11"	7' 3"	2' 0"	8' 6"
F	15' 0"	17' 6"	7' 6"	1' 9"	8' 6"
G	15' 0"	18' 0"	7' 6"	-	9' 0"
H	15' 0"	18' 0"	7' 6"	3' 0"	9' 3½"
I	15' 6"	18' 6"	7' 6"	3' 0"	9' 3½"
J	16' 0"	19' 0"	7' 6"	3' 0"	9' 3½"
K	16' 0"	18' 6"	7' 6"	3' 0"	9' 3½"
L	12' 0"	14' 4"	7' 6"	-	7' 0"
M	16' 0"	19' 0"	7' 9"	3' 5"	9' 6"
N	15' 6"	18' 6"	7' 9"	3' 0"	9' 3½"
O	14' 0"	17' 0"	7' 6"	3' 0"	8' 6'
P	14' 0"	17' 4"	7' 6"	3' 0"	8' 6"
Q	15' 0"	17' 6"	7' 6"	-	9' 0"
R	15' 9"	18' 6"	8' 0"	-	9' 0"
S	14' 10"	17' 10"	7' 6"	1' 9"	8' 0"
T	15' 0"	18' 0"	7' 6"	1' 9"	8' 6"
U	14' 6"	17' 4"	7' 6"	1' 9"	8' 0"
V	15' 0"	18' 0"	7' 6"	3' 0"	9' 0"

Withdrawals

Some information can be gleaned from references in various sources to the withdrawal of particular wagons. The Directors' Minute Books contain the following information: July 1937 - break up wagons 1, 11, 14, 16, 23 and 26; February 1942 - break up six useless wagons; 1943 - break up three wagons to value of new brakevan; February 1945 - scrap 10 wagons and purchase 10 replacements from Southern Railway (these were recorded as purchased in July 1945); 1947 - 12 wagons displaced. British Railways recorded the withdrawal of the following in 1948 - wagons 12, 15, 20, 22, 26, 28 and van 17.

The British Railways Inventory

British Railways made an inventory of rolling stock in March 1948 as follows: 16 open wagons, 3 timber wagons (not in use), 2 box vans, 3 brakevans (not in use) and 'the old Ashford breakdown crane'. On 3rd May, 1948 British Railways drew up the following note:

Wagon Stock

Nos. 1 to 10 open goods wagons are of Central section wood frame type and are in fair condition to work on the E.K. Section only. They will be marked accordingly.

Goods Brake No. 34 is also in fair condition for working on the Section. An additional goods brake will be selected by the Traffic Department and suitably marked.

LCDR Box Truck No. 33 used as a tool van will need replacement shortly if still required. The following vehicles will be withdrawn from traffic:-

Open Goods 12, 15, 20, 22, 26 and 28.

Box wagon 17.

Dumb buffered timber trucks 30, 31 and 32.

Cranes

Dumb buffered crane will be broken up.

This accords fairly closely with the March inventory except in the matter of brakevans. If the March figure was correct, albeit mistakenly including the North London brake as a goods vehicle, then the second LSWR brakevan was already present but if the May note is correct then the second LSWR van was not brought to the line until after Nationalisation. As we have mentioned earlier there is some doubt about the accuracy of the numbers ascribed to the timber trucks and the LCDR tool van.

Annual Reports

Except during wartime the railway was obliged to make a return of its rolling stock in its Annual Report and Accounts to shareholders. There is some evidence that this task was not always completed with great rigour. Mr G.W. Rogers, one of the EKR guards, recalled assisting Jim Smith, the railway's carpenter, to break up three wagons one Good Friday. Their labours were interrupted by the arrival of none other than Holman Stephens who pressed half a crown into Rogers' hand for his efforts. This may throw some light on the character of the Colonel but not on the Annual Reports which showed no reduction in the number of wagons during the period concerned. The wagon returns from the Annual Reports and the *Railway Year Book* and *Universal Directory of Railway Officials* are given at the end of this chapter.

Kent & East Sussex Wagons

An undated photograph of locomotive No. 6 shows at least two KESR wagons on the embankment at Shepherdswell. Ten of these 10 ton five-plank open wagons had been supplied new to the Rother Valley Railway in 1900 by Hurst, Nelson. They were normally only used for internal traffic on the KESR so their presence on the East Kent is something of a mystery.

Fortunately a brief glimpse of the use of these wagons is obtained from the pages of a Truck & Sheet Book kept at Shepherdswell from 12th April to 29th May, 1923. Their numbers are recorded as 3, 6, 7 and 9. On 30th April these wagons are listed on a note written on the back of the daily sheet under the heading 'Bunkers' along with seven South Eastern wagons. The location so described would have been part of the Tilmanstone Colliery complex. On the 4th May wagons 3, 6, 7 and 9 went from Eythorne to Ash Road (later Sandwich Road) loaded with coal after having come into Eythorne from Tilmanstone. On the 8th May 3, 6, 7, and 9 again went from Eythorne to Ash Road but this time their contents went unrecorded. They appear to have made the same trip again on 10th May and on several subsequent occasions. On the 16th May 3, 6 and 9 are listed under the heading 'Landsale' along with Tilmanstone wagons 107 and 120 and four South Eastern wagons. The Landsales wharf was located alongside the line to the Tilmanstone Colliery power house. Coal was collected here for local delivery by road.

It is apparent that the EKR was using these KESR wagons as part of its own internal fleet rather than for traffic between Shepherdswell and Headcorn. There is no official record of them being hired to the EKR so it is hard to know how long they remained here. Six KESR wagons were subsequently hired to the Shropshire & Montgomeryshire.

War Department Stock

It is known that the War Department brought a variety of rolling stock onto the EKR to service the rail-mounted guns but no details appear to have been recorded beyond the fact that this stock included German and French ferry vans.

Tilmanstone Colliery Wagons

Originally Tilmanstone operated a fleet of 7½-plank wagons of which Nos. 105, 110 and 120 can be identified from photographs. We have been unable to find out the total number and colour of these wagons or the duration of their operation. The Shepherdswell Truck & Sheet Book previously mentioned gives some details of their use. During the period covered by the book wagons Nos. 104, 105, 107, 110, 112, 114, 115, 117, and 120 are recorded in use. Nos. 105, 112, and 117 frequently appear together. Similarly Nos. 107 and 120 and Nos. 114 and 115 seem to have been operating as pairs.

Whilst little would be gained by listing every entry there are some interesting features worth mentioning. The first entry for 14th April records No. 110 outwards from Eythorne to Wingham. Its load is not recorded but its movement northwards from Tilmanstone via Eythorne suggests that the northern junction from Tilmanstone to the 'main line' had been taken out of use by this date. The Tilmanstone wagons seem to have been used quite indiscriminately alongside EKR wagons and wagons from the main line companies. No. 110 was accompanied to Wingham by EKR wagons 8, 6, 9, 1 and 11, though these last two were recorded as 'Eythorne for Sandwich branch'.

On 20th April Tilmanstone No. 110 again went from Eythorne to Wingham, its contents recorded curiously as 'black' as were those of accompanying wagon No. 31 owned by Hallett. The next wagons entered were Tilmanstone Nos. 107, 120, 105, 112, and 117 which all went loaded with coal to Ash Road, further evidence of the regular use of this branch for goods traffic well before its official opening two years later.

On the backs of a number of pages are separate entries for 'Bunkers' and 'Landsale'. On the 25th May Tilmanstone wagons 117 and 105 are listed respectively at these locations. It is not really clear why these apparently internal colliery movements should have been recorded or why they should have needed a separate location description from the more usual 'Til' for Tilmanstone.

It is disappointing that no further copies of Truck & Sheet Books appear to have survived to enable the earlier and subsequent career of these wagons and those of the EKR fleet to be traced. It is, however, remarkable that even this one volume has survived.

The colliery was also served by a wide variety of wagons from the main line companies and various coal dealers. During the 1920s the colliery purchased some ungainly ROD vans lettered ETAT which appear to have been used on the Richborough train ferries. It was intended to adapt these wagons for spoil removal but the experiment seems to have been unsuccessful. These wagons remained parked on the long siding adjacent to the old Tilmanstone North Bank Junction until scrapped in 1933.

Goods Rolling stock Returns

Year	Railway Year Book*	UDRO*	East Kent Railway Annual Report					
			Open	Box	Timber	Brake	Crane	Match
1911	-	-						
1912	-	4						
1913	12	4						
1914	30	140						
1915	30							
1916	30	140	-	-	-	-	-	-
1917	21	140	-	-	-	-	-	-
1918	21	140	-	-	-	-	-	-
1919	21		16	-	-	-	-	-
1920	30	140	15	1	3	-	-	-
1921	21	17	15	3	3	-	-	-
1922	20	17	15	3	3	-	-	-
1923	20	27	27	2	3	-	-	-
1924	20	27	30	2	3	-	-	-
1925	40	27	30	2	3	-	-	-
1926	35	35	36	2	3	-	-	-
1927	40	40	36	2	3	-	-	-
1928	41	41	36	2	3	-	-	-
1929	41	41	35	2	3	-	1	1
1930	41		35	2	3	-	1	1
1931	41		35	2	3	-	1	1
1932	41		35	2	3	-	1	1
1933	41		35	2	3	-	1	1
1934	41		35	2	3	-	1	1
1935	41		35	2	3	-	1	1
1936	41		35	2	3	-	1	1
1937	41		29	2	3	-	1	1
1938	34		29	2	3	-	1	1
1939	34							
1940	34							
1941								
1942			29	1	3	1	-	-
1943	26+2 brake		29	1	3	1	-	-
1944								
1945			29	2	3	-	1	1
1946	33+3 brake		28	2	3	-	1	1
1947	33+1 brake		16	2	3	1	1	1

Notes
* The *Railway Year Book* and the *Universal Directory of Railway Officials* were amalgamated in 1930.
Annual Reports were required not to include rolling stock details during wartime but the figures for 1942 and 1943 were obtained from manuscript records of assets for those years.

Not the incident in which No. 5 ran away through the end of the engine shed (*see page 372*) but a very similar one from the early 1920s. No locomotive appears to have been involved here but obviously a runaway train of wagons can do just as much damage without a locomotive on the front.   *Colonel Stephens Railway Museum*

The National Coal Board operated a very mixed collection of wagons at Tilmanstone during the early years of their ownership. Some of these were gradually engulfed by the spoil tips and a visit to Tilmanstone in September 1961 revealed the following wagons marooned by spoil: a 10 ton wagon NCB No. 3 (painted over 378) which bore plates reading 'Repair and advise Doncaster Wagon Co Ltd' and 'Gen Repaired Rigley LNER 1249 4-1948', an open wagon No. 130 lettered Bonnyside Fire Brick Works Bonnybridge, a 7-plank 10 ton open wagon No. 306271, a four-wheel Weltrol wagon, a 10 ton open wagon NCB No 90 and an open wagon No 95 lettered FOR MATERIAL and bearing a plate reading 'Gen Repaired by R & R Ltd LNW 42568 7-1945'.

There were extensive narrow gauge lines at Tilmanstone using standard four-wheeled tub wagons.

Kent & East Sussex wagons standing on North Bank siding in this greatly enlarged undated view which shows the tender of 0-6-0 No. 6 in the foreground.

No. 4 pauses for breath with a train of coal empties in the 1920s.

No. 6 labouring up the grade out of Golgotha tunnel with a loaded coal train in March 1937.

Chapter Seventeen

Running the Railway

Freight traffic

There are gaps in the official statistical returns for the railway during the periods of the two World Wars but with the exception of these periods it is possible to identify the main patterns of traffic over the line. The main source of traffic was always Tilmanstone Colliery and consisted primarily of the delivery of empty wagons and the dispatch of loaded wagons. The railway was also responsible throughout most of its independent years for shunting at the colliery and the internal movement of coal there, particularly the delivery of coal and 'Coaloid' briquettes to the Landsales wharf at the colliery where coal was sold for local use.

A limited amount of coal was taken by the railway from the colliery to other stations on the line for local merchants, but the bulk of the coal from Tilmanstone was taken to Shepherdswell for onward dispatch by rail over the main line. Coal traffic was closely tied to the varying fortunes of Tilmanstone Colliery and did not pass the 200,000 ton mark until 1923. It fell back again in 1924 and was badly affected by the Coal Strike in 1926 but never fell below 200,000 tons after that date. The opening of Tilmanstone's aerial ropeway did not actually reduce the railway's coal traffic from Tilmanstone, which remained quite buoyant despite the difficult economic conditions. The railway was also able to attract a certain amount of coal traffic from Snowdown to Richborough during this period with a peak of something like 30,000 tons in 1933. Although the Snowdown-Richborough traffic never justified the expense of the Richborough branch it must be remembered that this traffic was carried the full length of the railway, rather than just the two miles between Tilmanstone and Shepherdswell, and brought in more revenue per ton than the Tilmanstone traffic.

From unofficial figures the railway carried its heaviest known coal traffic in 1940, 330,684 tons, of which 328,271 tons had originated on the line and must have come from Tilmanstone. Traffic levels gradually dropped after that date but Tilmanstone was still supplying 255,658 tons of coal traffic in 1947. We have found few figures for coal traffic during the years of operation by British Railways, but understand that levels approached 500,000 tons after the modernisation of Tilmanstone Colliery.

Colliery traffic did not consist solely of coal from Tilmanstone. In the early years the railway was responsible for carrying construction materials for Tilmanstone, Guilford, Hammill and Wingham Collieries and continued to carry general supplies to Tilmanstone until August 1964. The carriage of pit props was another significant item and most of the traffic from Richborough Port consisted of Norwegian pit props for Tilmanstone and possibly Snowdown. There was also a small but steady coal traffic from other collieries to the various coal merchants based along the railway and to the Wingham Engineering Company and the Hammill Brickworks.

In addition to coal the railway carried other minerals. The nature of this traffic is unclear as the 'minerals' carried are not otherwise identified. It is known that fireclay and gravel were carried from time to time and there may also have been a market for colliery spoil. We understand that sugar beet was also classified as mineral traffic. The mineral traffic fluctuated wildly with a low of 248 tons in 1920 and an astonishing high of 16,032 tons in 1930.

The general merchandise traffic on the railway also fluctuated but usually came to something between 5,000 and 8,000 tons. This traffic rose to exceptional heights between 1942 and 1945, peaking at 18,366 tons in 1944, but had collapsed to 3,296 tons by 1947. This reflected the shortage of road competition during the war and its resurgence afterwards. The official statistics only identify the 'principal classes' of merchandise traffic carried and only took account of loads of two tons or more. On this basis there was a regular traffic in grain, vegetables and fruit. More intermittent traffic was recorded for bricks, a record 3,903 tons in 1930, potatoes, wool, hops and round timber.

For a line serving a primarily agricultural area, the EKR found little demand for livestock traffic. Seven cattle were carried in 1919, 13 in 1920 and two in 1921. No other livestock was carried until 1935 when 336 pigs were carried. A further 353 pigs were carried in 1936 and then the traffic ceased as abruptly as it had begun. There is no indication of any other livestock being carried and the railway never equipped itself with pens or vans to handle such traffic.

Passenger traffic

Although some of the EKR carriages contained first class accommodation there is no record of the railway carrying first class passengers. Instead the passenger statistics are divided into third class passengers and workmen. The latter were the miners at Tilmanstone whose trains were subsidised by the colliery. The withdrawal of this subsidy brought the service to an end in 1929. By this date the area was well served by regular bus services.

It is difficult to estimate the seriousness of this loss of workmen's traffic to the railway. Considerable numbers of miners used the workmen's trains, a maximum of 28,188 in 1922, but separate figures for the receipts from this traffic were only given in the railway's returns for 1927 to 1929 as follows:

	No. of Workmen	Receipts
1927	24,957	£334
1928	22,789	£532
1929	22,473	£502

There are no returns showing the expenditure on these services and it seems reasonable to assume that a fair proportion of these receipts were swallowed up by operating costs.

Ordinary passenger traffic declined much earlier than the workmen's traffic. This reflected both the development of bus services in the area and the reduction in services on the Railway. The problem with passenger traffic on the EKR was that few people actually wanted to travel between the places it served.

Those who lived in the area and wanted to go to Canterbury, Sandwich, Deal or Dover would find it quicker to travel to their destinations directly by bus, rather than by going to Shepherdswell and changing on to the main line services. A further disincentive for passengers hoping to travel from the unstaffed halts on the line was the reluctance of some train crews to stop at such halts however clearly they may have been signalled to stop. This has been explained variously as due to the need to reach the water supplies at Woodnesborough or Staple as quickly as possible (protracted shunting or other delays having depleted the limited capacity of the tank engines) or to the difficulties of starting the train again once stopped. From some accounts, though, the main reason appears to have been sheer cussedness on the part of particular drivers. By way of contrast it seems to have been the practice to pick up certain regular passengers at the lineside rather than put them to the trouble of making their way to a station.

By the 1930s it is a matter of wonder that anyone, enthusiasts apart, wanted to travel on the East Kent at all. The available statistics for passenger traffic tell a very clear tale:

Year	Passengers	Year	Passengers
1916	n/a	1932	1,873
1917	n/a	1933	1,360
1918	n/a	1934	1,276
1919	15,693	1935	838
1920	13,184	1936	745
1921	4,761	1937	933
1922	3,749	1938	1,049
1923	5,242	1939	n/a
1924	4,177	1940	n/a
1925	6,196	1941	n/a
1926	4,140	1942	n/a
1927	4,588	1943	n/a
1928	7,913	1944	n/a
1929	6,083	1945	985*
1930	3,375	1946	766*
1931	1,983	1947	556*

* Originating traffic only.

Although the figure for 1919 looks quite respectable in comparison with later years, a quick calculation reveals that it amounts to only slightly over 50 passengers per working day. By 1947 this had fallen to less than two passengers per working day!

We do not have passenger figures for World War II period but the figures for passenger train receipts for 1939-44 have survived and indicate that passenger traffic revived towards the end of this period. We have added the figures for 1933 to 1938 for comparison:

No. 6 terminates at Shepherdswell with the LSWR and Midland six-wheelers. Two passengers are happy to hang on for the photograph to be taken but the gent in the cap on the platform would prefer a chat with the porter.

The crew seems to be making some last minute adjustments to No. 8 before it can leave Canterbury Road with its mixed train in July 1932.

Pre-War Receipts		Wartime Receipts	
1933	£121	1939	£126
1934	£146	1940	£178
1935	£162	1941	£115
1936	£144	1942	£184
1937	£103	1943	£622
1938	£120	1944	£230

It should be noted that these are passenger train receipts rather than passenger receipts and therefore include parcels traffic and 'other merchandise carried on passenger trains'.

The reference to 'other merchandise carried on passenger trains' covers goods carried in a passenger vehicle rather than the contents of the goods wagons attached to the rear of the passenger trains. The EKR passenger had the additional pleasure of waiting at stations while shunting was carried out, or of actually participating in shunting manoeuvres whenever it was inconvenient or impractical to detach the passenger carriage before shunting commenced. This could lead to particularly long delays when trains had goods to collect or deliver at Tilmanstone Colliery, Poison Cross, Sandwich Road, Richborough Castle sidings or Hammill Brickworks. Trains purely for freight, apart from the traffic to Tilmanstone and Richborough Port, were only run when goods traffic was particularly heavy.

Timetables

The EKR does not appear to have issued Working Timetables and we therefore only have timetables for the railway's public passenger traffic. These trains would also carry the bulk of the line's goods traffic, apart from construction trains and the traffic to and from Tilmanstone and Richborough Port which appears to have been fitted into the timetable according to need. In 1948 British Railways recorded that there were five trains a day to and from Tilmanstone Colliery. Variables that might affect the non-passenger train traffic would be the extent of coal production at Tilmanstone, the availability of empty wagon traffic off the Southern which could rapidly exceed the capacity of Shepherdswell Yard, and the capacity of the locomotives working this traffic - if the more powerful locomotives were out of service then more trains would need to be run to handle the same amount of traffic.

Combining a report in the *Dover Express* and a timetable issued in October 1916 for workmen's trains it is possible to reconstruct the service operated by the railway when it opened to passenger traffic. The day started with a 5.13 am workmen's train from Shepherdswell to Eastry. This left Eastry at 5.42 am, stopped at Tilmanstone Colliery from 5.53 to 6.20, and arrived back at Shepherdswell at 6.30 am. There were then three Shepherdswell to Wingham trains setting out at 10.17 am, 1.38 pm and 5.17 pm and returning from Wingham at 11.35 am, 2.33 pm and 6.36 pm. On Saturdays there was a workmen's train from Shepherdswell to Eastry at 7.20 pm which left Eastry in the return direction at 7.50 pm, arriving back at Shepherdswell at 8.12 pm. On other weekdays this ran at 9.30 pm and only went as far as Tilmanstone Colliery whence it returned at 10.20, arriving back at Shepherdswell at 10.30 pm.

The first EKR timetable published in *Bradshaw* appeared in November 1916. This was a much simpler affair but omitted any mention of the workmen's service:

	am	pm	pm
Shepherd's Well	10.10	1.32	5.10
Eythorne	10.17	1.38	5.17
Tilmanstone Colliery	10.20	1.41	5.20
Tilmanstone Village & Knowlton	10.24	1.45	5.24
Eastry	10.31	1.52	5.31
Woodnesborough & Hammill	10.35	1.56	5.35
Ash Town	10.40	2.01	5.40
Staple	10.44	2.05	5.44
Wingham	10.50	2.11	5.56
Wingham	10.55	2.14	6.00
Staple	11.07	2.25	s
Ash Town	11.11	2.29	6.13
Woodnesborough & Hammill	11.15	2.33	6.16
Eastry	11.20	2.38	6.21
Tilmanstone Village & Knowlton	s	s	s
Tilmanstone Colliery	11.30	2.48	6.31
Eythorne	11.35	2.53	6.36
Shepherd's Well	11.41	2.58	6.42

It is apparent that the question of station names had not yet been settled. The longer return time between Wingham and Staple may have been to allow running round in the Wingham Colliery loop.

A more generous service was operating by July 1917 as follows:

	am	am	am	pm	pm	pm Mixed	pm
Shepherdswell	5z20	6.40	10.15	1z32	5z10	9z30	
Eythorne	5.27	6.50	10.22	1.38	5.17	9.37	
Tilmanstone Colliery	5.30	7.00	10.25	1.41	5.20	9.40	
Knowlton	5.34	s	10.29	1.45	5.24	9.44	
Eastry	5.41	7.15	10.36	1.52	5.31	9.52	
Woodnesborough Colliery		7.30	10.40	1.56	5.35		
Ash Town		7.40	10.45	2.01	5.40		
Staple		7.50	10.49	2.05	5.44		
Wingham Colliery		8.20	10.55	2.11	5.51		
				Mixed			
Wingham Colliery		8.50	11.00	2.14		5.55	
Staple		s	11.12	2.25		s	
Ash Town		s	11.16	2.29		6.07	
Woodnesborough Colliery		s	11.20	2.33		6.10	
Eastry	5z44	9.05	11.25	2.38		6z15	10z07
Knowlton	5.51	s	s	s		s	10.13
Tilmanstone Colliery	6.22	s	11.35	2.48		6.25	10.20
Eythorne	6.26	s	11.40	2.30	2z36	6.30	10.24
Shepherdswell	6.32	9.45	11.46	2.36	2.59	6.36	10.30

z Cheap workmen's tickets.   s Stops when signalled.

A number of interesting features emerge from this timetable. It seems that workmen's tickets were available, at least as far as Eastry, on the afternoon and evening Wingham trains but only on the evening return working. In later years the workmen's tickets were confined to the special trains between Shepherdswell and Tilmanstone. Another feature to disappear was the indication of one particular out and back working as Mixed, presumably all other trains shown at this date were for passengers only. The 30 minutes taken between Staple and Wingham by the mixed train would allow for shunting at Staple. Similarly, the first return working from Eastry had a generous allowance of time between Knowlton and Tilmanstone Colliery and may indicate that this train picked up stock from the northern junction to Tilmanstone Colliery. The 2.30 from Eythorne, possibly from Tilmanstone Colliery yard although not yet indicated as such, without a corresponding outward working from Shepherdswell is a common feature of later timetables.

By August 1918 the service had been reduced to early and late return workings to Eastry, morning and afternoon return workings to Wingham and a lunchtime return working to Tilmanstone. By May 1919 this had changed to an early return working to Eythorne, a morning return working to Wingham, a midday return working to Woodnesborough Colliery, an afternoon return working to Wingham and an evening return working to Eastry. As discussed elsewhere it is possible that the Woodnesborough Colliery should have been shown as an Eastry working. By July 1919 the midday working was extended to Wingham Colliery but was followed by a second midday return working to Tilmanstone Colliery Halt. This ran earlier on Saturdays than on other weekdays. A similar pattern was being worked in October 1919, except that the evening train to Eastry arrived back at Shepherdswell at 9.35 pm instead of 10.30 pm. With minor variations in times this pattern of three Wingham trains, early and midday workings to Eythorne or Tilmanstone and an evening Eastry train continued until 1921. In 1922 the midday Wingham train was cut back to Eastry on weekdays and this remained the pattern until 1925.

The opening of the Sandwich Road branch required a new timetable structure. The pattern of departures from Shepherdswell now consisted of workmen's services to Tilmanstone at 5.58 am and 1.22 pm, Wingham trains at 7.00 am and 5.20 pm (5.25 pm on Saturdays), Sandwich Road trains at 9.45 am and 3.10 pm on Saturdays only, an Eastry train at 8.00 pm extended to Wingham on Saturdays only and a final Saturday train to Eastry at 9.45 pm. For the people of Eastry this gave a generous service of six trains on Saturdays. 1925 also saw the first appearance of Eastry South in the timetable and Tilmanstone Colliery Halt had become Elvington.

In August 1926 a daily service to Sandwich Road was advertised in the mornings only, but by July 1927 this had changed to an afternoon service run on Wednesdays and Saturdays only. In 1928 two trains were running to Sandwich Road on Wednesdays and Saturdays and Poison Cross Halt was actually given a place in the Timetable; hitherto this had only appeared as a footnote, 'Calls at Poison Cross Halt between Eastry and Roman Road'. Poison Cross Halt's moment of fame was brief as the Sandwich Road service was abandoned at the end of October 1928. It is perhaps worth looking at the full timetable in operation in a typical month of that year. Note the extension of the weekday service to Eastry on to Wingham on Saturdays.

East Kent Railway July 1928

	Bb		WS			Bb	WS				Bb NS
	am	*am*	*am*	*pm*	*pm*	*pm*	*pm*	*pm*	*pm*	*pm*	*pm*
Shepherdswell	5.58	7.10	9.42		12.05	1.45	3.30	5.20	8.00		9.45
Eythorne	6.07	7.17	9.48		12.12	1.52	3.37	5.27	8.09		10.02
Elvington		7.20	9.51		12.15		3.40	5.30	8.12		
Knowlton		7.24	9.55		12.19		3.44	5.34	8.16		
Eastry South		Aa	Aa		Aa		Aa	Aa	Aa		
Eastry		7.32	10.02		12.27		3.52	5.41	8.24	8s24	
Poison Cross Halt			10.05				3.55				
Roman Road			10.08				3.58				
Sandwich Road			10.16				4.06				
Woodnesborough		7.38			12.31			5.45		8s29	
Ash Town		7.40			12.35			5.50		8s34	
Staple		7.43			12.38			5.54		8s39	
Wingham Colliery		7.48			12.43			6.00		8s45	
Wingham Town		7.51			12.45			6.03		8s48	
Canterbury Road		7.53			12.47			6.05		8s50	
Canterbury Road		8.30			1.40			6.10		8s55	
Wingham Town		8.32			1.42			6.12		8s57	
Wingham Colliery		8.34			1.45			6.15		9s00	
Staple		8.40			1.50			6.22		9s07	
Ash Town		8.43			1.54			6.26		9s11	
Woodnesborough		8.47	WS		1.58		WS	6.30		9s15	
Sandwich Road			10.21				4.10				
Roman Road			10.28				4.20				
Poison Cross Halt			10.32				4.23		NS		
Eastry		8.55	10.35		2.06		4.26	6.35	8.30	9s20	
Eastry South		Aa	Aa		Aa		Aa	Aa	Aa	Aa	
Knowlton		9.04	10.44		2.15		4.35	Aa	8.38	9s29	
Elvington	Bb	9.07	10.47	Bb	2.19	NSBb	4.38	6.48	8.42		NSBb
Eythorne	6.30	9.11	10.51	12s41	2.22	2.31	4.42	6.52	8.46	9s36	10.30
Shepherdswell	6.39	9.18	10.59	12s48	2.31	2.40	4.49	6.59	8.53	9s43	10.42

s Saturdays only   NS Not Saturdays   WS Wednesdays and Saturdays Only
Aa Stops when required   Bb Runs to or from Tilmanstone Colliery Yard when required

Following the ending of Workmen's trains the 1930 timetable consisted of morning, midday and late afternoon return trains to Wingham with an evening return working to Eastry that was extended to Wingham on Saturdays. In 1931 Austen had to make drastic economies and the service was reduced to two return workings to Wingham, one at midday and one in the late afternoon. With minor changes of times this remained the pattern until Autumn 1934 when the midday train was dropped and replaced by a morning working. This apparently satisfied the railway's requirements if not those of the steadily decreasing number of passengers. No further changes were made to this pattern until passenger services ceased in 1948.

Signalling on the East Kent

The East Kent was worked and operated as a single line. Not much is known about signalling during the construction period before 1916 except that second-hand semaphores were in use between Shepherdswell and Eythorne but not, apparently, beyond this point.

The Inspection Report of 1916 stated that the railway proposed to work the line on a staff and ticket system between Shepherdswell and Eythorne. The remaining part of the line then open, i.e. from Eythorne to Wingham Colliery, would be worked under the 'one engine in steam or two engines coupled together' system. The Report also stated that there were two ground frames in 1916. The first, at Shepherdswell, had three levers and controlled one up and one down starter. The third lever released the loop points which were worked by hand balance-weight levers in each case after being unlocked by the key on the train staff. The second frame, with four levers, was at Eythorne where there were stop and starter signals in each direction. The loop points at each end of the station were controlled by Annett's keys. As at Shepherdswell, interlocking was provided. There were telephone instruments at both these stations.

Further descriptions of the signalling methods in use were published by various sources in the years following World War I. From these it is clear that the points and signals beyond Eythorne were also interlocked, but by a singular method in which the points were controlled from ground levers which were in turn controlled by the keys which controlled the signals. In this way the signals had to be locked to match any movement of the point levers. This was said to be most economical since it did away with the need for point rodding and was claimed to be unique. It was claimed that it took only two minutes longer to shunt a siding using this method than would have been required by the use of conventional methods. Point rodding was, nevertheless, installed both at Eythorne, for the junction with the Tilmanstone Colliery branch, and at Eastry for the Sandwich branch junction.

A ground frame and point rodding had been installed at Eastry to control the loop and the junction of the Wingham and Sandwich Road branches when the arrangements here were inspected by Colonel Mount in 1925. This frame was reported to have been second-hand and did not meet with the Colonel's approval. Not only was it not fixed securely to the ground but the interlocking appeared to be defective. This may account for the habit of Wingham-bound trains taking the Sandwich Road branch in error.

By 1925 the section from Shepherdswell to Eythorne was being worked by Tyler's Electric Staff and the section between Eythorne and Eastry by Webb & Thomson Electric Train Staff. From Eastry to Wingham was also controlled by Electric Train Staff, possibly using Webb & Thomson equipment. There is less certainty about the methods in use on the Sandwich Road branch but it is known that two padlocked boxes were installed at Poison Cross Halt to hold whatever sort of staff or ticket was in use on the branch which was thus divided into two sections: Eastry to Poison Cross and Poison Cross to Sandwich and beyond. This would have enabled trains to make short workings as far as Poison Cross to pick up goods even if there was a train occupying the section

Right: Exchanging tablets at Eythorne. The starter signal at the rear was a replacement for one of the original signals damaged in a collision at the level crossing during World War II. *A.F. Pike*

Below: Double armed signal at Eastry in British Railways days. The upper arm governed access to the loop and has been taken out of use.

G.A. Hookham

Below right: Eythorne starting signal protecting the line to Shepherdswell. *G.A. Hookham*

beyond Poison Cross. Such occasions must have been rare and British Railways found that the whole section from Eastry to Richborough Castle was being worked on the 'one engine in steam' system when they inspected the line in 1948. The Eythorne to Eastry section was also being worked by this system as the Electric Train Staff equipment was out of order.

Long before 1948 it seems that train crews and station staff had begun to regard the semaphore signals beyond Eythorne as purely cosmetic reminders of the presence of stations as contemporary reports suggest that little attempt was ever made to set signals on or off. To make up for this the line abounded in speed restriction signs and whistle boards in recognition of the many ungated crossings and sections of trackbed of doubtful stability.

Permanent Way

Like the signalling equipment, the EKR track materials were second-hand. The reasons for this were twofold. Firstly, from 1914 everything was being diverted to the uses of war and this practice even went so far as to cause the lifting of several railways in the British Isles like the Bideford, Westward Ho! & Appledore Railway. Some of the materials from these lines were relaid in France whilst much went for salvage. Secondly, the chronic shortage of money ruled out the use of new materials. In view of the serious shortage of labour the company certainly deserved some commendation in getting a service to run at all.

When first laid the rail used was described as flanged, flat-bottomed and pinned to the sleepers without the use of sole plates. The general weight was recorded as 80 lb. to the yard but on gradients and at places liable to receive heavy traffic this weight was increased to 90 lb. In 1916 the Inspector described the track as having irregular expansion joints and, at some points, lacking in top ballast. Renewals were made after the war with the aid of surplus WD stock which Holman Stephens must have purchased in some quantity. This was of slightly different sections and types and if the carriage in which one was travelling suddenly gave a severe jolt this often indicated transition from one type of rail to another. The 1916 Report also stated that there were four varieties of flat bottom rail in use varying from 60 lb. per yard to 90 lb. These were 'fixed to cross sleepers by dog spikes and fang bolts'. The sleepers were made of creosoted Baltic fir and measured 9 ft by 9 in. by 4½ in. The ballast of 'colliery refuse, shale and ashes' was laid to a stated depth of 11 in. below the underside of the sleepers.

In 1924 Pearson & Dorman Long prepared a report on the railway which gave the following information. The line between Shepherdswell and Wingham Colliery was laid with flanged 80 lb. rail, with the exception of the section through Golgotha tunnel where it was increased to 90 lb. The rails were spiked to the sleepers except on curves where bolts and clips were in use. No sole plates were in use at all. From Wingham Colliery towards Wingham Town the weight was reduced to 60 lb. as was the branch from Eastry to Sandwich Road. In January 1925 a mention of the line was made in a Deal newspaper in which is to be found '. . . the main line is laid with 80-90 lb. rail capable of dealing with heavy traffic. The curves are easy'.

PERMANENT SPEED RESTRICTIONS

EAST KENT LINE.

A permanent Speed Restriction of **TWENTY-FIVE MILES AN HOUR** is in operation throughout the East Kent line, except at the undermentioned points, where lower speed restrictions are in force as indicated :—

LOCATION	LINE	MILE-AGE AT	SPEED RESTRIC-TION	SPEED INDICATION BOARDS PROVIDED ¶
		m. ch.	m.p.h.	
BETWEEN SHEPHERDS WELL AND EYTHORNE				
Shepherds Well Public Road Crossing	Single	72 4	5	150 yards Shepherds Well side.
BETWEEN EYTHORNE AND ELVINGTON				
Eythorne Public Road Crossing ...	Single	73 25	10	200 yards Canterbury Road side.
AT ELVINGTON				
Wigmore Lane Crossing	Single	73 47	10	220 yards Shepherds Well side and 88 yards Canterbury Road side.
Occupation Road Crossing	Single	73 77	10	200 yards Shepherds Well side and 150 yards Canterbury Road side.
BETWEEN ELVINGTON AND KNOWLTON				
Thornton Road Knowlton Halt Crossing	Single	75 12	5	120 yards Shepherds Well side and 200 yards Canterbury Road side.
BETWEEN KNOWLTON AND EASTRY				
Eastry South Halt Public Road Crossing	Single	76 57	5	250 yards Shepherds Well side.
			10	140 yards Canterbury Road side.
BETWEEN EASTRY AND WOODNESBOROUGH				
Drainless Drove Public Crossing ...	Single	78 11	5	200 yards Shepherds Well side.
			10	150 yards Canterbury Road side.
BETWEEN WOODNESBOROUGH AND ASH TOWN				
Ringleton Public Road Crossing	Single	78 31	10	200 yards Shepherds Well side and 160 yards Canterbury Road side.
BETWEEN ASH TOWN AND STAPLE				
Poulton Public Crossing	Single	79 70	10	180 yards Shepherds Well side and 150 yards Canterbury Road side.
Durlock Public Road Crossing	Single	80 21	5	220 yards Shepherds Well side and 110 yards Canterbury Road side.
BETWEEN STAPLE AND WINGHAM COLLIERY				
Occupation Crossing	Single	81 55	10	200 yards Shepherds Well side and 150 yards Canterbury Road side.
Danbridge Road Public Crossing	Single	81 69	5	140 yards Shepherds Well side and 300 yards Canterbury Road side.
BETWEEN WINGHAM COLLIERY AND WINGHAM TOWN				
Session House Public Crossing	Single	82 12	5	300 yards Shepherds Well side and 88 yards Canterbury Road side.
Adisham Road Public Crossing	Single	82 24	5	132 yards Shepherds Well side and 154 yards Canterbury Road side.

¶ The speed restriction indicators provided on the Kent and East Sussex and the East Kent lines are wooden boards 10 ins. by 10 ins., fixed to rail supports. The restricted speed in each case is indicated in white figures on a black background.

WATERLOO STATION,
20th July, 1950.   (R. 68,900/2).

S. W. SMART,
Superintendent of Operation.

British Railways table of speed restrictions on the East Kent, July 1950.

Ralph Gillam Collection

Of the Guilford branch trackwork little is known. The PDL Report had the following to say: '90 lb. rails, slightly defective. Spiked to sleepers. All in good condition. Practically no wear. Creosoted Baltic sleepers, placed 11 to 30 in. rail. About 15 per cent require immediate renewal. 90 lb. rails end about half mile from Eythorne, and 80 lb. rails commence'. One or two lengthmen recall that in 1927 and 1928 much of the branch was relaid with 60 lb. rails and the 80 and 90 lb. rails were used in the construction of Line 28 at Richborough.

Austen instituted a programme of track renewal between Shepherdswell and Tilmanstone Colliery in 1939 which proceeded intermittently until 1945 or 1946. The new rail appears to have included both chaired and flat bottom types and was of a heavier weight than used previously. Where flat bottom track rail was used, and on curves where the original rails were to be retained, Austen made use of sole plates to ensure even curvature of the tracks.

Tickets

Tickets were usually issued on the train by the guard but could be obtained from the station offices at Shepherdswell and Wingham Canterbury Road. It is probable that tickets were also issued at Eythorne and Eastry in the early days. If a train consisted of more than one carriage, or was made up of compartment stock as most of the carriages were, it was necessary for the guard to make his way along the train on the outside. It was not wise for the guard to leave the sale of tickets until the train stopped as the slow speeds on the EKR enabled delinquent passengers to alight between stations. This was a common problem at harvest times when the seasonal workers would see how far they could travel for free.

The main ticket stock of the EKR was on Edmondson cards printed by Williamson of Ashton but there were also some thinner issues on 'bell punch' stock. Most of the 'bell punch' tickets were blue, but the Edmondson tickets and some of the thinner tickets were colour coded to indicate the station of destination. Return tickets were printed in two colours. The colours used were:

Shepherdswell	White
Eythorne	Pink or Mauve
Tilmanstone Colliery Halt	White with red stripe or Orange
Elvington	Cream or Yellow
Knowlton	Green or Turquoise
Eastry and Eastry South	Blue or Grey
Woodnesborough	Yellow or Red
Ash Town	Dark Blue
Staple	Brown or Buff
Wingham	Orange or Pink

There were variations on the above. Examples include returns from Staple with both halves a light lilac blue and a return from Eastry South to Shepherdswell with the outward half cream and the homeward half green. A batch of yellow tickets intended for Elvington to Eythorne singles were mistakenly printed as 'Woodnesboro' to Eythorne' and were corrected by hand before issue.

East Kent tickets from the WEH-LYN collection. This collection is now housed at the Public Record Office.

It is not known what tickets were issued for the Sandwich Road branch and it seems likely that the stations on this branch made do with paper 'bell punch' tickets.

In addition to singles and returns the line issued a range of cheap day returns, weekend returns and privilege returns. Privilege singles do not appear to have been printed but could be produced by endorsing the homeward half as 'cancelled'. During World War II most reduced fare tickets were withdrawn but monthly returns were allowed to continue. Tickets for these consisted of old stocks of cheap day tickets rubber stamped 'MR' with the fare altered in pencil.

British Railways did not issue its own tickets for the line but used Southern Railway paper tickets on which the guard would enter the details in pencil. This was not a particularly onerous duty as very few passengers were travelling by this date.

EAST KENT RAILWAY.

FIRST CLASS FREE PASS No. 104

Expiring unless previously recalled.........................1945

Pass Mr..

between ....

....

....

NOT TRANSFERABLE.

Signature
of Holder ....

The holder of this Pass may also be required to give a specimen signature.

This Pass must be produced for examination when called for by the Officers of the Company, and upon the day of expiry must be returned to General Manager's Office, Tonbridge, Kent.

The Holder is subject to the same Rules and Regulations as other Passengers.

This Pass is granted upon the understanding that it is to be taken as evidence of an agreement that the Company over whose lines it is available are not to be held liable for any pecuniary or other responsibility to the Holder for loss of life, personal injury or delay, or for loss of or delay or damage to property however caused, that may be sustained by such person while using the Pass.

W. H. AUSTEN,
General Manager.

Issued by ....

East Kent first class free pass of 1945. By 1945 the chances of finding first class accommodation on the East Kent were slim.

Percy Buttifint (*left*) and Walter Clements (*right*) with locomotive No. 1 and carriage No. 1.
Colonel Stephens Railway Museum

In addition to passenger tickets the EKR issued white card tickets for 'one dog, bicycle, mailcart or article of luggage to any station on the East Kent Railway not exceeding 25 miles, 6d.'. There is some evidence of an intention to issue parcels stamps; the *Tenterden Terrier* for Spring 1978 illustrated two EKR parcels stamps. Parcels stamps were issued on several of the 'Stephens Railways' but these seem to be the only known examples from the EKR and there is no record of the railway receiving authority to issue such stamps. Curiously the two stamps shown both carry the same serial number '0499'. Railway philately is beyond our field of expertise and we shall treat this as another of the many unsolved mysteries of the railway.

Staffing

Staffed stations on the line were Eythorne, Eastry, Staple and Wingham. Shepherdswell was supervised by the office staff there in later years but may have had its own station agent or porter in the early years. Woodnesborough may have been staffed in the early years but the only recorded instance of this was when the staff from Staple were transferred to Woodnesborough after the arrival of the RAF at Staple.

There usually seem to have been three train crews, each consisting of a driver, a fireman and a guard but these were supplemented by fitters, apprentices and office staff when needed. The rest of the staff consisted of the engineering staff and carpenter at Shepherdswell, the clerical staff at Shepherdswell and the permanent way staff allocated to the different sections of line. The railway's needs were also served by the office and technical staff at Tonbridge and by the company's Secretary, Accountant and Solicitors at their respective offices.

Although the staff were poorly paid in comparison to their main line colleagues there seem to have been other compensations in working on the railway. Apart from the occasional flying visit from Stephens or Austen there was little rigorous daily supervision of work on the line and the staff seem to have been able to work at their own pace provided the job got done. Anecdotes abound of train crews stopping to play cards or dropping into a nearby tavern when they had time in hand, and of practical jokes played as a result of the rivalry between the engineering staff, the train crews and the lengthmen.

The longest serving employee on the EKR was Jim Smith, the carpenter and painter at Shepherdswell. He had joined the railway in 1916 and may have worked for the contractors before then. He was still hard at work at the age of 72 when British Railways took over in 1948. His work included carriage and wagon repairs, signwriting, locomotive painting, building and repairing stations and repairs to the timbers on the various bridges. Jim Smith was just one of a number of 'characters' working on the railway. Other 'larger than life' figures were drivers Reuben Griffin, Nat Sedgewick and Tom King, guard Percy Buttifint, Fred Carnell, the station agent at Staple, and Dick Harffey, the station agent at Canterbury Road.

Profit and Loss

The EKR was unique amongst the standard gauge railways managed by Holman Stephens and, later, W.H. Austen in that it was never actually declared bankrupt and never had to call in a Receiver. Admittedly, it sailed very close to the wind at times and its shareholders never received a dividend on their investment. The railway's survival was largely due to the Southern Railway's investment in the line and to the agreement of the debenture holders to accept payment of their interest partly in shares. It must nevertheless be pointed out that the EKR never made an operating loss on railway working and was able to supplement this with further income from rents, cartage and interest on its investments. This last source of income became particularly important from 1935 onwards when it regularly accounted for between one-third and one-half of the railway's profits. The investments had, of course, been made with the money put up by the Southern with the intention of financing the completion of the railway and its extensions.

We do not have details of the railway's receipts and working expenses before 1918 and only brief details for 1939 onwards. The worst year for the EKR between 1918 and 1947 was 1918 when the net income was only £219. The best year was 1920 when net income reached £4,143. The key factor in both these years was that the railway's expenses did not increase in direct proportion to the traffic carried. Once the basic cost of operating the services had been met it cost relatively little more to carry an increased traffic. Equally if traffic fell the costs of carrying that traffic would eat up a greater proportion of the receipts. The actual figures from 1918-38 are given below:

Year	Receipts from Rly working £	Expenses of Rly working £	Interest £	Misc. earnings £	Net income £
1918	5,885	5,741	-	76	219
1919	7,058	6,603	-	89	544
1920	12,936	8,903	30	79	4,143
1921	8,713	8,376	49	140	525
1922	10,032	6,897	16	85	3,236
1923	12,354	8,834	-	83	3,607
1924	11,073	8,200	-	80	2,952
1925	12,120	9,296	-	106	2,930
1926	8,532	8,214	-	295	613
1927	10,340	9,131	780	234	2,224
1928	10,471	10,183	668	166	1,123
1929	13,526	10,302	256	-89	3,390
1930	12,441	11,826	670	-150	1,136
1931	9,927	9,876	867	-17	897
1932	9,674	9,031	948	27	1,618
1933	11,267	9,636	941	29	2,601
1934	10,664	9,262	847	152	2,401
1935	10,913	8,852	1,103	178	3,343
1936	11,584	9,605	1,214	179	3,374
1937	10,924	9,089	1,354	164	3,353
1938	10,383	8,985	1,566	157	3,121

Even though the EKR was always able to show an excess of income over expenditure it must be said that this represented a very modest return on the money apparently invested in constructing the railway. By 1947 the railway had issued Ordinary Shares to the value of £505,609 but calls were in arrears on £1,395 of these shares and discounts on issuing the remaining shares amounted to £262,079. The Ordinary Shares therefore represented a value of £242,135. Similarly 5 per cent Debenture Stock had been issued to the value of £126,970 but discounts on this amounted to £20,624. The Capital Account therefore came to £348,481 rather than the £732,579 represented by the face value of shares and debentures. The capital assets of the railway were assessed at £332,655 consisting of £316,770 spent on Lines Open for Traffic, £5,688 for Rolling Stock, £7,913 for Land & Property not forming part of the Railway or Stations and £2,460 Stamp Duty on Additional Capital. This left a balance of £15,826 to be entered as a liability in the General Balance Sheet.

It is difficult to tell how accurate any of the above figures may actually have been. In the confused days when the EKR was just another pawn in the Kent Concessions Empire it was difficult to find out who had paid whom for what. Many of the debts incurred by the East Kent Contract & Financial Company had subsequently to be settled by the EKR and it seems possible that in some cases the railway paid twice for certain parcels of land, once in shares or debentures to the Contract company and then again in cash to the original vendor when the Contract company failed to complete the purchase itself. Record keeping at this stage appears to have been haphazard or even non-existent. Under these circumstances it is unlikely that it will ever be possible to say exactly how much was raised by the issue of shares or how much the railway actually cost to construct.

Viewed as an enterprise in its own right the EKR cannot be counted as a resounding success though it was certainly not the failure that many have claimed it to be. Viewed in the context of the Kent coalfield the railway was essential to the successful development of the chain of collieries from Guilford to Wingham. The failure of the coalfield to develop as it could have done cannot be blamed on the railway. It may be possible to blame the railway for not coming to terms sooner with Pearson & Dorman Long, but the railway's experience of the benevolence of industrial combines was hardly such as to inspire it with confidence. In the light of PDL's own difficulties in developing its enterprise it is unlikely that the railway would have fared any better under its control than under the paternal eye of the Southern Railway.

For the last word we shall return to the Prospectus for the railway issued on 1st April, 1912:

> Many more Collieries, besides Fireclay Works, will be planned and expeditiously established as soon as facilities are provided by these railways and their Extensions, and it is to this heavy and mineral traffic, and the traffic incidental to these Collieries, that the Directors look for their main revenues and profits. The traffic from Tilmanstone Colliery alone (with its three working shafts) when opened out should prove sufficient to return substantial dividends upon the small capital of the railways.
>
> Under the terms of the Orders the railways will be constructed to carry passengers, and a considerable tonnage of general goods and farm and market produce will pass over the line. The receipts from these sources, however, will be relatively unimportant.

Acknowledgements

We are grateful for the help of the following in producing this history. In the nature of a book that has been so long in gestation it is possible that some of those who have assisted with their experiences, knowledge or materials may have been omitted from this list. Please accept our apologies.

Dr I.C. Allen, G.W. Alliez, D.G. Ash, J.H. Aston, W.H. Austen, M. Baker, M. Barr, Bodleian Library, British Library, British Museum Newspaper Library, P.J. Bowden, C.C. Bowker, F. Brenchley, T. Burnham, R. Butler, Cambridge University Collection of Aerial Photographs, F. Carnell, R. Carpenter, R. Cash, H.C. Casserley, R.M. Casserley, G. Clements, Col Stephens Railway Museum at Tenterden, D. Cole, R.L. Coles, D. Collyer, T. Constable, P. Cooper, Professor E. Course, A.G. Crawshaw, A.W. Croughton, H.S. Dalston, L. Darbyshire, F.E. Elgar, K. Elks, M.R. Galley, R. Gardner, R. Gillam, D. Gough, K. Graham Barlow, G.W. Green, P. Harding, R. Harffey, Hayward Memorial Local History Centre at Lingfield, W.E. Heyward, L.M. Hobday, Dr J.R. Hollick, G.A. Hookham, Imperial War Museum, B. Janes, J. Jarvis, Dr W.J. Johnson, R. Jones, Kent County Council Library and Archives Service ,D. Kevan, R.W. Kidner, L. King, M. King, T. King, L. Lawrence, L. Layman, Locomotive Club of Great Britain, S. McAddie, Midland Railway Trust, J. Miller, A.L. Minter, T. Morris, W.B. Mottram, F.A. Munday, S.C. Nash, A. Neale, Mr Noakes, Mr Olley, A. Onions, G.V. Parker, B. Plummer, R.G. Pratt, Public Record Office, Railway Correspondence & Travel Society, P.J.T. Reed, R.F. Roberts, A.W. Robinson, G.W. Rogers, J. Scott-Morgan, P.D. Scurrell, N. Sedgewick, J.G. Sharland, P.D. Shaw, Simmons Aerofilms, J.L. Smith, A.W. Spratt, D. Stoyel, E. Tonks, E.B. Trotter, C.G. Turner, G. Weddell, A.G. Wells, H. West, Mr Whitaker, W.K. Williams, G.W. Wood.

We have not always been able to ascertain the photographer or copyright holder for a number of the photographs we have used. Please address any correspondence in this respect to Stephen Garrett, c/o Oakwood Press.

Bibliography and Sources

Books

The Kent Coalfield - Its Evolution and Development by A.E. Ritchie published by the Iron & Coal Trades Review 1919. Kent County Council Library Service has copies which might be able to be borrowed by your local library.

East Kent Regional Planning Scheme by Patrick Abercrombie and John Archibald. Survey published in 1925 and Report published in 1928.

The East Kent Railway by A.R. Catt published by Oakwood Press, 1970. A short history.

The Railways of Southern England: Independent and Light Railways by Professor Edwin Course published by B.T. Batsford in 1976. Chapter on EKR, history, extensions and operations.

The East Kent Light Railway by Vic Mitchell and Keith Smith published by Middleton Press in 1989. Wealth of photographs.

The Colonel Stephens Railways in Kent by Peter A. Harding published by himself in 1993. Short history includes EKR.

Memories of the East Kent Light Railway by Peter A. Harding published by himself in 1997. Many interesting reminiscences.

The East Kent Light Railway by Matthew Beddall published by himself in 1998. Short history.

Richborough Port by Robert Butler published by Richard Perry in 1993. Short history with rare photographs.

South Coast Railways - Ashford to Dover, South Coast Railways - Dover to Ramsgate and *Southern Main Lines - Faversham to Dover* by Vic Mitchell and Keith Smith published by Middleton Press in 1988, 1990 and 1992 respectively. Photographic histories with views of features related to EKR and coalfield.

The Colonel Stephens Railways by John Scott-Morgan published by David & Charles in 1978. Short section on EKR.

Railways of Arcadia by John Scott-Morgan published by P.E. Waters & Associates in 1989. Photographic review of Stephens' railways includes chapter on EKR.

Light Railways Explored - A Photographic Diary 1931-1938 by John E. Simpson published by Ross-Evans in 2001. Includes EKR.

The Locomotives of the South Eastern Railway, The Locomotives of the London, Chatham & Dover Railway, The Locomotives of the Southern Railway Volume 1 and *The Locomotives of the London & South Western Railway Volumes 1 & 2* all written by Donald Bradley and published by the Railway Correspondence & Travel Society. Comprehensive locomotive histories including details of classes used on EKR.

The Locomotives of the London & South Western Railway - The Early Engines and the Beattie Classes and *The Locomotives of the London & South Western Railway - the Adams Classes* both by Donald Bradley and published by Wild Swan Publications. Even more comprehensive details of Ilfracombe Goods, Saddlebacks and Adams Radials.

An Illustrated History of Southern Wagons ~ Volume 3 SECR by Bixley, Blackburn, Chorley and King published by Oxford Publishing Company in 2000. Includes photographs and details of LCDR and SER wagons that went to EKR.

Carriage Stock of the SE&CR by David Gould published by Oakwood Press 1976. Details of LCDR carriages of the types that went to EKR.

Magazines

There are many more articles about the East Kent or related topics than those that follow but over the years we have not kept details of every one. Where we have kept cuttings these have not always had the necessary details noted whilst in other cases the magazine concerned has not put its title or date on the relevant page. There must inevitably be some articles or references we simply never saw.

Railway Magazine December 1911 – Early plans of EKR and construction scenes
Railway Gazette November 1912 – progress on EKR
Railway Gazette May 1914 – not recorded
Railway Gazette January 1919 – Richborough Port
Railway Gazette December 1919 – Richborough Port
Railway Gazette September 1920 – Richborough Port
Railway Gazette October 1920 – Richborough Port
Railway Gazette April 1923 – EKR AGM
Railway Gazette February 1926 – Southern take shares in EKR
Railway Gazette March 1929 – Ropeway furore at Southern AGM
Southern Railway Magazine page 342 1935 – Journey over EKR by R.W. Kidner
Railway Magazine March 1937 – Extensive article on EKR by Klapper and Dalston
Locomotive Magazine August 1941 – not recorded
Railways February 1945 – A.P. Miall's journey on EKR in Letters section
Trains Illustrated January 1949 – not recorded
Railway World February 1959 – EKR Tickets
Trains Illustrated July 1960 – trial of diesel shunter on EKR
Railway World June 1962 – EKR in 1937
Model Railway News January 1969 – KESR 'Northiam'
Model Railway News September 1969 – Ilfracombe Goods locomotives as built.
Model Railway News December 1969 – KESR 'Hecate'
Model Railway News January 1970 - Pickering carriages (some errors)
Model Railway News June 1970 – LSWR Saddlebacks on EKR and KESR
Model Railway News January 1971 – NLR passenger brake on KESR
Model Railway News June 1971 – EKR locomotive No. 5
Model Railway Constructor January 1974 – LSWR 56'0" brake third carriages
Industrial Railway Record December 1975 – Pearson's Dover Harbour Railways
Royal School of Mines Journal No. 25 1976 – Kent Coalfield
Railway Modeller June 1984 – modelling Shepherdswell
Model Railway Constructor June 1987 – North London brakevan (EKR No.2)
British Railways Journal Summer 1988 – Ilfracombe Goods locomotives
British Railways Journal Winter 1988 – the East Kent at Wingham
Backtrack January-February 1991 – Shepherd's Well
Railways South East Winter 1991/2 – David Collyer History of EKR to 1931
Railways South East Summer 1992 – David Collyer History of EKR from 1931
Railway Bylines June-July 1997 – EKR in the 1940s

Enthusiast Journals

The following have contained a number of articles on the East Kent and will continue to do so.

The Tenterden Terrier – Journal of the Kent & East Sussex Railway, Tenterden Town Station, Tenterden, Kent TN30 6HE. Website www.kesr.org.uk

The Colonel – Journal of the Colonel Stephens Society, 131 Borstal Street, Rochester, Kent ME1 3JU. Website www.colonelstephenssociety.org.uk

East Kent Railway News – Magazine of the East Kent Railway Trust, Station Road, Shepherdswell, Dover, Kent CT15 7PD. Website www.eastkentrailway.com

The Railway Observer published by the Railway Correspondence & Travel Society has numerous reports of the East Kent from the 1930s to the 1950s when reports began to taper off as the line became less 'interesting'.

The Colonel Stephens Railway Museum posts articles on the Stephens railways, including the East Kent, on its website www.hfstephens-museum.org.uk. The Museum itself is custodian to a large collection of papers relating to the East Kent but these are only available for research by prior appointment. The Museum is run by volunteers with many calls on their time and cannot guarantee to be able to meet every request for access to the collection.

The Public Record Office

It is not proposed to detail all the relevant documents in the PRO archives but instead to explain the general principles. Having acquired your reading ticket from reception (check in advance what means of identification you will require) you then need to have a reader's seat allocated and to be issued with a pager. So equipped you can then select the documents you wish to order from a range of catalogues or indexes. Ordering documents is done on screen and you are initially allowed to order three documents at a time. You will then be paged when your documents are ready for collection. There is a procedure for having photocopies made but it is best not to leave this too late in the day. Large maps are viewed in a separate map room. Any notes you wish to make must be in pencil – pens are forbidden. There is a very helpful help desk in the room where the catalogues are held but you may have to queue. Refreshments are available as well as facilities for consuming packed meals. Bags and coats must be left in the cloakroom.

Some of the more relevant catalogues are as follows:

RAIL 175 – this is the catalogue prefix for the main East Kent Railway documents so that, for example, RAIL 175 1 contains the first volume of the Directors' Minutes, RAIL 175 18 contains the Contract between the East Kent Railway and East Kent Contract & Finance and RAIL 175 33 contains the Annual Reports.

MT58 – this is the catalogue prefix for Light Railway Orders so that, for example, MT58 495 contains the Reports of the Public Enquiries leading to the East Kent Light Railways (Extensions & General Powers) Order 1931.

MT54 – this is the catalogue prefix for files relating to unsuccessful applications for Light Railway Orders. The files have been pretty well filleted at some date before coming to the PRO but some maps and essential details survive. MT54 620 is the file for the Wingham & Adisham Light Railway application.

MT6 – this is the catalogue prefix for files of correspondence to the Light Railways Commissioners, later the Ministry of Transport. For each MT58 file there will be one or more associated MT6 files but there are MT6 files on many other subjects. The MT6 files have been exceptionally well catalogued and it is a relatively easy task to spot East Kent files in the Index. The returns to the Light Railways Investigation Committee are indexed amongst the MT6 files. Note for the unwary – most of these files must be read from the back to the front as papers were added on top of existing papers. There is often a useful summary on the front cover.

MT29 – Reports of Inspections of railways and works. Pringle's 1916 East Kent Inspection is MT29 78.

MT14 – the MT14 files contain carbon copies of letters sent out by the Light Railway Commissioners and require monumental patience since many of the letters are merely acknowledgements of letters received. Without the matching incoming letter it is often difficult to make out what the correspondence is about but occasionally gems come to light.

ZSPC11 327 – this is the W.E. Heyward collection of postcards, timetables, tickets, magazine articles and other ephemera relating to the East Kent. The PRO seems to have inherited the collection from the British Transport Archives at Porchester Road.

BT31 – The BT31 files contain papers relating to registered companies that have been wound up so that, for example, BT31 21588/130032 contains the papers relating to the Stonehall Colliery Company. The Catalogue was a little awkward to use but may have been updated since.

Newspapers

The main newspapers that have been consulted have been *The Dover Express*, *The Kentish Gazette*, *The Dover & County Chronicle*, *The Dover Times* and *The East Kent Mercury*. These are available at the British Museum Newspaper Library at Colindale and presumably at some other major libraries. We cannot claim to have read every issue of every newspaper but have homed in on significant dates. There are probably rich pickings still to be had in this area of research.

Video

There is almost a minute of locomotive No. 6 at Canterbury Road in 1938 on 'Pathe Railway Pictorial' produced by Video 125. Unfortunately the risky shunting manoeuvres are not shown.

The Corrugated Iron Shed

The round shed at Shepherdswell was the dumping ground for unwanted East Kent paperwork during the line's later years. Many enthusiasts helped themselves to random items of interest though the bulk of the papers simply mildewed away. From time to time an interesting titbit from somebody's collection comes to light and it is to be hoped that many more will do so.

Index